AUSTIN, CLEARED FOR TAKEOFF

D0933038

NUMBER FOURTEEN

JACK AND DORIS SMOTHERS SERIES
IN TEXAS HISTORY, LIFE, AND CULTURE

AVIATORS,

BUSINESSMEN,

AND THE

GROWTH OF AN

AMERICAN CITY

CLEARED

AUSTIN,

TAKEOFF

FOR

KENNETH B. RAGSDALE

 UNIVERSITY OF TEXAS PRESS, AUSTIN

Publication of this work was made possible in part by support from the J. E. Smothers, Sr., Memorial Foundation and the National Endowment for the Humanities.

Requests for permission to reproduce material from this work should be sent to Permissions, University of Texas Press, P.O. Box 7819, Austin, TX 78713-7819.

⊗ The paper used in this book meets the minimum requirements of ANSI/NISO Z39.48-1992 (R1997) (Permanence of Paper).

Library of Congress Cataloging-in-Publication Data

Ragsdale, Kenneth Baxter, date
    Austin, cleared for takeoff : aviators, businessmen, and the growth of an American city / Kenneth B. Ragsdale
        p.   cm.— (Jack and Doris Smothers series in Texas history, life, and culture ; no. 14)
Includes bibliographical references and index.
    ISBN 0-292-70167-5 (hardcover : alk. paper) —
ISBN 0-292-70268-X (pbk. : alk. paper)
    1. Aeronautics—Texas—Austin—History.   2. Austin (Tex.)—History—20th century.   1. Title   II. Series.
TL522.T4R34   2003
387.7'09764'31—dc22
                                          2003022172

ANOTHER ONE FOR JANET,
IN HEARTFELT APPRECIATION
FOR SIXTY YEARS OF COMPANIONSHIP.

CONTENTS

Illustrations on pages 9–16, 87–92, and 161–168.

It all began with a telephone call from fellow author Mike Cox, who asked the question that frequently initiates conversation between authors: "What are you working on now?" I explained I was between projects and suffering through an unusual lull in my life. And then he said it: "Why don't you do something on Austin aviation? Bobby Ragsdale is still around, and to many people he *is* 'Mister Austin aviation.'" Before I could accept the challenge, he continued: "Nothing much has been done on the subject and there should be plenty of material in local libraries." By then, my mind was already off and running. As a licensed pilot with a lifelong love affair with airplanes, I couldn't think of any subject I would rather explore.

And then there was another matter. I had never met Bobby (Robert L.) Ragsdale, although many times I had been asked, "Are you related to the Ragsdale that owns the airport?" The answer was no, and he doesn't. Although the Ragsdale name was emblazoned on various buildings, Bobby did not own Robert Mueller Airport. However, he had been a fixed base operator at that site since 1940 and so had witnessed vast changes in Austin aviation. Clearly, if I was going to write a book on that subject, meeting Bobby Ragsdale would be the logical place to begin. Our first interview, on November 26, 1996, launched a new friendship as well as a new research-writing project. During the next five years we met many times. As I gathered an abundance of information, Bobby seemed to relish the opportunity to relive his years in aviation, especially in partnership with his wife, Pearle. Our new friendship, however, presented a personal challenge; I had to remain ever vigilant that the ensuing narrative would be Ken Ragsdale's story, and not Bobby Ragsdale's. Considering the extensive data I was able to compile, I believe I have fulfilled that objective.

There were many others with memories to share. The Brownings, another Austin aviation family dynasty, began fixed base operations (FBO) in 1939. Robert M. Browning, his wife, Emma, son Robert M. Browning III, and daughter-in-law Mary Helen served the industry for more than four decades through flight training, aircraft sales, service, and charter operations. I never met Mr. Browning, but Mrs. Browning, Bobby Browning, and Mary Helen were always generous in sharing their aviation experiences. And thus a new round of friendships developed. It was essentially Bobby

Ragsdale and the Brownings, and, of course, Mike Cox, who launched me on a six-year research and writing adventure that yielded the following narrative. To each of them, and many, many more, I am deeply appreciative.

The Austin aviation story began on October 20, 1911, when Calbraith Perry Rodgers landed his Wright biplane in the Capital City on his pioneering coast-to-coast flight. That was the first airplane seen in Austin, and it ignited a wave of public enthusiasm for which there was no precedent. Most important, the kind of excitement exhibited by Austinites was an experience shared by citizens across the country. Wherever Rodgers appeared on his six-week, twelve-state coast-to-coast flight, he left in his wake a new awareness of manned flight, which helped implant in the minds and imaginations of millions of Americans a belief that aviation would become an increasingly important factor in their lives. From that time forward men with wings became the symbol of the country's progress into the future. "Between 1910 and 1950, two generations of Americans kept the faith with the winged gospel," wrote Joseph J. Corn. "They worshiped the airplane as a mechanical god and expected it to usher in a dazzling future, a virtual millennium."[1] In Austin, Texas, the celebration of flight closely paralleled that in other American cities.

Following a national pattern of public adoration, thousands of Austinites turned out on November 21–22, 1911, to see the Curtiss Exhibition Company's air show held at Camp Mabry and on November 23, 1915, to greet the arrival of Capt. Benjamin D. Foulois and the 1st Aero Squadron. After aviation assumed a role in combat, the University of Texas served national defense during two world wars by training young men and women for military air service. The School of Military Aeronautics opened on May 27, 1917, and the Civilian Pilot Training Program began in May 1940. Also, during World War I, the Austin Chamber of Commerce led a successful citywide endeavor to establish Penn Field, Austin's first landing field, where the University of Texas, in conjunction with the Army Air Service, established the Air Service School of Radio Operators. Following World War I, military-trained pilots flying war surplus Curtiss JN-4s ("Jennies") toured the nation, further spreading the gospel of flight. By the mid-1920s those "barnstormers" began establishing permanent bases of operation, forming the basis of the nation's emerging commercial aviation industry. In Austin, Mat Watson and Grace McClelland began flight operations at Camp Mabry in 1925, and a year later moved to a permanent site on Cameron Road. Also that year, Webb Ruff began fixed base operations at University Airport, located approximately one-half mile north of the present intersection of Airport Boulevard and North Lamar Boulevard on what was then known as the Dallas Highway.

The passage of the Air Mail Act of 1925 opened a new chapter in American aviation. Airmail service, initially a New York to Los Angeles operation with intermediate stops, did not reach Austin until February 6, 1928, and scheduled airline passenger service not until March 30, 1929. The expansion of commercial aviation led to the nationwide growth of municipal landing fields. Austin was no exception; Robert Mueller Municipal Airport opened on October 14, 1930. At that time, 133 airports were operating in Texas. With the general increase in air travel, manufacturers began building larger and faster multiengine aircraft, which were soon spanning the continent. The first ten-place Lockheed "Electra" landed in Austin on May 6, 1935; the first fourteen-place Douglas DC-2 on June 10, 1937; and the first twenty-one-passenger DC-3 in December 1939. Following the outbreak of war in Europe, the United States military began expanding its network of air bases. The opening of the Del Valle Army Air Base on September 19, 1942, stands as Austin's major aviation event during World War II.

Growth of postwar air travel, both private and commercial, soon rendered Mueller Airport inadequate, a circumstance the Austin City Council struggled with for years. After spending millions on a seemingly endless series of airport consultancies, the solution to the city's airport dilemma was reduced to three options: (1) enlarge Mueller; (2) seek joint use of Bergstrom Air Force Base; or (3) close Mueller and choose an alternate airport site. After nearly eight years of indecision, and with the first two options eliminated, the Austin City Council voted to establish a new municipal airport near Manor, Texas. The council, however, cancelled that plan when the Air Force announced the closure of Bergstrom, releasing that facility to the City of Austin. Construction on a new municipal airport began on March 6, 1995; city officials dedicated Austin-Bergstrom International Airport on May 23, 1999.

Briefly, that is the story for which I began gathering data on November 26, 1996, when I first met Bobby Ragsdale. He did, indeed, help launch the project, but many others joined me in ferreting out every possible piece of data that helped tell the Austin aviation story. I am deeply indebted to them for their commitment; without their help the story could not have been told. Where shall I begin?

My first stop on this new adventure was at the Center for American History at the University of Texas at Austin. In addition to having a host of friends on the professional staff, free parking was always available. (And to the research historian who constantly inhabits public repositories, free parking is a consideration.) Since I had researched previous books at that site, my welcome was warm and generous. Assistant Director Ralph Elder's knowledge of the Texas War Records greatly facilitated the initial research, while other staff members—Alison Beck, Katherine Fox, Evan Hocker, and Brenda Gunn—contributed greatly to this effort. I became such a "fixture" at the Center, they invited me to join them for the annual staff photograph.

High praise is also due Biruta Kearl, administrator of the Austin History and Records Center, where I enjoyed a new circle of friends. Jane Montz, Sue Soy, James Rust, and Margaret Schlankey each knew well the content of their special collections. And a special word of thanks to veteran Mary Jo Cooper, whose knowledge of the Center's aviation collections saved me hours of research.

At the Lyndon B. Johnson School of Public Affairs Library, Head Librarian Steve Littrell and his assistant, Margaret Flores, came to my rescue many times, as did Paul Rascoe, Government Documents Librarian at the University's Perry Castañeda Library. However, researching a topic as extensive as aviation led me down paths far removed from academia. And help was always waiting. Donaly E. Brice, Reference Archivist, Texas State Library and Archives Commission, aided me on numerous occasions—as he had for previous books—in locating state government documentation. So did Penelope Dukes-Williams, Legislative Reference Librarian. When I needed information on Austin City Council Minutes, Tonya M. Bell always had an immediate answer, as did Karen Winget, who provided extensive data on the University of Texas Department of Astronomy's unique Austin-Marfa airplane shuttle operation. And special words of appreciation for Jackie Mayo, Public Information Specialist, City of Austin Aviation Department, and Beth Youngdale, Professional Librarian, Tarlton Law Library, University of Texas at Austin. Thanks also to Kenneth Cox, longtime associate of Bobby Ragsdale, who aided me in documenting the Ragsdale fixed base operation, as well as to Jerry D. Oehler, with the Travis County Appraisal District, who identified land transactions relating to Austin airports. I am especially appreciative of Beth Gleason, Director of Marketing and Communications at Angelou Economics, who provided invaluable data on Austin area growth factors. Tom Hail, Air Force Historian, Texas Military Forces Museum, Camp Mabry, Texas, not only contributed important documentation on military aviation in Austin, but undertook a critical examination of that portion of the manuscript relating to the topic. Tom, a very special thank you.

Research, however, was not limited to Austin. Mike Miller, with the Texas History Division of the Dallas Public Library, and Larry Sall, Director, Aviation Collection, University of Texas at Dallas, provided background data on that city's aviation history. And when needing additional data on Federal Aviation Administration matters, the agency's historian Ned Preston (now retired) provided that information.

To all of the above, plus the some forty thoughtful individuals who contributed their time and information through personal interviews, a heartfelt thank you.

Researching this book has been a highly rewarding personal adventure. I not only made a host of new friends, but in the process accumulated a substantial body of data, which I believe adds a new dimension of understanding of the City of Austin and how it grew. My only regret is that Bobby Ragsdale did not live to see the project complete. I believe he would have shared the pride.

While all of the above contributed to this endeavor, it was my old friend and copy editor, Lois Rankin, whose special skill with words and ideas brought order and clarity to the manuscript.

Last, and above all, I want to express a deep personal indebtedness to my family, especially my two children, Keith Ellen and Jeffrey, who have contributed love and support for all my endeavors. But the one to whom I am most grateful is my wife of sixty years, Janet. Thanks to her success in the world of real estate investment, I was afforded the personal freedom to research this book, plus four others now in publication. She alone made this possible. And for that, Janet, a very special thank you.

I must also acknowledge the ongoing effort of Winston Ragsdale, a persistent yellow kitty cat, with whom I competed daily for the use of my desk. Winston won only part of the time.

K.B.R.

AUSTIN, CLEARED FOR TAKEOFF

INTRODUCTION

FRIDAY, October 20, 1911, marked a major milestone in Austin history. At 1:55 P.M., aviator Calbraith (Cal) Perry Rodgers landed his Wright EX Flyer in a vacant field near the present intersection of Duval and Forty-fifth streets. This was the first airplane to land in the Capital City. As the six-foot-four pioneer aviator stepped from his boxlike aircraft, excitement reached fever pitch; Austinites had just witnessed a phenomenon that, a few years previous, appeared impossible. Rodgers, unknowingly, had just ushered the City of Austin into the age of manned flight.

Of the roughly three thousand excited citizens who joined the celebration, few could fully comprehend what that event portended.[1] However, with the passage of time, their lives, their city, and their world would be changed dramatically. The airplane would deem it so. But when viewed in broad perspective, this was not a local phenomenon; the Austin aviation experience, in its many forms, would ultimately be repeated in every metropolitan center throughout America.

When Austin greeted Cal Rodgers, aviation was in its infancy. Only eight years separated Rodgers' arrival and man's first flight in a powered heavier-than-air aircraft. That occurred on the morning of December 17, 1903, on the windswept dunes of Kill Devil Hill near Kitty Hawk, North Carolina. With Orville Wright at the controls of the homebuilt, experimental aircraft, an attendant released the restraining rope, the machine gently moved forward, and suddenly became airborne. At that moment, the creative genius of two young men, Orville and Wilbur Wright, freed earthbound humans from terra firma and converted their world from two dimensions to three.[2]

The Wright brothers believed implicitly in the future of aviation. In 1907, in order to further their interests, they divided the territory. Wilbur toured France in an improved Wright Flyer No. 3, displaying the craft to the critical French Aero-Club, while Orville moved to Fort Myer, Virginia, to demonstrate the new Flyer at public trials conducted by the United States Army Signal Corps. Both endeavors were unqualified successes. In France, Orville won the Michelin Prize by establishing a world endurance record of two hours and twenty minutes; at Fort Myer Wilbur's performance far exceeded the Signal Corps' specifications.[3] There were immediate rewards. The Signal Corps placed an order for one aircraft, marking the beginning of military aviation in the United States. An ebullient press assured the nation, and the world, that manned flight was indeed a reality. "After 1910," wrote Walter J. Boyne, director of the National Air and Space Museum, "when the Wrights first publicly demonstrated their flying machines . . . the advancement of aviation took off exponentially."[4]

The success of the Fort Myer demonstration came at a price. Orville Wright experienced tragedy, as well as triumph, for Lt. Thomas E. Selfridge, a passenger on one of Orville's flights, was killed when their machine crashed from a height of seventy-five feet, thus becoming aviation's first fatality. Sadly, death would be an ongoing theme in the early history of aviation. That single tragedy, however, failed to dampen public interest. While comparatively few people had ever seen an airplane (an "aeroplane," in early reports) or could conceive its ultimate potential, subsequent press coverage of flying demonstrations fired the nation's imagination. "Increasing numbers took to the air," explained aviation historian Eileen Lebow. "In 1909, there were twenty men flying in America; by the end of 1910, there were 100 aviators."[5]

Hoping to stimulate the growth of aviation, as well as civic pride, through the promotion of air shows, civic leaders in many American cities began organizing aero clubs. Their efforts quickly gained public attention. Thousands flocked to designated sites to witness man invade the once-exclusive space of birds in flight. More than twenty meetings were held in Europe, while in the United States air shows continued to attract unprecedented attendance. In January 1910, Los Angeles sponsored the first international air meet held in the United States. Some twenty-five thousand people converged on Dominguez Field to see "a variety of events that tested the proficiency of the pilot and the responsiveness of his machine."[6] The following May, the *New York World* offered a $10,000 prize for the first flight between New York City and Albany. Glenn Curtiss, flying a biplane of his own design, claimed the prize after making refueling stops at Poughkeepsie and Spuyten Duyvil. It was the first long-distance flight in the Western Hemisphere.[7]

Other important air shows include the Harvard-Boston event in September 1910 and the New York air show staged at Belmont Park on Long Island in October. "The Belmont Park meeting merits special attention," explained Charles Howard Gibbs-Smith, "as its quality and venue attracted influential attention from American financial, military and social spheres: it was also an international occasion, with overseas teams from England and France, and helped—more than any other occasion   to popularize flying in this country, as well as stimulating technical development."[8]

Calbraith Perry Rodgers was one of the growing number of individuals who took to the air. A New York socialite and motorcycle enthusiast, young Rodgers exhibited a special fondness for thrills and excitement. Flirting with danger was an inherited trait. His father, an army captain, was killed fighting Indians in Arizona; Commodores Matthew Calbraith Perry and John Rodgers, his great-grandfathers, were United States naval heroes.[9] When the navy selected Calbraith's cousin John Rodgers, an Annapolis graduate, to learn to fly, Cal joined him at the Wright flying school in order to investigate the opportunities in aviation. It was a great revelation. Rodgers discovered the thrill of flying far exceeded anything a motorcycle or automobile could provide.

When John Rodgers reported to the Dayton flying school in March 1911, his classmates were two young army officers destined for outstanding military careers: Henry "Hap" Arnold and Thomas Milling. Cal subsequently registered as a civilian, paid his $850 fee, and embarked on a new and exciting career. When he passed his tests the following August 7, the Aero Club of America issued him license number forty-nine; he had earned the title *aviator*. John Rodgers, who had passed his tests four days earlier, joined his cousin in purchasing an airplane. They chose a Wright Model B two-place biplane, powered by a four-cylinder water-cooled engine and capable of speeds up to fifty miles an hour in still air.

Civic pride is a competitive impulse. When a group of Chicago business men proposed hosting an air show in that city, they believed that, if the New York air show had switched the focus of aviation progress from Europe to America, an even bigger show in Chicago would establish that city as the nation's premier aviation center. The idea enjoyed wide support. Industrialist Harold McCormick headed a planning committee that included the cream of Chicago's business elite, as well as the Aero Club of Illinois. They chose Grant Park as the location for the Chicago International Aviation Meet and offered $80,000 in prize money, the largest sum ever offered for a competitive air show. Thirty-two pilots registered for the event, including Calbraith Rodgers. Bolstered by approximately one week's experience as a licensed aviator, he eagerly accepted the challenge.

When the eight-day show opened on Saturday, August 12, it appeared the committee had planned wisely; more than one hundred thousand people jammed Grant Park to witness the spectacle. They were well rewarded; the following day attendance soared to an estimated six hundred thousand. All came to see the newest phenomenon of the age. Young Rodgers began earning prize money from the opening cannonade. By the time the show closed on August 19, his earnings totaled $11,285, more than twice the original cost of the plane. And, in addition to a love of flying, Rodgers also relished the heroic status accorded flyers by an adoring public. The daring young men in their flying machines became instant celebrities. Fellow pilot Tom Sopwith, a bachelor, "was greatly admired by the ladies who wrote him love notes and waited to catch a glimpse of him." [10]

The Chicago air show was indeed a major event in the early history of aviation. The show established Chicago as the nation's most important aviation center in the pre–World War I era, and Cicero Field, the airport Harold McCormick and the Aero Club of Chicago created for the air show, was at that time "the most complete flying facility in the world." [11] The aviation success factor also caught the attention of Chicago publisher

William Randolph Hearst, who, according to contemporaries, became obsessed with aviation. Hearst, however, supported a more practical aspect of flying. He believed better engineering and improved airframe design would yield a product that would benefit American society, especially business and industry. To further that movement, Hearst shocked the American public with an almost unbelievable offer: a $50,000 prize to the first aviator who could fly across the United States in thirty days. The contestant could embark from either coast and choose any route, but the flight had to be completed within thirty days and include a stop at Chicago.[12]

Hearst's offer gained the approval of America's most famous flyers, including the Wright brothers and Glenn Curtiss. When Rodgers learned of the projected transcontinental flight, he seized the opportunity. He realized, however, that such a flight would require resources far beyond his means, which, he believed, were available within the Chicago business community. Rodgers' recent celebrity status caught the attention of meat packing executive J. Ogden Armour, whose company was launching a marketing campaign promoting its new grape soft drink, Vin-Fiz. The two met and quickly came to terms: Rodgers' Wright biplane would be converted into a flying billboard, the Vin-Fiz. In addition, when flying over urban areas, Rodgers would release hundreds of small cards bearing the name and price of the soft drink.

In exchange for Rodgers' endorsement, the company would pay all expenses, including bonuses of five dollars for every mile flown east of the Mississippi River and four dollars for every mile west of the river. In addition, Armour would provide a special train with two cars, one for staff accommodations, plus a "hangar" car, which contained a spare Wright B aircraft, two spare engines, a machine shop, plus a six-cylinder Palmer-Singer touring car to transport Rodgers from each landing site to the train. The agreement included accommodations for his mechanics, Rodgers' wife and mother, his personal manager (Fred Wettengel), and members of the Vin-Fiz publicity staff. Rodgers, however, would pay for his fuel, oil, repairs, and spare parts, as well as his mechanic's salary.

All pieces of the complicated business mosaic were beginning to fall in place; the future, it seemed, belonged to Calbraith Rodgers. The projected transcontinental flight, if completed, would insure his stature as a pioneer in American aviation, as well as in the virgin field of celebrity endorsement. All that remained was launching the project. On Sunday afternoon, September 17, some two thousand spectators paid admission to witness

Rodgers' takeoff from Sheepshead Bay, New York, in pursuit of the Hearst prize.[13] It was, indeed, a festive occasion; spectators cheered as a young girl christened the plane with a bottle of Vin-Fiz. As the applause subsided, Rodgers, with his ever-present cigar clamped between his teeth, reversed his cap, donned his goggles, and took his seat—*sans safety belt*—beside the 35-horsepower, water-cooled engine. After checking his only flight instrument, a weighted string tied to a cross wire to indicate the plane's attitude in flight, his mechanic started the engine. At 4:22 P.M. Rodgers took off, gained altitude, circled Coney Island, dropped leaflets advertising Vin-Fiz, and turned west toward California.

During the hype and publicity that surrounded the flight's preparation, the magnitude of that unprecedented undertaking was seemingly overlooked. At that time there were neither designated airways nor airports (except Chicago's), road maps were scarce and inaccurate, and, according to journalist Tom Mahoney, "the farthest anybody had flown had been 1,155 miles. That had been Harry Atwood's 11-day St. Louis to New York flight with many stops."[14] California lay some four thousand miles ahead of Rodgers' Wright B pusher,[15] and in order to follow a predetermined course, he elected to rely solely on railroad tracks for guidance.

As the Hudson River disappeared behind Rodgers, he could see the long panels of white cloth placed between the Erie Railroad tracks marking his initial route. He was on course. He followed the tracks to Middletown, New York, where at 6:07 P.M., he landed in an open field. Some ten thousand people were waiting to greet the now-famous aviator with the first of many ovations. He had flown 104 miles in 105 minutes.[16] Rodgers arose early the following morning, rode to the field in the Palmer-Singer touring car, took his seat on the Vin-Fiz, and waved to the cheering crowd. "The Vin-Fiz bumped along the field and rose into the air," Eileen Lebow reported. "The crowd's cheers turned suddenly to screams as the plane rose slightly, then plummeted to earth. . . . Just thirty seconds had passed, but the birdlike machine was a twisted mass of splintered wood, broken wire, and shredded fabric."[17] Rodgers survived the crash with only minor bruises and immediately began supervising the repairs.

The Middletown crash marked the beginning of a tragic scenario that would be repeated some sixteen times before Rodgers reached California. He nevertheless moved forward with dogged determination. Three days later, the repairs complete, he was again airborne for Chicago. After some twenty stops, including two more major crashes, Rodgers landed in Chicago, fulfilling one condition of the Hearst prize. There were, however, other matters of concern. With the expiration date of the $50,000 prize only two days away, he applied for an extension. Hearing nothing, he moved forward with his plans anyway. Taking off from Grant Park, Rodgers pointed the Vin-Fiz on a southwesterly heading, determined to reach California with or without Hearst's prize money.

When Rodgers reached Marshall, Missouri, on October 10, he had flown 1,398 miles, farther than any pilot in the world, yet his elation was short-lived. On alighting from the Vin-Fiz, he received a telegram bearing Hearst's response: there would be no extension. "Fading hope for the $50,000 strangely enough increased public interest in Rodgers," Mahoney wrote. "The crowds became bigger, their cheers louder."[18] Despite the loss of the anticipated prize money, Rodgers remained resolute in his determination to reach California. He was, however, still receiving Armour's five-dollar-per-mile bonus, and his advance agents began negotiating lucrative contracts for flying exhibitions at towns along the remaining route.

To the sound of packing house whistles, Rodgers landed in Swope Park in Kansas City. From there he followed the Missouri-Kansas-Texas (Katy) Railroad tracks south across Oklahoma, and shortly before 9:00 A.M. on Tuesday, October 17, the Vin-Fiz crossed the Red River into Texas. Later that day he arrived in Fort Worth, and continued on to Dallas for a two-day appearance at the State Fair of Texas. On October 20, Rodgers again took to the air, located the railroad tracks, and headed south toward Waco. The Waco Young Men's Business League had negotiated a contract with Roger's manager for him to circle the city several times to ensure that all citizens had an opportunity to see the famous Vin-Fiz.

Anticipating a fifty-mile-an-hour gale while flying unprotected at two thousand feet, Rodgers had taken additional precaution against the cold blast. He wrapped his upper body with newspapers before donning his usual business suit, leather coat, and knee-high boots. When he arrived at Waco's Gourley Park, a crowd of excited spectators was gathered to see the celebrated aviator. At 11:45 A.M., to the fanfare of sirens, factory whistles, and the crowd's applause, Rodgers took off, circled the city, and headed south. In less than three hours, if all went well, he would reach Austin for a prearranged landing at the Ridge Top Annex.

C. P. Rodgers in "Vin Fiz" Flyer, leaving Sheepshead Bay, N. Y., Sept. 17th, 1911, in Hearst $50,000 ↞n to ocean flight.

Courtesy Photography Collection, Harry Ransom Humanities Research Collection, University of Texas at Austin.

Calbraith (Cal) Perry Rodgers taking off from Sheepshead Bay, New York, on September 17, 1911, in his Wright Model B biplane on the first leg of his historic coast-to-coast flight. Rodgers reached Austin, Texas, on Friday, October 20. His was the first airplane to land in the Capital City.

Source: Austin History Center, Austin Public Library, PICA 20568.

On October 20, 1911, some three thousand Austin citizens witnessed the first airplane landing in Austin. Calbraith Perry Rodgers (right), flying a Wright EX Flyer, included Austin on his historic coast-to-coast flight. That event ushered the Capital City into the age of manned flight.

Source: Texas War Records Collection, CN 11537. The Center for American History, The University of Texas at Austin.

Source: Texas War Records Collection, CN 11536. The Center for American History, The University of Texas at Austin.

United States Army Curtiss JN-4 trainers at Penn Field. Established on 318 acres south of Austin, Penn Field was Austin's first airport and represented the initial effort of the Chamber of Commerce to bring aviation to the Capital City.

With Curtiss JN-4 trainers in the background, Austin citizens meet with United States Army officers at Penn Field. Community effort helped develop Penn Field; on Sunday, April 20, 1918, some 689 citizens gathered at the field to help remove rocks that were damaging aircraft.

11

Source: Texas War Records Collection, CN 11538. The Center for American History, The University of Texas at Austin.

Wearing helmets, goggles, and leather flying jackets, United States Army pilots pose before a Curtiss JN-4 trainer at Penn Field. The airport served as an intermediate stop on formation training flights between Kelly Field near San Antonio and other Central Texas military fields.

Courtesy Smithers Collection, Harry Ransom Humanities Research Center, University of Texas at Austin.

Capt. Benjamin D. Foulois, commander of the 1st Aero Squadron, standing beside a Curtiss JN-3 at Fort Sam Houston, following his 1915 historic flight from Fort Sill, Oklahoma. The Curtiss JN-3 was the forerunner of the venerable JN-4 "Jenny." During the 1920s thousands of these World War I surplus aircraft were flown by "barnstormers" throughout the nation and became the symbol of the coming air age.

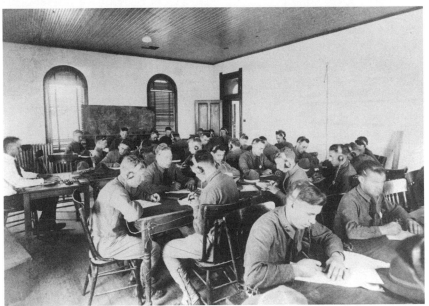

Cadets practicing Morse code at the University of Texas School of Military Aeronautics during World War I. Using headsets, cadets transcribe messages sent by the instructor at left.

School of Military Aeronautics cadets practicing aerial observation using a "flight simulator." As a map of Belgium slowly rolls before them, they attempt to identify strategic locations, which, in combat, they would relay by radio to a military command center.

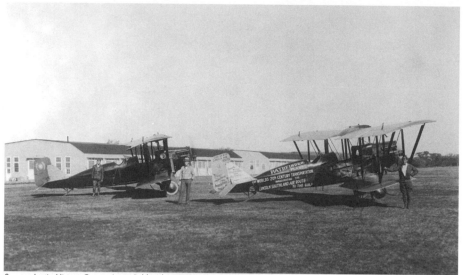

Source: Austin History Center, Austin Public Library, PICA 19199.

In 1925, Mat Watson and Grace McClelland offered one-dollar airplane rides in two five-passenger Lincoln Standard LS-5 biplanes, operating from the parade ground at Camp Mabry. The former cavalry post, located in northwest Austin, served as Austin's second landing field.

Source: Austin History Center, Austin Public Library, PICA 19200.

Accidents were an integral part of the early history of aviation. This United States Army Air Corps Curtiss A-3 attack plane made an emergency landing on a farm near Austin and was demolished. The two-man crew survived.

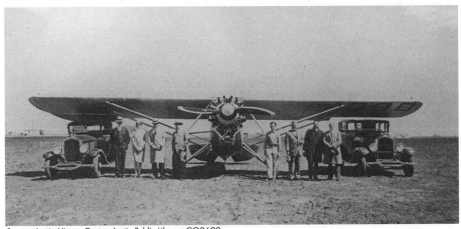

Austin city officials greet airline executives at the inauguration of scheduled airline passenger service on March 30, 1929. The Texas Air Transport Travelair 6000 cabin monoplane operated from Dallas to Brownsville, with intermediate stops at Waco, Austin, San Antonio, and Corpus Christi.

A ten-passenger Long & Harmon Airlines Ford Tri-Motor, the first multiengine aircraft to serve Austin, takes off from University Airport. The company inaugurated airliner service on February 23, 1931.

Source: Austin History Center, Austin Public Library, CO3144.

Visitors inspect United States Army Air Corps bombers at the dedication of Robert Mueller Municipal Airport on October 14, 1930. One year later Texas had 133 municipal airports. By 1932, that number had increased to 141.

Source: Austin History Center, Austin Public Library, PICA 03771.

A Braniff Airways Lockheed "Electra" parked at Austin's first airport terminal, located on East Fifty-first Street. The ten-place, 190-mph "Electra" represented the airline industry's increasing use of safer and more efficient multiengine aircraft.

CHAPTER 1

CAL, GLENN, BENNY, AND THE ORIGINS OF AUSTIN AVIATION

IT was an odd conglomerate; excitement pervaded the onrush of humanity. Some came walking, while others arrived on horseback and in buggies, hacks, and carriages; a few drove automobiles. By mid-morning they had begun filling up the open spaces of Ridge Top Annex, north Austin's newest real estate development.[1] All came to witness the newest phenomenon of the twentieth century—a man flying an airplane.

News accounts of Calbraith Rodgers' transcontinental flight had fascinated Austin readers since he departed Sheepshead Bay, New York, on September 17. As he flew west toward Chicago, the *Austin Daily Statesman* reported his progress crash by crash. And by the time Rodgers reached Kansas City on October 11, further local news coverage had heightened the interest of Austin readers. With Rodgers following the Katy Railroad tracks southward to San Antonio, his route would take him over Austin. So the city waited.

A hastily arranged meeting between Lawrence Peters, Rodgers' representative, and members of the Austin Business League assured the celebrated aviator's Austin visit. It was a meeting of common interests; Rodgers needed money and W. T. Caswell Jr. wanted to sell some city lots. For a $200 fee raised by Caswell and other Austin business leaders, Rodgers agreed to land at the Ridge Top Annex.[2] The guarantee thus assured Rodgers' appearance in Austin, if only briefly. He would land the Vin-Fiz at the real estate development, refuel the aircraft, have lunch, make a brief public appearance, and continue his flight. That alone would be sufficient to satisfy the people's desire to see an airplane, something they had never seen before.

To accommodate what was estimated to be the largest public gathering in Austin's history, the Austin Electric Railway Company scheduled twenty-three extra streetcars on the Hyde Park line, to run at six-minute intervals. Most spectators exited the cars at the Avenue G and Forty-third Street intersection and hurriedly embarked on the half-mile walk to Ridge Top Annex. To manage the excited throng, the Austin mayor dispatched to the landing site a cadre of police, who, by noon, began herding the spectators into a huge rectangle, protecting a large area in the center of the annex for Rodgers to land the Vin-Fiz. And still they waited.

The local telephone companies, in cooperation with the *Statesman,* positioned representatives along the in-coming route to report Rodgers' progress. Carried forward at the rate of sixty-five miles an hour by a light tail wind, he flew over Temple and landed at Granger for a brief fuel stop. At approximately 1:15 P.M., the whistle at the water and light plant heralded Rodgers' arrival at the Capital City. He approached the Ridge Top site, made several wide circles, identified the landing area, and glided gracefully to the earth. Instantly masses of people swarmed in from every direction. "It was a race from all sides of the compass," the *Statesman* reported, "with the man-bird and his craft as the goal." Austin businessman C. N. Avery rescued Rodgers from the onrush and welcomed him to Austin.[3]

Avery immediately became the envy of everyone in a wall of humanity fifteen-feet deep, each clamoring for a closer view of the "man bird" and the machine that bore him to Austin. When it appeared the fragile craft might be crushed by the onslaught, half a dozen policemen forced their way through the throng and roped off the craft to avoid damage. Rogers, not known for his verbosity, quickly warmed to his audience and provided some details of his incoming flight. From time to time, total strangers would force their way to the celebrated aviator and grab his hand for a personal introduction.

Subsequently, when two men with large gasoline cans began refueling the aircraft, the crowd realized Rodgers' visit was nearing an end. Armed with his $200 check, he completed his preflight inspection of the Vin-Fiz, climbed into his seat, and signaled to his mechanic to start the engine. As the police forced the reluctant crowd to a safe distance from the Vin-Fiz, the aircraft was wheeled to the west side of the landing area and pointed east. At approximately 3:15 P.M., Rodgers again took to the air and, after climbing to about four hundred feet, circled back over the crowd and headed south toward downtown Austin. Reaching an altitude of approximately two thousand feet, he circled the Capitol building, turned south once again, and disappeared against a dark cloud bank.

As Rodgers flew southward toward San Antonio, had he been clairvoyant, he might have read into the ominous overcast a dark premonition of what lay ahead. An all-too-familiar scenario was about to repeat itself. Some fifteen miles south of Austin, Rodgers heard a loud bang. His engine began vibrating violently, and then stopped. Flying over fairly level terrain, he managed to glide to a comparatively safe landing in a cotton field. However, damage to the engine was substantial. Rodgers' mechanic worked most of the night without success and finally decided to replace the damaged engine with a spare one carried on board the accompanying train. When that engine did not function properly, maintenance continued throughout the following day. Finally, on Sunday morning, October 22, when everything appeared to be ready, Rodgers took off from the cotton field and continued on his transcontinental flight.

During the course of his coast-to-coast flight, Rodgers, probably unknowingly, was spreading the gospel of flight among hundreds of thousands of Americans who had never before seen an airplane. Once they did, their enthusiasm was as great as that generated in Austin, Texas. A minister observing the public's reaction to the first airplane to fly over Chicago wrote, "Never have I seen such a look of wonder in the faces of the multitude. From the gray-haired man to the child, everyone seemed to feel that it was a new day in their lives." [4] For the next half-century, the nation would be adjusting its lifestyle in an ever-changing society conditioned by a growing dependence on the airplane.

In American culture, no innovation gave rise to as much public fascination as men flying airplanes. The excitement of seeing the first train or the first automobile was far less thrilling than the initial vision of men in flight. The very act of a human being leaving the earth under supplementary power was, in itself, almost beyond comprehension, and, with the likelihood of failure—falling to one's death—added to the equation, it touched on one of the strongest elements of human response, self-preservation. Thus, when the masses of earthlings looked skyward to the courageous young men in their fragile flying machines, they vicariously experienced the thrill and danger of flight while still enjoying earth's security. And so, wherever men with wings appeared, an enthusiastic crowd was sure to follow.

The business and civic communities quickly recognized the economic potential of the public's fascination with aviation. William Randolph Hearst, J. Ogden Armour, as well as W. T. Caswell Jr., all reaped the benefits of using the airplane to market their products. Inevitably, an opportunist would envision the flying exhibition as itself a marketable commodity. Glenn Hammond Curtiss was an inventor, a mechanic, a designer and builder of airplanes, an accomplished pilot, and an enterprising businessman. In September 1910, he launched the Curtiss Exhibition Company to capitalize on the interest of an eagerly awaiting public. According to a business associate, the company grossed over $1 million in three years.[5] The *Austin Daily Statesman,* whose publisher foresaw opportunity in co-sponsoring a flying exhibition, became one of the company's clients. Joining the Austin Girls' Co-Operative Home in a fund-raising project, the *Statesman* signed a $2,500 contract with the Curtiss Exhibition Company for a two-day show to be held at Camp Mabry on November 21 and 22, 1911.[6]

Austinites first read of the forthcoming event on Sunday, November 5. The front page headline states, "Two Curtiss Flyers Will Give Exhibition Under Auspices of the Statesman." For the next nineteen days, the upcoming exposition dominated local news coverage. Subsequent issues focused on aviation's emerging personalities (such as Beckwith Havens, the youthful glamour boy of the Curtiss troupe), their stunt repertoire (dives, loops, turns, and spins), the dangers of flying (the Curtiss staff was losing a pilot a month), the airplane's potential for carrying the United States mail, and Camp Mabry as possibly Austin's future landing field (the term "municipal airport" was not yet in current use).

Advance members of the Curtiss Exhibition troupe began arriving in

Austin early Monday morning, November 20. The mechanical staff embarked immediately for Camp Mabry and began uncrating and assembling the aircraft for the first show the following day.

Because Camp Mabry was then well outside the city limits, public access posed a problem. However, the International and Great Northern Railroad provided the most convenient form of transportation. On opening day, hours before the first scheduled flight, crowds were standing in line at the Congress Avenue railroad station to purchase tickets for the three-mile ride to Camp Mabry. The early arrivals headed immediately for the two aircraft, parked beneath two huge oak trees. There was great excitement, and to add interest to the event, Curtiss aircraft mechanics were present to answer visitors' questions, like "How does this thing work?" But an even greater thrill came with the arrival of the two aviators. Much to the spectators' surprise, they discovered that pilots Charles F. Walsh and Beckwith Havens "are much the same as other men in general characteristics . . . Havens smokes cigarettes and Walsh persists in wearing goggles when he aviates. Both men enjoy automobile riding and wrestling matches, and are like other humans in their likes and dislikes."[7]

On this particular day as the time drew near for the first flight, the crowd began moving toward the grandstand, where the aircraft had been moved pending the beginning of the show. It was indeed a festive event; Texas governor Oscar Colquitt attended the exhibition to officially welcome the two aviators to Austin. Following his official greeting, the pilots announced they were ready to begin the flights. Essentially, this was a bad omen; by then it was nearly four o'clock, but the flying was originally scheduled to begin forty-five minutes earlier. In that time, the sky had become overcast and the wind was gusting to twenty miles per hour. For light aircraft—and these were light aircraft—such conditions are hazardous. However, the air show went on, but not as the *Statesman* had predicted. Turbulence and low ceilings greatly restricted the flight plans. Beckwith Havens made no aerial carnation drops to the ladies, there was no airmail demonstration, nor were any new aviation records established. It had not been a good day for flying.

In view of the exhibition's disastrous beginning, someone in authority, hoping to financially salvage the project, apparently decided to marshal local forces and succeeded in securing widespread cooperation. For the show's final day, the post office cancelled all afternoon deliveries so that carriers and other postal employees could attend the exhibition. Superintendent of Schools A. N. McCallum announced that classes would be dismissed an hour early to allow both teachers and students to take advantage of the rare educational opportunity, and several local businessmen declared a half-holiday. The newspaper itself announced half-price admission for the final show. Those combined efforts might have helped salvage the event, but the weather did not cooperate: low clouds, fog, and light rain blanketed Camp Mabry the following day. According to the *Statesman,* the final show was limited to only fifteen minutes of "aerial caper-cutting."

And so the highly publicized Camp Mabry flying exhibition came to a close, and according to the newspaper, "Everybody was pleased with the big show."[8] There was no follow-up assessment of the exhibition, but it presumably fell far short of its financial goal and certainly failed to provide the numerous aerial escapades promised in the advance publicity. Nevertheless, it was a worthwhile endeavor, achieving a margin of success. In 1911, simply seeing an airplane either on the ground or in flight was a stimulating and enlightening experience, and the citizens of Austin and Central Texas also emerged with a new awareness of aviation and the airplane's potential in an unforeseeable future. But most important for Austin aviation, praise of the Camp Mabry field by the Curtiss Exhibition staff implanted in the minds of many civic leaders the idea of using it as the city's permanent landing site, an idea that would continue to generate interest for years to come. Unquestionably, the *Austin Daily Statesman* flying exhibition of 1911 touched many lives in many ways. It would be long remembered.

Four years passed before Austin citizens would again see the sights and hear the sounds of men in flight.[9] In the meantime, aviation remained a primary topic of interest; *Statesman* headlines regularly alerted its readers to ongoing aerial activities, especially those ending in tragedy.

Phil Parmalee Falls 400 Feet to His Death (6/2/1912)
Two Army Men Crushed When Airship Falls (6/12/1912)
Another Aviation Accident in the Army School (6/25/1912)

Amid the specter of tragedy, civic leaders remained cognizant of aviation's public appeal. On January 6, 1913, the *Statesman* announced a proposed cooperative undertaking between the Austin and San Antonio chambers of commerce: "Aviator Hamilton" would fly from San Antonio to Austin, "circle over the city at 3,000 feet, land in some central place and later give some exhibition flights. The matter has been referred to the carnival committee."[10] Since nothing further was heard of "Aviator Hamilton," it can be assumed the matter remained in committee.

During the three years that separated the Camp Mabry air show and the outbreak of war in Europe, military strategists began defining new roles for aircraft. The Europeans, locked in political unrest, led the way. "A decade after the Wrights flew at Kitty Hawk only the Germans . . . were mass producing airplanes for war," wrote aviation historian C. V. Glines. When Germany declared war, it had 500 military aircraft in inventory, whereas "England had only 200 planes and only a portion were convertible for war purposes. German performance was equally advanced." With the development of 200-horsepower engines, German airplanes could fly a distance of 600 miles at altitudes of up to 13,000 feet, with a top speed of 200 miles per hour.[11] Thus, the following items gleaned from *Statesman* front page stories bore slight resemblance to what readers had observed at the Camp Mabry air show. The airplane had acquired a new role, warfare.

Germans drop bombs in Paris . . . A German aeroplane flying at the height of 6,000 feet over Paris dropped a bomb into the city 1:30 o'clock this morning. The bomb struck near L'Est railway station not far from military hospital, but did no damage. (8/31/1914)

Aeroplanes in battle high above Paris . . . two French machines engage three Germans but without casualties on either side. (9/3/1914)

Aerial raids on England are expected.(10/14/1914)

The activity of German aeroplanes over Paris has brought up their value in warfare and a recital of thrilling aerial duels between French and German machines. (10/15/1914)[12]

Understandably, the *Statesman* report on November 22, 1915, that the 1st Aero Squadron of the United States Army Signal Corps would arrive in Austin the following day created much excitement. Local citizens, well aware of the airplane's military application, were eager to see for the first time an aircraft bearing the United States insignia. That arrival was both a historic event and part of a historic mission. Based temporarily at Fort Sill, Oklahoma, the 1st Aero Squadron received reassignment to a permanent base, at Fort Sam Houston, Texas. When the six Curtiss JN-3 airplanes took off from Fort Sill on the morning of November 19, 1915, the event initiated "the first squadron cross-country flight in the history of the United States . . . a distance of 439 miles."[13] The officer leading the flight, Capt. Benjamin D. Foulois, and the aircraft he flew, the Curtiss JN-3, also would etch their marks in aviation history. Foulois had first flown with Orville Wright on July 30, 1909, during the initial army flight tests at Fort Myer, Virginia. Electing to remain with the aviation section of the army, he was assigned to Fort Sam Houston, along with "Aeroplane No. 1," under the remarkable orders to "evaluate the airplane" and "teach yourself to fly."[14] He did both, later advancing to the rank of major general and eventually becoming chief of the United States Army Air Corps.

The airplane Foulois flew, a Curtiss JN-3 two-place biplane, was the half-sister of the Curtiss exhibition aircraft that appeared at Camp Mabry. Britisher B. Douglas Thomas, a former Sopwith engineer, joined the Curtiss company in 1914 and helped develop the JN series of aircraft. The new tractor-type biplane (as opposed to the pusher type) combined the best features of his "J" design and the traditional Curtiss "N" model. "By the end of the war," aviation historian C. R. Roseberry explains, "it was said that 95 percent of the U.S. military pilots had handled the controls" of the venerable "Jenny."[15] In the post–World War I era, thousands of barnstormers acquired surplus Curtiss "Jennies," which, to millions of Americans, became the ubiquitous symbol of civil aviation.

Captain Foulois designated Fort Worth, Texas, as the first intermediate stop on the historic cross-country flight. From there, after refueling the six JN-3s, the squadron departed for Fort Worth by way of Waco on the morning of November 22, taking off at five-minute intervals. The lead aircraft arrived over Waco approximately one hour later. The welcome the city's citizens accorded the 1st Aero Squadron rivaled that extended to Cal Rodgers some four years earlier. The siren whistle of the Young Men's Business League announced the squadron's arrival, and spectators crowded the tops of buildings, hoping to get a better view of the airplanes. Some one thousand others had traveled out to the landing site, located about two-and-one-half miles west of the city, to welcome the aviators in person. Following their welcome by the public, the flight crews enjoyed a luncheon hosted by the Rotary Club. They remained in Waco overnight, departing for Austin the following day.

Another warm reception awaited the 1st Aero Squadron in Austin. Shortly after dawn Tuesday, November 23, people began arriving at the designated landing site, an eighty-acre field located north of the "State Asylum for the Insane."[16] Arriving in automobiles and buggies, and many on foot, they quickly lined the east and west fences that enclosed the landing area, eager to see the first military aircraft to land in the Capital City. Soon Mayor A. P. Wooldridge, four members of the city council, and Walter E. Long, secretary of the Austin Chamber of Commerce, joined the crowd, estimated at between fifteen hundred and two thousand. Together they waited, and at approximately ten-thirty, the first JN-3 came into view, closely followed by a second. They circled the field, landed, and as the pilots stepped from their aircraft they were quickly surrounded by an enthusiastic throng of well-wishers. Restrained by roped enclosures, they crowded around the two aircraft to get a closer look at the Curtiss JN-3s. Only one group of spectators was permitted inside the rope enclosures: fifty-two blind boys from the adjacent State Institution for the Blind who arrived in pairs, the partially sighted leading those totally blind. The latter, depending solely on their sense of touch, were permitted by the guards to feel the airplanes. A member of the squadron escorted the students, answering questions and explaining the function of various parts of the aircraft.

By one o'clock, when only two of the six aircraft had arrived in Austin, enthusiasm gave way to concern. According to the flight plan, all six aircraft, departing at six-minute intervals, should have already arrived in Austin. With a maximum flying time of two-and-one-half hours, the four overdue JN-3s were obviously on the ground at some unknown location. The *Statesman* launched an immediate telephone search. Staff members soon learned that one of the missing airplanes had landed at Kingsland, Texas, and two others at Lampasas; there was no news of the fourth aircraft.

A *Statesman* reporter, noting the apparently ideal flying weather, pressed one of the pilots, Lt. Thomas Milling, the last to see the missing JN-3s in flight, for an explanation of the lost aircraft. "His presumption was that the machines were swept far off their course by the strong east wind, and discovering how far off the route they were, the pilots thought best to land."[17] That incident, occurring at this early stage of military aviation, demonstrates the deficiency in basic airmanship skills. Lacking valid preflight wind data, unskilled at plotting wind correction angles, and relying on thirty-year-old geological maps for navigation, the fledgling pilots found themselves at the mercy of a strong and unexpected east wind and drifted some fifty miles off course.

Although there was apprehension in Austin for the missing aircraft, the unscheduled landings brought pleasure to many remote villagers who had never seen an airplane. The *Statesman* reported the excitement at Kingsland:

One of the aeroplanes of war flying squadron landed here today about 11:45 A.M. in a field about a half mile from town. It was the first airplane that ever flew through this country and it created quite an excitement. Everybody dropped their work and school broke up in confusion and all ran to see it. The aeroplane was driven by First Lieutenant J. C. Carberry.[18]

Lieutenant Carberry, incidentally, was the flight leader.

Eventually, with the last of the delayed aircraft safely on the ground, Mayor A. P. Wooldridge extended Austin's official greeting and announced plans for a banquet honoring the squadron members that evening in the Driskill Hotel. Following the formal dinner in the Crystal Ballroom, the mayor introduced two members of the squadron, who addressed the group. Lt. Thomas Milling spoke first, on flight safety, and Captain Foulois addressed the topic foremost on the minds of most Americans, the war in Europe and the prospects of United States involvement. The captain explained that "army men were less in favor of war and more in favor of adequate defense than the average citizen." He then alluded to the political regionalism that was currently impeding passage of a military appropriation bill in Congress, noting that "the only real opposition which is developing against preparedness is in the Middle West, where people feel secure against the effects of a possible invasion."[19]

When the squadron flight crews arrived at the field the following morning and prepared for takeoff, they experienced another problem that will plague aviation as long as anyone flies airplanes—the weather. Faced with a fifty-mile-an-hour southwest head wind and a blanket of low hanging clouds, Captain Foulois delayed the departure. The *Statesman* announced the delay in nautical terms: "Aviators Postpone Sailing." That was a great disappointment for the crowd who arrived at the field early to witness the takeoff. Captain Foulois told Mayor Wooldridge, present also for the expected departure, that he would get in touch with him at least one hour prior to takeoff. The mayor received no word from Captain Foulois that day, nor the following day; the inclement weather continued. Finally, on Friday morning, November 26, the announcement came. At eight o'clock, the squadron took off on the final leg of its historic cross-country flight. Lieutenant Carberry, the flight leader, landed on the Fort Sam Houston maneuver field at 9:20 A.M. The remaining five JN-3s soon followed.

The cross-country mission complete, Captain Foulois' date with history was far from over, his tenure at Fort Sam Houston unexpectedly brief. On March 11, 1916, three days after Francisco "Pancho" Villa raided Columbus, New Mexico, Captain Foulois received orders for the 1st Aero Squadron to join Pershing's Punitive Expedition into Mexico. As the proving ground for military aviation, the JN-3s fell far short of expectations. Terrain, altitude, and aridity all took their toll on the underpowered aircraft. After one month in Mexico, none of the eight original "Jennies" were flyable.[20] The operation, however, was not without merit; Captain Foulois stated he considered "the experience of our eight-plane air force to have been a vital milestone in the development of military aviation in this country."[21] The Mexico assignment also hastened the appearance of the venerable Curtiss JN-4 as the replacement of the ill-fated JN-3.

The administrative skills Captain Foulois exhibited, especially during the Pershing Expedition, led to his being reassigned to Washington to help reorganize the United States Army's aviation section. Facing the likelihood of this nation's involvement in the European war, he returned to Texas on a priority assignment to locate a permanent facility for organizing, training, and operating new air units. He chose a site near San Antonio, which became Kelly Field. Following the declaration of war, the University of Texas responded to the national emergency by establishing the School of Military Aeronautics. As the program developed, Kelly Field and the Curtiss JN-4, two enduring reminders of General Foulois' military vision, emerged as important factors in that undertaking.

CHAPTER 2

AUSTIN, THE UNIVERSITY OF TEXAS, AND WORLD WAR I

C APT. Benjamin D. Foulois' experience with the 1st Aero Squadron in Mexico served mainly to reinforce what he already knew: United States military air power was virtually nonexistent. This fact, when viewed within the growing prospect of war, created deep concern among the members of the Aviation Section of the Army Signal Corps. Unfortunately, they represented a minority; the United States still languished in a state of isolationist bliss.

The Atlantic Ocean provided both a real and a psychological barrier against the war in Europe. In August 1914, when President Woodrow Wilson proclaimed U.S. neutrality, he in essence enacted the will of the people. "The American people, with few exceptions, took it for granted that they would have no part of the war," wrote historian Ernest R. May. "Most Europeans agreed. . . . What made America's situation exceptional was the country's geographical remoteness, pacifist and isolationist traditions, and enormous latent power."[1] Geographic remoteness probably provided the greater psychological security. Texas congressman Martin Dies articulated that perspective: "Europe is on fire all right, but there is about 3,000 miles of Atlantic Ocean between us and the conflagration."[2]

Europe had indeed experienced the fire of battle. Five million men had died in two-and-one-half years of fighting, and four million remained burrowed in trench works that stretched from the English Channel to the Swiss border. After repeated attack and counterattack, the battle lines appeared immovable. Viewing this stalemate from afar, President Woodrow Wilson, walking a diplomatic tightrope, attempted to negotiate a "peace without victory" among the belligerents. The proposal received both British and German endorsement. However, Germany concurred, with a condition: unrestricted submarine warfare would continue. So did the war. Such was the political environment that greeted Captain Foulois when he arrived in Washington.

Gen. George O. Squier, the army's chief signal officer, called Foulois to Washington to serve as his deputy in September 1916. As the only senior flight officer with tactical field experience, Foulois' primary assignment was to aid General Squier in reorganizing the Aviation Section of the Signal Corps. They faced a formidable task. "It is almost impossible to realize now the utter unpreparedness of the United States in 1917," Foulois wrote later. "Germany had entered the war with nearly 1,000 planes, France with about 300, and England with about 250. We not only had less than 100, but ours were already obsolete and not a single one was suitable for combat."[3] As international tension mounted, Congress, after years of neglect, faced the task of trying to buy time with money—much money, $640 million. While Congress grappled with that unprecedented aviation appropriation, Foulois encountered his strongest and most intractable opposition in the War College Division of the General Staff. "They were tied to the ground forces," Foulois remembered, "had never seen the airplane in a combat role, and had no conception of the uses to which an airplane could be put to assist in the ground war."[4]

While Congress debated and the American people enjoyed the protection afforded by the Atlantic Ocean, the United States drifted toward the inevitable. The pace quickened, however. The turning point in Wilson's diplomatic crusade came when he received a copy of a secret telegram, deciphered by the British, that German foreign minister Arthur Zimmermann sent to his ambassador in Mexico. It proposed Mexico join Germany in war against the United States in return for restitution after the war of territories lost to Mexico in New Mexico, Texas, and Arizona. "The President thus had before him a document of unquestionable authenticity," wrote May, "indicating that Germany preferred war to abandonment of the U-boat campaign."[5] On February 3, 1917, President Wilson severed relations with Germany. The national war psychology was quickly changing. Publication of the Zimmermann telegram on March 1 launched a nationwide demand for war with Germany. Still Wilson hesitated; he was the president "who kept us out of war."[6] However, when German U-boats sank three United States merchant vessels with a huge loss of life, Wilson had no choice but to act. On April 6, 1917, the United States declared war on Germany. Seventeen days later W. F. Durand, chairman of the National Advisory Committee for Aeronautics, invited presidents of six major universities to a conference on the education of officers for the United States Air Service.[7] Dr. Robert E. Vinson, president of the University of Texas, accepted the invitation.

The military's appeal to academia was the call of a nation in crisis. The United States was at war, yet sadly lacked the men and material with which battles are won. It was a period of great awakening. News from Europe continued to document the growing importance of the airplane in modern warfare, yet the military had neither staff nor facilities to train young airmen for war. In that moment of crisis, the United States looked to Great Britain for a solution. The Royal Flying Corps (RFC) had taken over the University of Oxford for the preliminary training of Air Service officers and had established a similar program in Canada at the University of Toronto. The meeting Dr. Vinson attended in Washington, D.C., on the morning of April 30, 1917, focused on the University of Toronto program. The six university presidents heard the proposal and responded positively. Each agreed to send three representatives to Toronto to take a one-month course at the RFC ground school. Then they would return to their respective campuses and establish similar programs to prepare United States Army Air Service cadets for flight training.

President Vinson moved with dispatch. That night, April 30, he telegraphed F. W. Graff, secretary of the University of Texas, informing him that the university would establish an aeronautics school in cooperation with the Southern Department of the United States Army. Dr. Vinson requested that Graff select six faculty members to report to him in Washington, prepared to go immediately to Toronto for one-month intensive training in elementary aeronautics. He added that the training would not involve actual flying and all expenses would be refunded by the government.[8] Dr. Vinson subsequently changed his directive. Instead of six representatives, he selected only three, and, rather than report to him in Washington, D.C., they were to proceed directly to Toronto.

The three professors selected to represent the University of Texas were S. L. Brown, adjunct professor of physics; J. M. Bryant, professor of electrical engineering; and T. S. Painter, adjunct professor of zoology.[9] They departed Austin on May 2, 1917, and reported to RFC headquarters in Toronto on Monday, May 7. Col. Hiram Bingham, former Yale University professor and chairman of the United States Commission to the Toronto Royal Flying Corps, greeted the eighteen university representatives. He explained they were temporarily appointed as aeronautical engineers, as well as official members of the commission. Each representative received a copy of a letter from W. F. Durand that outlined the objectives of the conference. The professors quickly realized they were treading on virgin soil. As academics with no knowledge of aviation, it was their responsibility to develop a course of study to train Air Service cadets. And there was another problem: because of the wartime emergency, the original month-long session had been reduced to only three days.

During the ensuing seventy-two hours, the professors were barraged with unfamiliar materials and information. Tremendous responsibility lay ahead. They, as civilians, had to create a learning environment designed to launch thousands of young student pilots on military assignments fraught with inestimable danger. Thus, their daily regimen in Toronto encompassed all phases of Air Service technology: aerial reconnaissance, map reading, artillery observation, bombs and bomb sights, machine guns, radio telegraphy, aircraft engines, aircraft rigging, aerodynamics, theory of flight, and military discipline. In addition, they were to select textbooks, plus other instructional material, which in many cases was still in the elementary stages of development. In designing that course of study, Colonel Bingham insisted that the participating universities strive for uniformity in both instruction and evaluation.

The stringent regimen the delegates followed included serving on various committees and subcommittees, visiting RFC training facilities, and attending seemingly endless lectures. At one session a Major Allen of the Royal Flying Corps, who was addressing the delegation on Cadet Wing Organization, commented on the time constraints of ground school: "You must stuff the boys, you cannot educate them properly." A Lieutenant Pack, in charge of the Cadet Course at Toronto, explained the testing and evaluation policy. The Royal Flying Corps required a 60 percent average for passing, and if a cadet "does not pay attention, listen to his instructors, keep up in drill, etc., drop [him]." The lieutenant, emphasizing the necessity for discipline, issued a specific word of warning to the visiting professors: "American boys are accustomed to run their families and must be broken of this." Colonel Bingham added that the "high-strung, nervous type that easily gets rattled," the immature type, and the "fresh, smart, overconfident men" should be considered ineligible for flight training.

In choosing instructors for the university-sponsored ground schools, Lieutenant Pack recommended supplementing current faculty members with military personnel. In response to questions from delegates about compensation for military personnel, Colonel Bingham explained that it would be paid by the government. He requested the university delegates provide immediately the number of military personnel that would be required by each program and the earliest date they should report for duty. He emphasized that their presence at the outset was essential since the initial teaching responsibilities would be in the areas of military drill, physical drill, and army regulations.

Urgency remained the dominant theme of the Toronto conference. The army currently had a backlog of between three and four hundred cadet candidates awaiting ground school assignment, while some six hundred others were presently being qualified. Dr. Bryant reported the University of Texas could begin instruction almost immediately. He telegraphed President R. C. Vinson at the end of the second day of the conference, "Have offered the War Department twenty-five enlisted men [cadets] per week immediately after our return." [10] When questioned about the availability of instructional material, Colonel Bingham explained instruction could begin without textbooks, but military drill books were available. To supplement the training manual, the colonel urged the delegates to obtain copies of lectures, mimeographed notes, and similar materials compiled during the three-day conference.

The final meeting was held in the King Edward Hotel at eight o'clock on the evening of May 9, 1917. Each committee gave its summary report, and the meeting adjourned shortly after nine. The Texas delegation returned to Austin on May 14 and met immediately with President Vinson. He appointed Dr. Bryant chairman of the University of Texas School of Military Aeronautics and relieved all three professors of other academic responsibilities.[11] The president further empowered them to begin making the necessary arrangements to open the new school. That included cadet housing, food service, classrooms, laboratories, and drill facilities, plus assembling a teaching faculty. A formidable task lay before them.

Within twenty-four hours of his appointment, Dr. Bryant had established headquarters for the new school in the Engineering Building and assembled a fourteen-member civilian faculty. He was to serve as dean of instruction and instructor in Theory of Flight, Dr. Painter was to teach Map Reading and Artillery Observation, and Dr. Brown to head the division of Wireless and Signals. The remainder of the civilian staff was drawn from the University faculty roster. Capt. Ralph D. Cousins, whom the army assigned as military commandant, arrived on campus on May 18. Percy Pennybacker, recently discharged from the Texas National Guard, became Officer in Charge of Drill. He was later replaced by L. Theo Bellmont.[12] With staff and temporary facilities in place, all that remained was the arrival of the first cadet. On May 19, just five days after the delegates returned from Toronto, Edgar G. Tobin presented his credentials to Captain Cousins. Tobin would be the first of 5,958 cadets admitted to the ground school of the University of Texas School of Military Aeronautics.[13] At that moment, Cadet Tobin, probably unknowingly, achieved a small niche in the annals of Texas aviation history.

Cadet Tobin's moment of glory was short-lived. The school opened officially on May 21, 1917, but instead of the twenty-three cadets expected, only eight joined Tobin in the School of Military Aeronautics. That was welcome relief for Dr. Bryant, who still faced a multitude of problems. With University facilities already occupied by civilian students, the School of Military Aeronautics had to seek alternate accommodations. University officials arranged for the nearby Presbyterian Theological Seminary to temporarily quarter and feed the first three squadrons. In addition to the housing problem, cadet clothing had not been received, nor had the allotted cots and bedding, and Captain Cousins reported a lack of government forms required to report and monitor the operation. And there were other shortages. "The University did not receive the expected equipment or instructional matter from the Government promptly," Dr. Bryant reported later. "On June 7th we had received no engines or airplanes, though Senior Wing work was to start June 11th. Happily, three engines and two airplanes arrived Saturday, June 9th, and the first class unpacked these and began work on scheduled time." Machine gun equipment did not arrive until one week later; consequently, that instruction had to be omitted by the first squadron.

Space allotment continued to be a problem. With the spring semester already under way, the University administration reassigned to the ground school many classrooms, laboratories, and offices previously occupied by civilian students and the general faculty. The matter was easily resolved, as everyone was eager to sacrifice personal convenience for the war effort. Cadets reported for academic instruction in the Electrical Engineering Building and attended laboratory sessions in the University gymnasium and the Power Building. On June 9, when University students vacated Brackenridge Hall for the summer, the problem of living accommodation appeared temporarily solved: that facility became the regular cadet barracks. Amenities, however, were limited. The cadets had to take showers in the University gymnasium, while the YMCA offered the use of their swimming pool and reading room in the YMCA building. When the cadet population later exceeded "B" Hall capacity, the University provided additional accommodations in the Zoological Shack—"L" Hall—and in the Law Building.

By June 11, 1917, when the first squadron entered the Senior Wing, most of the difficulties had been resolved, though not the lack of equipment and a civilian teaching staff generally unskilled in some subject areas. However, the school curriculum proved to be the instructors' immediate ally. Because the first three weeks of ground school were devoted largely to military instruction, the civilian instructors had an opportunity to collect additional data for lectures and secure equipment for laboratory demonstration. Also, the government gained more time to deliver the much-needed equipment to the school.

As the United States' commitment to the war effort increased, so did the need for additional manpower in the military. Ground school enrollment reflected that need. Originally, the School of Military Aeronautics was to receive 25 cadets each week for an eight-week course, with 200 cadets in each squadron. By early June, the number of cadets in ground school was 235, the weekly enrollment having risen to 35. Apparently taking note of the school's progress, Colonel Hiram Bingham on July 26 telegraphed Captain

Cousins that "your school will be gradually enlarging up to 400 and should reach that total by September 8. You may expect about 50 men per week commencing August 6."

Space remained an ongoing problem. When "B" Hall could no longer accommodate the growing cadet population, President Vinson appealed to the Texas legislature for use of the former State Blind Institute facility, a group of vacant structures located two blocks east of the University campus. The legislature, in turn, gave the University free use of the facility. Renovation began in August, and on September 21, 1917, the School of Military Aeronautics moved to what became known as "Little Campus." [14] The original plan was to house 500 cadets at the new facility; however, on September 18, three days before the planned transfer, Colonel Bingham telegraphed President Vinson, "Can you . . . receive [125 cadets] per week beginning November [17] . . . Please wire reply." On September 20, the president replied, "Contracts for necessary additions [to Little Campus] have been let. Preparations will be completed in time for additional men November [17]." The president fulfilled his promise; by mid-January some 1,130 cadets were registered in the ground school.

Fluctuating class size created another headache for the teaching staff. On January 19, 1918, for example, 150 cadets entered the school, but only 28 men reported one week later. For the next six weeks, excepting the week of February 16, the number of new arrivals exceeded the 125 mark. However, beginning on March 23, weekly entrants fell short of that mark by some 50 to 75 men. Therefore, maintaining an adequate teaching staff with ever-changing class sizes created a scheduling problem for Dr. Bryant. Also, the lack of teaching equipment for the various departments remained a source of great frustration. On July 21, 1917, with 235 cadets enrolled, the instructional staff was limited to one Lewis machine gun, three Curtiss OX-5 engines, two Martin airplanes, and miscellaneous parts of a third airplane. As Dr. Bryant wryly observed, "The difficulty of teaching a class of 50 students the mechanism of the Lewis Machine Gun with only one gun will be readily appreciated." By early September, additional equipment began arriving, including nine Lewis machine guns, an additional Curtiss engine, and another airplane (a Curtiss). On October 1, the school received twenty-eight additional Lewis machine guns.

Air Service cadets led a busy life at the University of Texas. During the first three weeks of the course, the cadets drilled four hours each day, except Saturday and Sunday, and spent half an hour each day doing calisthenics and a similar amount of time in military ceremonial formations. On reaching Senior Wing level, they drilled only one hour each day, although calisthenics and ceremonials continued as before. Their course work, which consisted of both lecture and laboratory sections, included engines, theory of flight, cross country and general flying, signals (Morse code), gunnery, and aerial observation. For the latter course, the instructional staff developed a unique teaching tool, designed to give cadets a simulated experience in aerial observation. Since probably none of the cadets had ever flown in an airplane, the undertaking was challenging, yet one that, with all its limitations, better equipped the young airman for the task that lay ahead. The so-called flight simulator consisted of a rolling map of a portion of Belgium as seen from an altitude of five thousand feet. The map measured 12' × 19' × 38' and was mounted on rollers turned by an electric motor. The "simulator" operated as follows:

> Plumb bobs were suspended from the ceiling and hung over various parts of the country [Belgium]; each cadet was assigned to one particular plumb bob, which represented his airplane. As the country rolled under him, so to speak, the cadet was required to plot the course his airplane followed, and to pinpoint all cross roads, or objects which he observed . . . When his airplane entered a "cloud," the direction was changed so that the cadet had to orient his man [pilot] anew. This rolling map was a very valuable model for Map instruction.

The size of the instructional staff varied with the ever-changing number of cadets. During the some twenty months of operation, nearly 170 different instructors taught in the ground school. Of that total, just over 100 were military personnel (mostly privates or noncommissioned officers) and the rest civilians. Peak activity occurred between December 1917 and September 1918, when the School of Military Aeronautics staff averaged 113 instructors. By January 1919, just before the school closed, teaching personnel had decreased to 46. Because of age, physical disabilities, or dependents, none of the civilian instructors were subject to call by the draft; all had received deferred classification by their respective draft boards. To improve staff proficiency, the Academic Board dispatched various instructors to other ground schools or neighboring flying fields for in-service training. However, during periods of apprenticeship, instructors received no salary. The School of Military Aeronautics compensation, when viewed from a contemporary perspective, appears pitifully small; instructors received $100 a month (some received less), and division heads, $250. In the case of army privates, the University paid the difference between their military pay and what they would have received as civilians.

Whether in class, in the dormitory, at mess, or on the drill field, the School of Military Aeronautics cadet lived an ordered and highly disciplined life, following a well-defined schedule of events. Passing from Junior Wing to Senior Wing brought a major change in the cadet's life. The long-anticipated Saturday night pass marked the rite of passage. Cadets possessing it could attend movies at the YMCA and swimming parties at either Barton Springs or Deep Eddy, with picnic supper provided by the mess officer. Music and laughter also became part of Senior Wing life. Cadets wrote, produced, and performed in vaudeville shows, and each day at the end of calisthenics, the entire cadet corps assembled around a platform on the drill field, where a song leader led group singing. Following retreat, the entire cadet body sang "The Star Spangled Banner." Some former School of Military Aeronautics cadets long remembered the nameless "B" Hall bugler who provided his individual brand of humor for the cadets. Since he frequently played reveille in early morning darkness, he omitted the usual necessity to dress, giving his unpopular performances in the nude. That unusual spectacle went undetected until an early-rising professor took careful note of the source of reveille. Subsequent performances were given in full uniform.[15]

Cordial relations developed between the student body and the Austin community. Various private clubs were open free to the men, and church and community groups offered programs to entertain the cadets. That mutual bond of affection was well demonstrated during periods of emergencies. On February 1, 1918, when fire broke out in the adjacent Austin Sanitarium (now Brackenridge Hospital), cadets were released to aid in the evacuation of patients and equipment from the burning building.

At last came the day for which all cadets had waited—graduation. Amid the pomp and ceremony conducted according to military tradition, the cadets spent their final days in celebration. It all began on Friday evening of graduation week with an elaborate ceremony in which a member of the cadet corps presented the post commandant with a pictorial crest representing the spirit and thought of that particular squadron. For the Senior Wing, that event signaled the end of ground school. The following day the graduating class, led by the Drum and Bugle Corps, marched to the train station to depart for Kelly Field near San Antonio, where the primary flying school of the Army Air Service was located. Kelly Field became the destination for most School of Military Aeronautics graduates.

With the rapid growth of aviation and radio technologies, it was inevitable that they would play increasingly important roles, both singly and together, in the ongoing conflict. The School of Military Aeronautics curriculum reflected that technological bonding; Air Service cadets were learning to send and receive radio messages by Morse code. When the source of technical manpower failed to keep pace with the nation's increasing troop commitments, the government called for an additional fifteen thousand radio operators. The University of Texas responded by establishing a radio night school course, offered through the Engineering Department and especially for men subject to being called into military service. To stimulate enrollment, the University allowed students to drop other courses in order to take the radio course. The school opened on December 10, 1917. Dr. S. L. Brown, who transferred from the School of Military Aeronautics, headed the instructional staff; Dean T. U. Taylor of the Engineering School administered the program. The course was free and classes met at 7:30 P.M. daily except Monday. By December 22, the course had an enrollment of 193 students.[16]

The University was destined to play an even larger role in the war effort. On January 19, 1918, University president Robert E. Vinson and presidents of one hundred twenty other colleges and universities met jointly in Washington with representatives of the Federal Board on Vocational Education and the War Department. Simple economy again prompted the government to turn to colleges and universities, with their established staffs and facilities, to help in wartime training. When informed the government needed some three hundred thousand mechanics and technicians for military service, President Vinson offered to take twelve hundred vocational students, who would be drawn from military draft rolls.[17] That new wave of trainees fell within two categories: automobile mechanics and radio technicians. On March 19, 1918, a Captain Moderhak arrived in Austin to serve as commanding officer of the new government radio school, the Air Service School for Radio Operators, which became part of the School of Military Aeronautics. Instruction began on Monday, April 1, with 109 cadets in the initial class. Enrollment in the eleven-week course was expected to reach 300 by that weekend. Instruction focused on operating radio equipment installed in military aircraft.[18]

The Air Service School for Radio Operators was well underway by June 22, when 190 students in wireless telephone and ground telegraphy reported to 29 instructors. One week later the ratio of students to instructors had reached 299 to 31, and by August 31 it was 470 to 48.[19] Dr. Brown, president of the Academic Board, faced problems similar to those he encountered initially in organizing the School of Military Aeronautics: lack of equipment and uncertain weekly enrollment. However, in his July 8 Weekly Progress Report to the commanding officer, he cited a new problem—student incompetence. Dr. Brown noted that performance tests administered to new students indicated they were unable to perform the work beyond the fourth week of the course. In addition, the school was grossly short of instructional material; they needed more head sets for code practice, more microammeters, and more radio ammeters. Dr. Brown also complained to the commanding officer that the teaching staff was greatly handicapped in advance planning: "they do not know whether they should plan for three hundred or three thousand [students]."

The low achievement level of incoming students remained Dr. Brown's primary concern. In the July 27, 1918, entering class, he noted, only one student had attended college, four were high school graduates, seven reported some high school work, one attended grammar school, and one had had no schooling. As a professional educator, Dr. Brown turned to remedial methods to aid the less competent, which resulted in a measure of success. On July 15, he had projected radio school graduation figures as follows: fifty men on July 20, fifty on July 27, thirty on August 31, thirty on September 7, twenty-five on September 14, fifty on September 21; and fifty on September 28. Considering the total number of entering students, the attrition rate remained substantial.[20]

By that time, Austin citizens were well accustomed to the noise of aircraft engines. The presence of military aircraft, closely allied with the University's wartime mission, resulted primarily from the work of Austin Chamber of Commerce manager Walter E. Long and other Chamber members. Motivated by practical as well as patriotic purposes, Long envisioned the postwar commercial application of aviation as an essential element of urban growth and prosperity. He also recognized the benefits of pursuing those goals in conjunction with University president Vinson. Their initial collaborative achievement was the School of Military Aeronautics, later identified by the War Department as "one of the most successful (university-sponsored programs) in the country."[21] Other cooperative ventures would follow.

Walter E. Long also recognized that establishing a landing field was the initial step in bringing aviation to Austin. Acting for the Chamber, he had secured options on some 1,700 acres of land south of Austin, near what was then St. Edward's College. That plot of land included 318 acres sufficiently level for a landing field.[22] In September 1917, General Squier, as chief signal officer of the United States Army and accompanied by Col. Clinton G. Edgar, inspected the site and approved it as an alternate landing field for military aircraft on cross-country flights. Although military aircraft began using the unimproved field almost immediately, negotiations continued. On April 17, 1918, Long sent five copies of lease for the south Austin landing field to Lt. Newell Thomas at Fort Sam Houston, Texas.[23]

Long's decision to establish a military-use landing field was not without precedent. By the time the first airplane landed at the new field near Austin, seven other military-related fields were already in operation near four other Texas cities. In 1914, Dallas civic leaders purchased 600 acres of land some five miles northwest of the city, on which they persuaded the United States Air Service to establish Love Field for flight training. That same year the United States Army opened Meacham Field, five miles north of Fort Worth, as an airways station for military aircraft. In 1915, Katherine and Marjorie Stinson established Stinson Field on 500 acres of ranch land six miles south of San Antonio, where they taught Canadian students to fly. The following year the City of San Antonio took over that field as a civilian aviation facility. In 1917, the Canadian Royal Flying Corps opened Hicks Field, originally named Taliaferro Field, fourteen miles northwest of Fort Worth to train pilots for World War I. And after the United States entered the war, that field was taken over by the United States Army for flight training. Also in 1917, the army established two military fields, Brooks Field and Kelly Field, in the San Antonio area, and Ellington Field near Houston.

The Austin field, which would be named for Eugene D. Penn, a former School of Military Aeronautics graduate, had no official designation, no facilities, and some very obvious problems, specifically, an abundance of rocks and acres of corn stalks.[24] Consequently, military aircraft landing there sustained minor damages—blown tires and holes torn in the fabric covering of wings and fuselages. To solve these problems, Long turned to the Austin community, where help was immediately forthcoming. First, the city commissioners appropriated one thousand dollars, with which the Chamber of Commerce engaged local farmers to level the field with horse-drawn equipment. The surface, however, remained strewn with acres of flint rocks. For help in correcting that problem, the Chamber again appealed to the citizens' patriotic and civic pride through a newspaper item:

"All good citizens desiring to lend a patriotic hand are requested to appear at the aviation landing field south of St. Edward's College on Sunday morning at 8 o'clock with their lunch and a rake or shovel or a grubbing hoe and help make the field the safest, the best and most inviting in the country for our flyers. Old clothing and working gloves will be in order."[25]

The community responded. Max Bickler, chairman of the Chamber's aviation committee, directed the volunteer labor of 689 citizens, including farmers, ranchers, bankers, city and county officials, and school children, including 161 Boy Scouts and 246 boys from the State School for the Deaf. Together they removed 317 truckloads of rock from the field.[26]

By early 1918, the airfield had become a regular intermediate stop on formation training flights between Kelly Field and another military field near Waco. Two squadrons, comprising fifteen to twenty planes, scheduled weekly landings at the new facility. On February 24, Lt. John A. McCurdy, commander of Advanced Cross-Country and Formation Flying at Kelly Field, led a twelve-plane formation on a flight to Austin. After becoming lost in fog, eleven planes returned to Kelly Field. The other pilot, losing sight of the leader, climbed above the overcast hoping to rejoin the squadron. When that failed, he "lowered in an effort to get a glimpse of the ground through the thick haze, when suddenly two tall smoke stacks loomed through the fog ahead. The machine barely cleared the top of them and the pilot decided he could fly without seeing the ground."[27] When the fog cleared, the pilot made an emergency landing at a site north of Austin. He telephoned Walter Long for directions to the airfield, and landed there at half-past ten that morning. By one o'clock, five planes in all had landed at the new field. A reception committee headed by A. W. Griffith escorted some of the crewmembers into the city for refreshments. Subsequently, air traffic to the new "lighting field" remained brisk. According to the Austin Chamber of Commerce 1918 Report, the number of aircraft arriving from Kelly Field each day varied from six to twenty-five.[28]

University president Vinson and Chamber of Commerce manager Walter E. Long combined efforts to broaden the scope of Air Service training at the University of Texas. On July 31, 1918, the *Austin Statesman* reported that "Penn Field . . . will soon be turned into a flying field . . . This will be done in connection with the enlargement and extension of the University Radio School."[29] The following day President Vinson signed a contract between the University of Texas and the United States Army Signal Corps, authorizing the University to "provide, properly equip and maintain at or near the University of Texas . . . a Radio School, including a Flying Field of sufficient size to train and instruct such students as may be designated by the Director of Military Aeronautics." The Penn Field project represented the University's largest commitment to the wartime emergency. General contractor J. F. Johnson's $322,800 bid included eight airplane hangars of frame construction, plus six barracks buildings, one mess hall, and an administration building, all of brick construction. The University was to be reimbursed for all "reasonable expenditures," plus $2.12 per day for each man under instruction at the school and $1.00 per day for each enlisted man receiving mess and quarters at the field. Col. C. G. Edgar signed for the Signal Corps; the contract could be terminated by either party with thirty days notice.[30] In retrospect, the last provision conveyed ominous overtones.

In making his announcement, President Vinson paid silent tribute to the work of Walter E. Long and the Austin Chamber of Commerce in establishing Penn Field. Defining the school's' training mission, Dr. Vinson explained the artillery officers would be given actual experience in receiving radio messages in flight to enable them to better direct ground operations. He added that commissioned flight officers would be based at Penn Field to participate in that program.[31] There remained, however, one obstacle to launching the University's most ambitious wartime training program—money. Confronted with a $500,000 minimum budget to erect a new facility to accommodate from five hundred to two thousand additional students, Dr. Vinson sought outside funding. He turned instinctively to the University's most generous benefactor, Major George W. Littlefield. Banker, cattleman, philanthropist, and member of the University Board of Regents, Major Littlefield had previously advanced the University $300,000 to erect buildings at Camp Mabry for the University's School of Automobile Mechanics. In early September, Dr. Vinson, accompanied by H. A. Wroe, president of the Austin Chamber of Commerce and an officer in Major Littlefield's American National Bank, traveled to Baltimore to consult with the hospitalized philanthropist. They were richly rewarded for their effort. Major Littlefield loaned the University Liberty Bonds valued at a half-million dollars, which Wroe personally carried to New York to establish the loan.[32]

With funding assured, construction on the new facility was well underway when Wroe and Dr. Vinson returned to Austin. In his September 15 Weekly Progress Report, Dr. Brown noted that construction at Penn Field was being rushed with greatest possible speed. The foundations for four barracks were completed and the walls and framework of the mess hall nearly complete, as was the city water line to the field (previously, water had been hauled to the construction site). It is important to note that the use of brick in the construction of temporary wartime buildings was rare indeed. That material was selected at the insistence of Austin Chamber of Commerce manager Walter E. Long, who envisioned postwar commercial use of the structures.[33]

Expecting enrollment to more than double with the opening of the new radio-aviation school at Penn Field, the president of the Academic Board embarked in early October on a faculty-recruiting trip. Dr. Brown, however, left the campus at a most inopportune time. The October 7 Weekly Progress Report, filed by assistant W. L. Eyers, stated that the "Spanish Influenza made its first appearance at the school during this week, and class work was seriously affected. Many men, being in the hospital, failed to attend class, others attended only a day or two." By October 10, conditions had improved somewhat. "There have been no deaths for twenty-four hours," the *Austin Statesman* reported, but "forty-three new cases of influenza have developed, and seven pneumonia cases."[34]

The epidemic notwithstanding, construction at Penn Field moved rapidly ahead. By October 29, two barracks buildings were ready for occupancy, while two others were almost complete. Although the mess hall still lacked doors and windows, the kitchen equipment had been delivered and awaited installation. However, construction on the airplane hangars had not begun. The October 27 Weekly Progress Report stated that construction at the airfield had been rushed during the last week and contractors were using as many workmen as could be recruited. With no unexpected interruptions, four barracks and one school building and the mess hall would be completed by November 1, the date set for moving the school to the new location. By the time Dr. Brown filed his November 3 report, some one thousand radio students were attending class at the new school. School Building No. 29, Barracks No. 37, the mess hall, and Barracks Nos. 34, 35, and 36 were ready for occupancy. Work on the 5,500-foot railroad spur connecting the International, Great Northern Railroad with Penn Field was fast moving forward; some 150 men were driving thirty-five teams of mules grading the railroad right-of-way.

As workmen, staff, and students gave maximum effort in completing the wartime emergency project, *Austin Statesman* headlines in the fall of 1918 seemed to warn that it might be all for naught.

"Both Austria and Germany Are Ready to Yield" (10/28)
"Allies Break Last Lines of Resistance" (10/29)
"Another Big Drive Made by Americans" (11/3)
"Armistice Not Yet Signed" (11/7)
"Emperor Wilhelm Abdicated" (11/9)
"Hohenzollern Dynasty Is Dead" (11/10)

Then, on November 11, 1918, came the news for which the world had been waiting: "Wilson States the Armistice Terms." With that announcement, postwar psychology swept the nation. The Penn Field project felt the impact almost immediately; construction work terminated at five o'clock the following day. Dr. Vinson received orders that "no further construction will be carried on and no further obligations incurred except such as may be ordered by the Director of Military Affairs . . . The [Air Service School for Radio Operators] remains at a standstill awaiting developments."[35] A similar mood fell over the University main campus; instruction in most military subjects ended immediately. The quick change to peace was further dramatized on Saturday, November 30, when more than 2,800 members of the University's Student Army Training Corps made its farewell march down Congress Avenue.

Although construction at Penn Field was at a standstill, instruction continued, but with some difficulty. Because of military reassignments following Armistice, Dr. Brown reported he never knew the actual number of officers and enlisted instructors currently on the staff. Also, the autumn weather created more problems. In his November 30 Weekly Report, he further noted that during the week, with the heating plant unfinished, classrooms were so cold instruction had to be interrupted. In addition, with the roads and sidewalks still under construction, muddy conditions during the wet weather made it impossible to walk between buildings. And following Armistice, student apathy emerged as another persistent problem. "Many complaints have come from instructors that it is impossible to get the men to put any effort into their work," Dr. Brown reported. "Their only interest concerns when they may be demobilized and sent home." The latter, at least, was soon forthcoming; the men received holiday passes and classes were discontinued from December 21 to January 6, 1919. That, for all practical purposes, marked the end of the short life of the Penn Field operation. When the men returned on January 6, some were discharged, while others received reassignments to other Air Service stations. A token military staff remained on duty at the south Austin facility.

Of the three military schools operated by the University of Texas, the School of Military Aeronautics was the last to close. On February 20, 1919, the one remaining cadet was transferred to another school. As the University's first and largest military school, 5,958 cadets entered the program in eighty-one different classes, 1,285 either failed or were transferred, and 4,663 graduated and entered primary flying school. Charged with patriotic zeal, the young cadets embarked on that new adventure with boundless enthusiasm, not fully aware of the dangers that lay ahead. Military aviation during World War I was in its infancy, the methodology largely experimental, the aircraft untested and unproven, and the techniques of airmanship limited by inexperience with aircraft whose response was often unpredictable. Thus, many pilots paid the ultimate price. When Dr. J. M. Bryant filed his final report on July 10, 1919, he listed 68 graduates who gave their lives for their country. Significantly, all deaths occurred in 1918, the final year of the war; only 12 are listed as "killed in action." All other fatalities occurred during primary training, while 2 cadets succumbed while still at the University. There were, however, significant successes. Twenty-four graduates received special honors for their military service. Edgar G. Tobin, the first cadet to enter the University's ground school, received the Distinguished Service Cross.[36]

With the war over and the University-sponsored military schools closed, all that remained was a financial settlement with the government. The final balance sheet reflects the terms of the contractual agreement; the ground schools would yield no profit for the participating universities, nor would they be a financial liability. Against $38,668.80 in receipts, disbursements totaled $715,330.79. On May 19, 1919, the United States government reimbursed the University of Texas in the amount of $76,661.99. That closed the School of Military Aeronautics account.[37] Settling the Penn Field claim, however, evolved as a far more complicated matter. Since the University of Texas and the United States Army Signal Corps developed the project jointly, there were no well-defined terms of agreement under which a resolution could be easily reached.

In the meantime, President Vinson turned to other priorities. He obviously relished the University's new role in military training, a mission he hoped to expand further. He discussed establishing an Air Service Academy at Penn Field, with Lt. Col. H. A. Drague, assistant director of Military Aeronautics. Drague's response was not encouraging. The timing was not right, he explained, especially with the Air Service's postwar role undecided; consideration of an Air Service Academy would probably receive a very low priority. By early May, however, the Penn Field settlement again became Dr. Vinson's primary concern. With the next University Board of Regents' meeting scheduled for June 9, the president began planning his report. On May 5, 1919, he appealed to Col. A. L. Fuller, the current director of Military Aeronautics, for a settlement of the military Penn Field account. "The University has some $700,000 or more tied up" in unresolved government accounts, he argued, "upon the major portion of which we are paying interest at the rate of six percent, which, of course, is keeping the available funds of the University so occupied as to make them of little use to us." [38] Since the response Dr. Vinson hoped for was not forthcoming, the responsibility for negotiating the settlement ultimately fell to Dr. Bryant, then chairman, Board of Control, U.S. Army Schools at the University of Texas.

In early June 1919, Dr. Bryant spent some two weeks in Washington discussing the Penn Field settlement with members of the Air Service administration. His proposal that the Air Service salvage the Penn Field property and pay the University the total amount of the claim had been recommended favorably by every branch of the Air Service. Since that method of settlement involved the purchase of the Penn Field land by the United States government, chief of Air Service Gen. C. T. Menoher refused to present the proposal to the secretary of war. The general's hesitancy was understandable. The land purchase power Congress granted the secretary of war during the wartime emergency was temporary. [39] Dr. Bryant next suggested that the two parties determine the salvage value of the property, which the University would, in turn, offer for sale. Further negotiations placed the salvage value of Penn Field at $91,650, against actual costs of $626,938.91. Gen. Menoher again refused to accept the agreement and insisted that a board of arbitration be selected to resolve the matter. With that agreement, the two parties moved one step closer to settlement. [40]

Prior to Dr. Bryant's departure for Washington, D.C., Leo C. Haynes, secretary of the University of Texas Board of Regents, instructed him to agree to a value of not more than $30,000 on the land and not more than five percent of the original gross costs of the buildings. Dr. Bryant fulfilled his assignment. In early July 1919, the University advertised Penn Field for sale to the highest bidder. When the bidding closed at 10:30 A.M. on July 17, 1919, Dr. Vinson had received seven bids ranging from $50,000 to Austin businessman Sam Sparks' successful offer of $107,555. [41] Three weeks later

Dr. Vinson received the following memorandum from the Commanding Officer, Air Service School for Radio Operators, Penn Field, Austin, Texas: "You are hereby advised that Penn Field has this date been abandoned."[42] That cleared the way for a final settlement. On September 3, 1919, Dr. Vinson received a check from the War Department for $484,376.54.[43] That resolved the United States government's wartime commitment to the University of Texas.

Thus, one era in Austin aviation history had come to an end, making way for another. During the wartime emergency the community had coalesced, establishing a pattern for urban cooperative enterprise. Aviation had emerged as a central theme of that undertaking, a theme that was destined to grow within the coming years. With the availability of surplus military aircraft in the immediate postwar years, the sound of aircraft would become increasingly familiar to Austin citizens. And with aviation emerging as an integral part of civic growth, the community would again be drawn together to help establish Austin as part of a future network of aerial commerce. Thus Austin, as well as the entire nation, was about to embrace the gospel of flight.

CHAPTER 3

BARNSTORMERS, BUSINESSMEN, AND HIGH HOPES FOR THE FUTURE

THE postwar euphoria that followed the armistice eventually ran its course. With the new year came a plethora of national problems: labor strife, racial unrest, prohibition, and controversy over the Versailles peace settlement. Those issues were a lesser concern in Austin, Texas, where its 34,876 citizens nevertheless addressed a number of local matters: unpaved streets, an escalating number of automobile accidents, a proposed streetcar fare increase from five to seven cents, and people legally shooting doves within the city limits. However, two individuals, Walter E. Long, manager of the Austin Chamber of Commerce, and Max Bickler, chairman of the Chamber's Aviation Committee, looked primarily beyond current issues to the future. They both viewed aviation as synonymous with urban progress. With that industry still in its infancy, they based their strategy to bring an aviation presence to Austin more on desire than substance, plus a large measure of civic boosterism.

The Army Air Service, statistically a military minority, emerged from the recent war with greater visibility than any other military force, thanks largely to media coverage, a situation that maximized its combat role in the public perception. The pursuit pilots—later known as fighter pilots—became foreign journalism's glamour creation. Those with five or more victories over the enemy became celebrated "flying aces." By war's end such well-publicized pilots as Rickenbacker, Luke, Lufberry, and Bishop had achieved higher identity factors than the generals who commanded them. That disparity did not go unnoticed. "The final tally of damage inflicted during the war by the American Air Service is not impressive," concluded aviation historian Glines. He noted that 650 airmen destroyed 781 enemy planes and 73 balloons, whereas some 150 bombing missions released 275,000 pounds of explosives on German targets. "While these achievements contributed considerably to the final victory," Glines adds, "other statistics show the penalty that had to be paid for unpreparedness." He further notes, "On Armistice Day American units had 740 planes assigned, of which only 196 were American made. Two hundred thirty-seven American officers and men had been killed in air battles, many of whom could have been saved if they had been required to wear parachutes. Two hundred eighty-nine planes and forty-eight balloons were lost, including fifty-seven planes flown by American pilots assigned to British, French and Italian air forces." [1]

By whatever measure the Air Service's contribution to victory is evaluated, one fact remains abundantly clear: preparing for the conflict advanced the fledgling aviation industry manifold, and accorded the airplane a utilitarian function.[2] With the return to peacetime, the American nation possessed a huge inventory of aircraft, mainly Curtiss JN-4 two-place trainers, and some ten thousand pilots trained by the military to fly them. By war's end the government had produced approximately six thousand JN-4s, plus an overrun of two thousand planes, produced before contracts were cancelled but never put into military service. With these war surplus "Jennies" selling for as little as three hundred dollars, many returning airmen elected to continue flying. Strapped securely in the rear cockpits of their fragile biplanes (the front cockpits were for paying passengers), those World War I veterans created a new industry and a new term in the contemporary vernacular—"barnstorming."[3]

Flying from town to town and landing in any convenient open field, the young pilots began selling airplane rides to fascinated individuals for whatever the traffic would bear: as much as $12.50 in the early 1920s, as little as $1.50 in the Depression years. It was not an easy life; future income at best was unpredictable. Yet thousands of military-trained pilots were able to earn a living in aviation. Costumed in helmets, goggles, and flowing white scarves, those daring young men introduced millions of people in thousands of towns and villages to the thrill of flying. Their impact far exceeded in dollar value their monetary reward for risking their collective necks. They, unknowingly, were exploring aviation's potential as commercial enterprise. The results would be far-reaching.

Soon after the Wright brothers made history at Kitty Hawk, farsighted men began considering the airplane's commercial application. The one aspect discussed most frequently was flying the mail, then the most common form of communication. Consequently, in many pre–World War I air shows, demonstrations of aerial mail carrying, even for short distances, became popular attractions. The idea gained currency during the war, and some seven months before the armistice, the United States Post Office Department launched the nation's first airmail service. On May 15, 1918, Lt. George L. Boyle, flying a new Curtiss JN-4H "Jenny" training plane, took off from the Washington, D.C., polo grounds bearing a cargo of some sixty-six thousand letters bound for New York City via Philadelphia. But a funny thing happened on the way to Philadelphia. Lieutenant Boyle, relying on a malfunctioning compass, turned south instead of north, and some two hours later landed in a pasture near Waldorf, Maryland. Despite this inauspicious beginning, the Post Office Department ushered the nation into the era of commercial air transportation. By 1919, the department had extended the service west from New York City to Chicago, and a year later war-surplus DeHavilland DH-4 biplanes were flying coast to coast carrying an ever-increasing payload of the nation's mail.[4] Almost immediately civic leaders in other sections of the country began scrambling to have airmail service extended to their communities. In Austin, Max Bickler, who had served on the Austin Chamber of Commerce Aviation Committee since 1917, represented his constituency with dogged determination in pursuing his ultimate goal, bringing airmail service to the city. In the interim, however, the sight and sound of flying aircraft became integral factors in his effort to promote Austin's economic growth and civic pride.

Since Penn Field remained temporarily active, flight crews maintained proficiency with frequent flights over the city in their Curtiss JN-4s. When banker H. A. Wroe launched a campaign to sell Victory Liberty Bonds, the Penn Field commander offered the use of two aircraft to promote the sale. On May 2, 1919, Wroe, flying with Lt. N. D. Brophy, dropped a much-publicized letter from the plane, entitling the finder a $50 bond. The promoters scheduled the event at four o'clock in the afternoon so school-children could see the aircraft and have a chance to find the order for a bond. At press time no one had claimed the free bond, yet to the astute observer, the event conveyed an emphatic message: in postwar America, aviation events had wide public appeal.[5] The gospel of flight was indeed sweeping the country. Max Bickler took careful note of these and other aviation activities across the nation and developed a multifaceted program promoting Austin aviation. Establishing a permanent landing field was the first step in ensuring Austin's aviation future. With the Penn Field property being developed commercially, Bickler and his committee began looking elsewhere; Camp Mabry seemed a logical alternative. "The continual use of airplanes has necessitated the preparation of some accurate data regarding the best landing field . . . near Austin," the Chamber reported. "This landing field is on the parade grounds of Camp Mabry."[6]

In July 1922, Bickler's committee, in association with Miller Blue Print Company, prepared more than one hundred blueprint maps of Camp Mabry showing the "smooth ground suitable for landing" airplanes, with a "wind funnel" mounted atop the Quarter Master building. Those maps, accompanied by Bickler's cover letters, served as Austin's official invitation for aviators to visit the city. On March 13, 1923, Bickler sent a copy of the map to Lt. Robert D. Kapp, Air Service Headquarters, Fort Bliss, Texas, pointing out that the Camp Mabry parade ground "is amply large to accommodate a whole formation of ships at one time." He added that a ground crew is always available at the Quarter Master building to service transient aircraft.[7] Four days later Bickler sent two copies of the map to Capt. Burdette S. Wright, Chief, Airways Section, in Washington, D.C., suggesting that a hangar be located at Camp Mabry for the service and convenience of military aircraft. Although Bickler's request for a hangar was not immediately fulfilled, his continued map barrage yielded results. On April 23, 1923, he wrote Charles J. Glidden, editor of *Aeronautical Digest*, that a squadron of nineteen bombing planes from San Antonio recently landed at Camp Mabry. Glidden, in turn, encouraged Bickler to move forward in his effort. He also offered to provide Bickler complimentary copies of *Aeronautical Digest,* a publication advocating "establishing a municipal landing field in every community . . . The gravity of the situation requires prompt action so that your city may be on the National Airways," a projected airways system promoted by that publication. Bickler requested fifteen copies.[8]

Although Bickler's immediate objective was establishing a permanent landing field, his ultimate goal, achieving airmail service for Austin, continued to elude him. Nevertheless, he moved forward, pursuing the matter through both military and political channels. On May 21, 1923, he invited Maj. H. H. Hickman at Kelly Field to address the Austin Kiwanis Club on June 11 on the potential uses of "aerial mail." That same day Bickler wrote Paul Henderson, Second Postmaster General in Charge of Air Mail, requesting his assistance in providing airmail services to Austin. Henderson was less than encouraging. He explained that according to the current law, airmail was limited to one route, specifically the transcontinental line linking New York City with San Francisco. To expand or extend that service, additional legislation would be required. Henderson, however, concluded with a mild note of encouragement, "It is certainly interesting to note that Austin, Texas, is planning the establishment of an air field."[9]

By the mid-1920s "barnstorming" had partially run its course and many of the young businessmen-aviators had established permanent bases across the nation. They became what is known as fixed base operators, or FBOs. Austin was no exception. In 1925, Mat Watson and Grace McClelland, using two biplanes, began flight operations at Camp Mabry. A year later, when they moved to a 62-acre site on Cameron Road (presently I-35 at East Fifty-first Street) and established Austin Air Service, Jerry Marshall and Webb Ruff occupied their original location at Camp Mabry and launched the Marshall and Ruff School of Flying. Apparently that partnership was short-lived. In 1926, Webb Ruff moved his operation to a 138-acre field north of Austin on Fiskville Road (North Lamar Boulevard) and established University Airport. At that location Ruff sold Waco (pronounced WAH-co) airplanes, offered charter service, gave flight instruction, and featured airplane trips to all out-of-town University of Texas football games.[10] The fixed base operators became the wellspring of Austin's commercial aviation industry.

With aircraft readily available, Austin business firms began exploring the commercial benefits of aviation. At noon on February 2, 1926, the city received an unexpected introduction to Orbit chewing gum; an airplane flew over the downtown section dropping ten thousand samples of the new product, prompting hundreds of surprised citizens to scramble for the free gum. The following day a local theater executive, taking note of the interest generated by the gum drop, chose aerial display to promote the Majestic Theater's current attraction. At five o'clock that afternoon an airplane dropped thirty tickets over downtown Austin, each admitting the holders to a showing of *Vanishing American*. The pilot painted the film's title on the lower wings of the aircraft, while the name of the theater appeared on the bottom of the fuselage. That plane was operated by representatives of the Lincoln Standard Airplane factory of Lincoln, Nebraska, who were in Austin taking up passengers at Camp Mabry.

The *Statesman* editor also recognized the benefits of aerial promotion and launched a tie-in campaign with Austin Air Service. The Monday, April 20, 1926, edition contained Statesman Flying Week coupons, with instructions to "Present this coupon . . . at the Austin Air Port [Austin Air Service] located on Cameron Road . . . with $1.50 cash and receive a $2.50 ride over the city of Austin." According to the Austin Air Service, the readers responded almost immediately to the offer. On the first day of the campaign, visitors began arriving at the landing field as soon as that issue of the *Statesman* was on the street. The campaign ran from Monday morning, April 20, to Sunday evening, May 2. Apparently all parties benefited from the offer. The *Statesman* sold some newspapers, the Austin Air Service sold some flying time, and a segment of the Austin community experienced the thrill of an aerial view of the city. The newspaper also supplemented the "Flying Week" campaign with an additional aerial promotion. At noon on April 28, pedestrians along Congress Avenue were startled to see an Austin Air Service plane overhead with the slogan Read the Statesman painted under the wings. According to the *Statesman*, "The business section of Austin had to stop and look—in spite of the fact that a plane is now a common event."

Judging from the combination of paid advertisements and general news coverage that appear in subsequent issues of the *Statesman*, the fixed base operators were indeed acquainting Austin residents with the new mode of travel. Competing for public participation, the Marshall and Ruff School of Flying and the Austin Air Service chose different strategies to lure customers to their respective fields. On April 28, the *Statesman* announced that the following day Jerry Marshall would give a free exhibition of aerial daredeviltry at Camp Mabry. Marshall planned to turn off his engine at three thousand feet, do a complete loop and five tail spins, and land on a small white circle on the parade ground. The stunt, Marshall claimed, had never been performed in Austin, and was both difficult and dangerous. Five days later the Austin Air Service offered a unique combination to promote its business—a free airplane ride and a free chicken dinner. In that bizarre promotion, the air service stated it planned to release a number of live chickens from an airplane and the persons catching the chickens would get a free airplane ride over Austin, plus keeping the chickens.[11] In the absence of a humane society, it may be assumed that several Austin citizens enjoyed both a free chicken dinner and a free airplane ride.

Subsequent ads placed in the *Statesman* by the two fixed base operators were less sensational and more businesslike. On Sunday, June 6, 1926, the Marshall & Ruff School of Flying offered "One Dollar Rides" in "Two Brand New $5,000 5-Passenger Airplanes" at Camp Mabry. The company repeated the ad on Friday, June 11, with the additional inducement of a "Sensational Parachute Jump." Two weeks later, the Austin Air Service countered with the added appeal of "Moonlight Rides—See Austin at Night from the Air." On September 19, the company repeated the offer with a romantic nocturnal appeal: "Take her up in a plane in the moonlight—Talk about your romance and thrills—A moonlight ride by airplane over beautiful Austin will furnish them a-plenty . . . $1.50 per trip."

When not flying local passengers for hire, the Austin fixed base operators were frequently joined by their colleagues from Kelly Field for some weekend aerial high jinks, performed for their, as well as the city's, personal enjoyment. "Austin aviators and the general public were supplied with thrills Sunday [August 9] by two army aviators from San Antonio who seemed bent on establishing new low altitude records for flying," the *Statesman* reported. Those aerial games took an unexpected turn when Lt. John I. Moore, a passenger in one of the aircraft who unfortunately had released his safety belt, fell out of the plane at an altitude of only five hundred feet. Lt. Moore averted tragedy by quickly pulling the parachute's ripcord and landing safely with only minor scratches. The plane's pilot, seated in the front cockpit and unaware of his passenger's fate, returned to Kelly Field, where an unexpected surprise awaited him. During the impromptu air show Grace McClelland and other pilots from the Austin Air Service joined their military visitors in the air, and according to the *Statesman*, "Pedestrians and autoists were thrilled while the pilots went through a series of stunts near the ground." Other citizens, however, took opposing views of the matter, which they articulated to City Manager Adam R. Johnson, who, in turn, notified Police Chief J. N. Littlepage "to order all airplane operators to stop their stunt flying over the city."[12]

In place of the independent aerial cut-ups, the air show concept emerged as a timely, well-organized phenomenon of the mid-1920s and early 1930s. The promoters marketed the events with a twofold objective: luring people to the field and selling them airplane rides. The system worked. Sensationalism—stunt flying, wing walking, and parachute jumps—brought the multitudes to the landing fields, and many exhibited the raw courage to purchase their first ride in an airplane. New segments of society were discovering the thrill of flying.

Locally, the Austin Air Service led the way by staging what was probably Austin's first postwar air show. The June 13, 1926, event featured stunt flying by Benny Howard, a daredevil pilot from Houston, and $1.50 airplane rides over the city. The following July 11, the company staged a second "Aerial Exhibition," again featuring Benny Howard, "Ace of Stunt Flyers," this time teamed with Matthew Watson, "The Airplane's Master," who performed "the Air Charleston" at the Cameron Road field. To encourage the $1.50 airplane rides, the pilots agreed to do "no stunt flying with passengers unless requested."[13]

Encouraged by the success of these events, the Austin Air Service staged "Austin's First Air Circus" the following year. The two-day event began on September 3, 1927, with the arrival of about fifteen out-of-town pilots to compete for the one thousand dollars in prize money provided by Austin merchants. With no admission charge, some six thousand Austin citizens visited the field to witness "daredevilry in the air such as has not been seen over the city before." The "daredevilry" included loops, falling leaf tailspins, barrel rolls, and other challenges to the pilots' airmanship. The show's sponsors designated opening day as "Governor's Day," when a Martin bomber from Brooks Field, San Antonio, gave a demonstration especially for the governor's benefit.[14]

The following day attendance doubled, even without the governor's presence. More than twelve thousand people arrived at the field to witness such an aerial spectacle that Paramount News assigned a camera crew to record the event. Speed races, altitude races, dead-stick (without power) landings, acrobatic flying, upside down flying, and a free-for-all speed race highlighted the afternoon. Pilot Shorty Reddack of Dallas provided the spectators one of their biggest thrills by crawling "all over a swiftly-moving plane at a dizzy altitude, and hung by everything except his teeth." Reddack ended his performance with a spectacular parachute jump. However, the day's events were marred by near tragedy when "Stud" Stratton, a student pilot from Waco, made an unauthorized flight to the show in a new Curtiss "Jenny." Because of his lack of flying skill, instead of landing into the wind, Stratton attempted a downwind landing and overshot the field. "Seeing a crash threatening," the *Statesman* reported, "Stratton tried to rise again, but hung his plane in the telephone wires across the road from the field. The Jenny [then] drove into the earth a few feet distant, and was completely demolished. Stratton and his passenger emerged from the wreckage unhurt, trembling a bit, but smiling." [15]

In spite of the sensationalism associated with air shows, Max Bickler continued to view that city's three airfields—Camp Mabry, Austin Air Service, and University Airport—as stepping stones to Austin's aviation future. And the increased air traffic the air shows generated seemed to forecast an era in which the airplane would play an increasingly important role in American society. With the mail already being flown coast to coast, Bickler envisioned a time when Austin would also receive that service. Although the actual reality of local airmail service was beyond Bickler's immediate reach, it was destined to occur.

When the United States government first launched the airmail operation, it was considered a temporary arrangement. "There was no thought . . . that this enterprise, once established on a sound footing would remain permanently under Federal auspices," wrote aviation historian Nick A. Komons.[16] By demonstrating the practicality of air commerce, government officials believed commercial interests would ultimately take over the operation. When Calvin Coolidge signed into law the Air Mail Act of 1925 on February 2, it set in motion a process that eventually brought airmail to all regions of the United States, including Austin. Conceived as an instrument "to encourage commercial aviation," the act authorized the postmaster general to contract with private firms "for the transportation of air mail by aircraft between such points as he may designate at a rate not to exceed four-fifths of the revenue derived from such air mail." [17] This legislation, and the subsequent passage of the Air Commerce Act on May 20, 1926, established the legal cornerstone for the development of civil and commercial aviation in the United States.[18] The impact was both immediate and far-reaching. The commercialization of air transportation created new sources of investment capital for the fledgling industry. During the summer of 1925, businessmen throughout the nation began shifting stock issues to ensure themselves a role in an anticipated aviation boom. This led to the development of new types of aircraft that could fly faster, farther, and carry greater payloads.[19] But Austin still remained far removed from the single airmail operation that linked the two coasts.

In less than a year, however, Texas and the Southwest began to reap the benefits of the Air Mail Act. On May 13, 1926, the National Air Transport Company established service to Dallas and Fort Worth. The first northbound flight carried almost a ton of mail, 486 pounds of which was transferred to the New York–bound plane in Chicago.[20] With Dallas and Fort Worth serving as southern co-terminals of an airline linking that region with Chicago and the East Coast, airmail service existed within two hundred miles of Austin. This development further accelerated Bickler's efforts. During 1926, the Aviation Committee met nine times, mainly to acquaint the Austin business community with the advantages of airmail. Drawing a historical analogy, committee speakers pointed out that "the city which is not alive to aerial transportation today, may, in the future, be in the same position as the town which ignored the railroad."[21]

There were, however, encouraging developments. At eleven o'clock on the morning of April 29, 1926, three U.S. Army planes carrying six representatives of the Dallas Chamber of Commerce arrived at the Austin Air Service field. Before continuing on to San Antonio, the visitors discussed with members of the Austin Chamber of Commerce welcoming committee the benefits of the airmail service then available between Dallas and New York City. Another purpose of the visit was to exhibit the new types of aircraft then carrying the mail. One was a Curtiss "Carrier Pigeon," a new high-wing, twin-engine monoplane with a one-thousand-pound cargo capacity, designed especially for transporting the mail. The other ships were World War I DeHavillands, the aircraft used initially in the airmail service. The newspaper account notes that before the visiting aircraft arrived in Austin, pilots Jerry Marshall and Mat Watson gave welcoming committee members Max Bickler and Sam Sparks complimentary flights over the city. Neither had ever ridden in an airplane.[22]

One month later when Bickler and his committee attended the annual meeting of the Texas Postal Supervisors in New Braunfels, Texas, they received more encouraging news. W. B. Luna, Dallas assistant postmaster and keynote speaker, predicted the extension of the airmail service to Austin and San Antonio within the coming year. He cautioned, however, that "the extension will not be made until sufficient use of air mail service to justify the extension is definite." Adolph Koch, Austin superintendent of mails, reported that Austin was then dispatching between twenty-five and thirty airmail letters and parcels each day. Luna noted further that the speed of the airmail planes (averaging one hundred miles per hour, depending on the wind) was also attracting shippers of small parcels containing perishable items—baby chickens, queen bees, small alligators, and horned frogs.[23]

With the prospect of local airmail service brightening, Bickler returned to Austin to face two critical issues: increasing the business community's use of airmail and selecting a landing field fulfilling the requirements of the airmail service. C. B. Brown, Texas Air Transport division traffic manager, visited Austin on September 15, 1926, to address the first problem. "The object of my visit is to create more interest in the use of air mail," Brown explained, "and to solicit the business men and citizens generally to increase their patronage." He added, however, that Austin patronage is "rather light" due to the lack of knowledge of the service. "Air mail is simply the latest contribution of man's ingenuity to the business world," Brown continued, "and the progressive businessmen of the country are adopting the use of the air mail as a regular method of doing business."[24]

When airline executive William P. Brown arrived in Austin on June 17, 1926, to inspect the available landing sites, Bickler submitted descriptions of the three fields: Camp Mabry, the Austin Air Service field on Cameron Road, and Webb Ruff's University Airport on Fiskville Road. After Brown evaluated the assets of each, he decided the Cameron Road site best fulfilled the airline's requirements. Located 4.1 miles from the post office, it contained sixty-two acres of well-sodded, well-drained land with takeoff distances of eighteen hundred feet east and west and twenty-four hundred feet north and south and had a 75′ × 140′ metal hangar with fueling and servicing facilities already in place.

Continuing his mission to bring airmail to Austin, Bickler scheduled seven meetings of the Aviation Committee during the year. Success, however, was even closer than he realized. On the morning of May 20, 1927, a shy young pilot named Charles A. Lindbergh took off alone from New York bound for Paris, an unprecedented undertaking. All odds favored failure. However, some thirty-three hours later, when the wheels of his Ryan monoplane touched down in Paris, the man and the event ignited a worldwide explosion of adoration. The airplane suddenly assumed a new role. Acknowledging the significance of his flight, Lindbergh wrote later, "The airplane has now advanced to the stage where the demands of commerce are sufficient to warrant the building of planes without regard to military usefulness . . . Undoubtedly in a few years the United States will be covered with a network of passenger, mail and express lines."[25] The impact of Lindbergh's achievement was immediate. "Suddenly in the summer of 1927," wrote aviation historian R. E. G. Davis, "the United States was caught up in a wave of enthusiasm for aircraft and aviation which increased the momentum at an astounding rate."[26]

The Lindbergh Syndrome became an all-pervasive phenomenon, touching all segments of society, including the United States Post Office Department. On June 15, 1927, the department issued an invitation for bids on a Dallas–San Antonio airmail route, with intermediate stops at Waco and Austin. A Laredo extension would be activated once the Dallas–San Antonio service was established. The department required each bidder to post a two-thousand-dollar bond, to state the number of planes that would provide the service, plus "the number in reserve for each plane in the air," and to describe the planes, "showing number of motors, horsepower, speed, and cruising radius." The successful bidder would operate one daily round trip. In submitting the successful bid of $2.89 per pound for airmail carried, Fort Worth attorney Seth Barwise, acting for Texas Air Transport, received authorization for two airmail routes in Texas, one serving Houston and Galveston from its Dallas base, the other a Dallas–San Antonio operation with Waco and Austin as intermediate stops.[27] When the news of this projected service reached Austin on August 1, 1927, there was rejoicing. The *Statesman* reported, "Awarding of the contracts for air mail service to Austin is seen by members of Austin's aviation committee, headed by Max Bickler, as a reward for five years of work to secure the service for the capital city."[28]

Prior to inaugurating the service, Texas Air Transport purchased six new Pitcairn "Mailwing" aircraft, designed especially to carry the mail. With a cruising speed of approximately one hundred miles per hour, this two-place biplane could carry five hundred pounds of mail six hundred miles without refueling. Austin citizens first viewed this new aircraft on December 28, 1927, when two new "Mailwing" planes landed at the Austin Air Service field on a route familiarization flight. A committee of Austin civic leaders, including Max Bickler and Walter Long, met the planes to greet the three pilots, accompanied by Texas Air Transport vice president Temple Bowen. After examining the local facilities, the company representatives departed for San Antonio and Laredo.[29] From that day forward, all planning focused on February 6, 1928, the date set for Austin to receive its first airmail.

Max Bickler and Austin postmaster J. Lynn Hunter quickly marshaled local forces to produce a celebration commensurate with the importance of the event. All segments of Austin society—state, city, and county officials, all local civic organizations, and the entire citizenry—were accorded a role in the forthcoming event. Austin High School principal T. A. Gullett assigned the high school band to help welcome the inaugural flight, and merchants along Congress Avenue erected flags and colorful bunting to give the city a gala appearance. Bickler's committee invited Gov. Dan Moody to ride as a passenger in a United States Army plane scheduled to escort the airmail plane from Austin to San Antonio, while Travis County sheriff Horace E. Burleson and City Manager Johnson assured Postmaster Hunter adequate police protection for both morning and afternoon airmail deliveries.

And then came that magic day, Monday, February 6, 1928. The double-deck banner headline in *The Austin Statesman* dramatized the importance of the event: FIRST AIRMAIL PLANE ON TIME DESPITE RAIN AND HEAVY FOG. At 10:35 A.M., Texas Air Transport pilot L. S. Andrews glided "City of Waco," his Pitcairn "Mailwing," to a historic landing on the rain-soaked Austin Air Service field. As he taxied to the hangar, the Austin High School band played patriotic selections while a police and sheriff's cordon restrained the surging crowd.

In a brief twelve-minute ceremony, pilot Andrews delivered the mail pouches, containing some ten thousand letters, to Postmaster Hunter and Superintendent of Mails Adolph Koch. They embarked immediately for the downtown post office in a specially decorated Lincoln automobile escorted by a detachment of motorcycle police. Arriving at the south entrance of the Capitol grounds, the American Legion Drum and Bugle Corps joined the motorcade, which they escorted down Congress Avenue to Sixth Street, and thence west to the post office.[30]

Meanwhile, the celebration continued at the Austin Air Service field. When pilot Andrews took off from Austin, a six-plane escort followed the airmail plane to San Antonio. These included five army planes from Kelly Field (no mention is made of Gov. Moody), while city commissioner D. C. Reed and Max Bickler flew in Reed's plane, piloted by Mat Watson. When they returned to Austin escorting the northbound flight, they discovered the afternoon crowd "was equal to the throng of the morning, but included in its numbers [were] hundreds of school children eager to watch the 'flying post office' in action."[31]

The extension of airmail service to Austin partially fulfilled Max Bickler's civic mission. However, one level of service—airline passenger service—remained, and that was shortly forthcoming. At 11:45 on the morning of March 30, 1929, a Texas Air Transport Travelair 6000 cabin monoplane landed at University Airport, inaugurating Austin's first passenger service. In addition to the present airmail service, this new passenger service linked Dallas and Brownsville, with intermediate stops at Waco, Austin, San Antonio, and Corpus Christi. Significantly, this inaugural arrival in Austin bore scant resemblance to the first airmail service celebration. Gone were the bands, the hordes of school children, the police cordon, and the surging crowds. The welcoming committee consisted of only Mayor P. W. McFadden, Postmaster Lynn Hunter, Max Bickler, and Walter Long. After receiving Austin's official greeting, Texas Air Transport president A. P. Barrett responded briefly, "This is only the beginning."

And a beginning it was, but one more symbolic than substantive. Austin had indeed entered the modern air age, receiving daily airmail and passenger service, but, whereas government subsidy ensured the airmail contractors a fair return on their investment, passenger service carried no such guarantee. Profit from this phase of the business depended entirely on passenger load, and in 1929 passengers were comparatively few. The problem stemmed primarily from two aviation-related factors: early airline policy and a widespread fear of flying.[32] When the initial airmail contractors began operation, "many airline executives did not want to bother with passenger traffic" because mail was more profitable. For the major carriers, developing passenger traffic became incidental to the business of transporting the mail. However, with an increase in passenger interest along the New York–Chicago route, pilots were allowed to carry "one passenger per trip provided there was no interference with mail or express." At any point along the route, "the pilot had the authority to replace a passenger with mail or express [small parcels]." And to further discourage passenger traffic, one operator increased the one-way New York–Chicago fare from $200 to $400.[33]

Fear of flying was an even stronger deterrent. In the early days of aviation, accidents occurred with frightening regularity, which newspapers sensationalized, employing a special terminology. Whereas trains and automobiles had wrecks, airplanes *crashed!* In covering the 1931 airline accident that killed football legend Knute Rockne, the *American-Statesman* reported, "the crippled ship hit with tremendous force . . . [The] six passengers and two pilots met death instantly. Five bodies were thrown from the plane and the others, broken and mutilated, were found in the wreckage." Nor did Austin newspaper editors feel restricted by location. The story following a page-one headline, "13 Killed in Plane Crashes," cited accidents in seven states, none in Texas. Another headlined story, "Skull Fractured, Leg Broken In Crash, Aviator Crawls 5 Hours to Aid," carried a Pennsylvania dateline.[34] Even foreign accidents received the catastrophe treatment. When an airliner crashed at Penhurst, Kent, England, the *American-Statesman* headline read: "Plane Bursts Into Flames, 7 Persons Die; Paris-London Air Liner Crashes in Spectacular Accident; All On Board Killed: Three Women Among the Five Passengers Who Perished."[35] The evidence was clear: airplanes kill people. Unquestionably, fear of flying was prompting many travelers to avoid airplanes altogether. As one civic leader noted, "The Air Mail Service has attained such efficiency and reliability that no business man now hesitates to send his most valuable papers by Air Mail, though perhaps he could not possibly be induced to take a ride in an airplane on account of the real or fancied dangers."[36]

A. P. Barrett had indeed entered an economically challenging field, and like many other businessmen attracted to aviation in the 1920s, he also possessed the financial resources to maintain operations until airline passenger traffic improved. In addition to owning Texas Air Transport, he was president and major stockholder of Southern Air Transport. Barrett also held executive positions in several utilities companies and owned Dixie Motor Coach Corporation. According to his son, Hunter Barrett, Texas and Louisiana Power and Light Corporation primarily generated the funds that his father reinvested in his faltering airline operations. Monthly deficits sometimes reached eighty thousand dollars. Struggling to maintain the passenger operation, "My father actually paid people to ride in the Texas Air Transport planes," Hunter Barrett added. "He would have them photographed boarding the plane, which he would use for publicity purposes."[37]

The problems Barrett faced with his Austin operation did not go unnoticed. Frank Taylor, who worked as a mechanic's assistant at University Airport when Texas Air Transport flights first landed there, noticed that "very few" people arrived by plane; even fewer departed. Taylor also recognized other deterrents to local air travel, airport location especially. Situated some five miles from the heart of the city, departing passengers objected to the long drive to the airport, and on arriving there, complained of the lack of passenger accommodations. They could choose between waiting for their flights in Webb Ruff's cramped airport office or in his "filling station," located some thirty yards north of the hangar on Fiskville Road.[38]

The airport inconveniences experienced by Austin citizens were, however, destined for change, as were the operating deficits A. P. Barrett faced with Texas Air Transport. Barrett soon launched a reorganization plan, inviting C. R. Smith, a young accountant with Texas and Louisiana Power and Light Company, to join his company and "attempt to establish some 'fiscal responsibility' within his airline interests."[39] This proved to be a most astute decision. In January 1930, they, with the aid of the Lehman Brothers investment firm of New York, formed The Aviation Corporation, a holding company that began acquiring small airlines throughout the United States. Under Smith's leadership, they merged the component units, including Texas Air Transport and Southern Air Transport, into a coordinated system that became American Airways, and later American Airlines.[40] Barrett benefited greatly from this corporate reorganization. His Travelair monoplanes that continued to land at University Airport ultimately would carry the American Airways insignia.

Other changes were also in the offing. Public concerns about the inadequacies of Austin's airport facilities were an ongoing issue. On August 19, 1927, the *Statesman* addressed the matter editorially, admonishing the city government, claiming that *"Austin officially has done nothing to further aviation"* [italics added]. The editor notes further that cities that have established municipal airports are finding "satisfaction in the thought that they are individually doing their part in keeping the nation foremost in the world's fight for aerial progress."[41] Less than a year later, a feature story appearing in the March 4, 1928, Sunday edition of the *American-Statesman* reminded the readers "Austin is the only town on the airway between St. Louis and San Antonio that does not yet own their own field." This item undoubtedly reflected community concern, as the Austin City Council had already called for bids on ten parcels of land under consideration for a municipal airport. Mayor McFadden voiced his support of the matter, claiming "Austin is virtually assured of having a municipal field."

To fund this and other proposed city projects, the city commissioners submitted a $4.2 million bond issue to the voters that included $75,000 to purchase land for an airport. (The Austin Chamber of Commerce had requested $150,000). Returns from the May 18 election indicated all issues passed; the big winner was the municipal airport with 4,501 votes for and 2,032 against. Some observers felt the vote also carried specific philosophical overtones; Austin citizens viewed aviation as synonymous with civic progress. The *Statesman* agreed editorially: "The voters have placed in the hands of their city administrators, present and future, the working tools . . . to lay the foundations for future growth." [42] One of the "foundations for future growth" would be a municipal airport.

In passing the airport bond issue, Austin voters obviously were expressing civic pride, rather than supporting a municipal project that would benefit them individually. In the late 1920s, comparatively few people used airmail service, still fewer purchased airline tickets. "Airports did not [become] a major part in the lives of Americans or a truly vital part of the urban infrastructure until the post–World War II period," wrote aviation historian Janet R. Daly Bednarek. In Austin, however, Walter Long and Max Bickler had successfully spread the gospel of aviation, and their many converts came to the polls to ensure their city's future role in aviation. Long and Bickler were not alone in their effort. "Many cities had their aviation champions for whom airport development was personally quite important," Bednarek observed. "In most cases they were able to ensure enough attention from local governments to promote airport projects successfully." [43]

With airport funding assured, Mayor McFadden moved quickly to expedite the matter. On the afternoon of July 13, 1928, the mayor invited Max Bickler and his aviation committee to join members of the city commission to inspect the prospective airport sites. This was a huge undertaking. A total of twenty-eight parcels of land had been offered the city. These varied in size from the 265.53-acre G. A. Bahn property to a plot of land 400 yards wide and extending along a highway "as far as the city might choose." Prices ranged from $50 an acre to the $75,000 asked for the present University Airport. [44] While there is no record of the committee's July 13 itinerary, it is apparent they neither visited all of the locations nor arrived at any conclusion. To take the next and final step, the commission extended that responsibility to Max Bickler. Since the military conducted the majority of flying in the 1920s, Bickler sought the advice of Army Air Corps commanders in the San Antonio area. The person recommended most highly to aid in making the site selection was Lt. C. L. Chennault, Operations Officer, Brooks Field, Texas. [45] On July 20, 1928, after inspecting several of the more probable sites, Lt. Chennault submitted his recommendations to Mayor McFadden.

The Chennault report, a comprehensive analysis of municipal airport requirements, remained as valid seven decades later as it was in 1928. Lt. Chennault considered the following factors:

1. *Accessibility.* "The chief value of air transportation is its speed. . . . The most valuable airport is the one that lies near the center of business and has easy, rapid means of ground communication with that center."

2. *Size.* "The airports of today must be planned of sufficient size to care for large, heavily loaded airplanes of the near future. . . . Land can be purchased very cheaply now in comparison to the price that will be required in the future . . . [I]f more than enough land for the actual operation of the airport is purchased now, the surplus can be disposed of later at a profit and with such restrictions as will prevent the erection of structures near the port."

3. *Soil.* "A well drained, gravelly soil permits the use of the field in all weather without the necessity of building runways. However, . . . a well sodded field with one or two runways for use in the worst weather is usually preferable."

4. *Topography of Field.* "The field should be nearly level . . . and of sufficient size to permit of landings from all directions."

5. *Location.* "The airport should be located as near the center of the city as possible and as is consistent with safety to life and property. It should have easy, rapid communication facilities . . . The necessity for landing and taking off over inhabited areas should be avoided."

6. *Cost.* "The original cost of the property is the last and least consideration. The municipal airport is an investment for the future . . . Emphasis should be placed on location and suitability rather than upon purchase price."[46]

In applying these criteria to the land available, Lieutenant Chennault chose first a 145.58-acre site known as the Matthews farm, located some three hundred yards east of the current Austin Air Service field on Cameron Road. He also advised acquiring the adjacent Bascom Giles property.[47] The city commission apparently accepted the Chennault report verbatim; six weeks later airport land acquisition was underway. On September 13, 1928, the city acquired the Matthews property, and four days later purchased an additional 45 acres from S. F. Nolen. On September 3, 1929, James Bascom Giles deeded an additional 146.51 acres to the City of Austin, bringing the potential airport landing area to 337.09 acres.[48] Responsibility for developing the property fell to City Manager Johnson. During the following year the Public Works Department removed fences, leveled the landing area, graded and graveled a 100' × 1,000' runway, installed flood lights for night landings, built access roads, and erected a small terminal building on the east side of the property. By September 3, 1930, with the facility almost ready for operation, Bickler visited the site at night to witness the preliminary test of the lighting equipment. He found it "most satisfactory. The beacon, floodlight, and border lights functioned very well, and the City Electrician hopes to have the flicker code beacon and the ceiling light placed by the 14th." [49]

The mayor and the city commission set October 14 for the formal dedication of Austin's first municipal airport. Again Max Bickler's assignment was to plan and direct the event. The initial problem he faced was location. Just two years previously, the airport site was a working cotton field situated some two miles beyond the city limits, lacking direct access routes to downtown Austin. Faced with other important issues, Bickler assigned the problem of crowd control to a Chamber of Commerce committee. He next addressed the matter of celebrity guests. By 1930, aviation personalities—speed pilots, stunt pilots, and long distance flyers—enjoyed a high identity factor and attracted wide attention wherever they appeared. Col. Charles A. Lindbergh, recent trans-Atlantic flyer and world celebrity, topped Bickler's invitation list, followed by speed-record holders Maj. James H. (Jimmie) Doolittle and Capt. Frank Hawks and the assistant chief of the Army Air Corps, Gen. Benjamin D. Foulois. All, including Texas governor Dan Moody, declined Bickler's invitation. He did, however, receive a positive response from Brig. Gen. Charles H. Danforth, Commander, Air Corps Training Center, Kelly Field, Texas. The general also agreed to provide a contingent of military aircraft, providing they performed no combat maneuvers. That event, originally scheduled, had to be deleted from the program, as aerial acrobatics performed by army pilots required the posting of a bond, which the city was unable to fund.

With the approach of October 14, all facets of the local community united to ensure a successful airport dedication. First, there was the weather; October 14 dawned bright and clear with not a cloud in the sky. By early morning out-of-town visitors began arriving by train; all lines serving Austin offered reduced round-trip fares for the dedication. To provide transportation to the airport, the Austin Street Railway Company operated buses every fifteen minutes from Congress Avenue at Sixth Street. And to aid local motorists, Chamber of Commerce representatives placed signs along streets and roads leading to the airport, and on the day of the dedication both the *Statesman* and the *American* carried maps directing motorists along a circuitous route that many had never traveled before. [50]

The airport dedication program followed a pattern that would apply to hundreds of similar functions throughout the United States in the 1930s. First came the arrival of visiting aircraft (military, private, and commercial), then a formal luncheon with a visiting speaker (usually a military officer), airplane rides, aerial acrobatics, and a band concert, and finally the formal dedication. At 4:00 P.M. on October 14, Mayor P. W. McFadden welcomed the visitors to the new airport and introduced the platform guests.[51] Following General Danforth's address, the mayor introduced Mrs. Robert Mueller, widow of the late Austin city commissioner for whom the airport was to be named, and their three sons. That event marked the emotional high point of the ceremony. As the three young men jointly raised the United States flag in honor of their father, the band played "The Star Spangled Banner." Over the sound of the National Anthem came the roar of the Air Corps planes as they took off in formation, circled the airport, and continued on to Kelly Field, the Corps' home base. The Aviation Ball held that night at the Stephen F. Austin Hotel roof garden concluded the celebration.

And so Austin, Texas, had indeed entered the modern air age. By 1931, Texas had 133 urban landing facilities; one year later that number had increased to 141.[52] The development of municipal airports and landing fields was fast becoming a sign of urban growth and an expression of civic pride. When comparing Austin's Mueller airport with municipal airports in other Texas towns of comparable size, a general uniformity in size, location, facilities, and safety factors emerges. Austin's official 175-acre landing area was smaller than either Amarillo's 480 acres or Brownsville's 251 acres, but larger than Beaumont's 55-acre facility. All facilities were five miles or less from the civic centers (Beaumont's was closest at one-and-one-half miles), all except Beaumont's had a rotating beacon, and all provided day and night service. Runways varied in their construction: Amarillo's had both graveled and paved portions; Austin's was sod; Beaumont constructed two shell runways; and Brownsville, two graded, caliche runways. Peripheral obstructions—buildings, utility lines, trees, fences, ditches, light poles—surrounded the airports.[53]

As a landing facility for a growing urban center, Robert Mueller Municipal Airport also possessed some additional shortcomings: no maintenance facilities, no hangar space, no hard-surface runways, no radio communication, and no control tower. Those, of course, would come in time. Yet, by comparison, Austin had indeed made an auspicious beginning. The city was located on a federal airway system and received daily airline mail and passenger service. And to accommodate transient aircraft, the Chamber of Commerce Aviation Committee had placed air markers on the roofs of two downtown buildings directing the pilots to the new airport. In addition, the Capital City possessed the basic essentials for economic growth—an integrated transportation system, the seats of county and state government, the state's major university, and a civic leadership committed to progress and growth. Civilian, commercial, and military aviation, as represented by Mueller airport, was part of the city's growth concept. However, when examined in broad perspective, aviation emerges as a strange anomaly in history. At the very time the fledgling industry was experiencing substantial growth, the worst economic depression in modern history paralyzed the country. As economic indicators continued to fall, President Herbert Clark Hoover attempted to reassure a frightened nation that "prosperity was just around the corner." Businessmen throughout the country, and especially those who had labored to see Robert Mueller Municipal Airport reach fruition, looked to the day when the nation would turn that all-important corner.

CHAPTER 4

A BRIGHT SIDE OF THE GREAT DEPRESSION

WHEN the citizens of Austin gathered for the airport dedication on October 14, 1930, the initial shockwaves of what came to be known as the Great Depression had already reached the Capital City. The ensuing economic indicators brought scant hope for quick recovery. During the first six months of 1932, the number of Texas firms going into bankruptcy reached 532, and business failures were occurring at a rate of fifteen a week.[1] To further cloud the economic horizon, unemployment became widespread and retail sales fell 53 percent below the 1929 level. Yet the airplanes continued to land at Robert Mueller airport.

Contrary to the general economic downturn, aviation remained a growth industry. Scripps-Howard Washington correspondent Ernie Pyle noted that, during the first six months of 1930, nearly as many new airlines began operation as had during the entire year of 1929.[2] Texas fell within the growth cycle. In February 1930, two San Antonio–based air carriers inaugurated scheduled service between that city and San Angelo and Laredo. Cromwell Air Lines, operating one Lockheed and two Stinson monoplanes, provided daily round trip service to San Angelo, while Maj. Frederick Long, a former World War I pilot, launched a Laredo operation with Bellanca cabin planes. A planned extension of the Laredo service to Saltillo, Mexico, with connections to Monterrey and San Luis Potosí, was pending.

The expansion of regional air service reflected a national trend. "Although the business depression has for a time crushed all the meaning from the term 'prosperity,'" observed another journalist, "it has failed to deprive the airlines sufficient vitality to continue growing." In January 1930, airfare reductions by eight of the nation's leading air carriers suddenly made air travel affordable for a greater number of business clients. According to *Aero Digest,* the industry's leading publication, the California "state controller of finance notified all employees of the state that he would approve expense vouchers for air travel." With more people choosing air travel, starting an airline gained investor appeal. That growth factor would ultimately be felt in Austin, Texas.

Dallas-based Long & Harmon Airlines became the second scheduled air carrier to enter the Austin market. (The first, Texas Air Transport, had been serving the Capital City since March 30, 1929.) The Long & Harmon inaugural flight arrived at the Austin municipal airport at noon on February 23, 1931. The airline's president, William Long, and general manager, H. E. Harmon, emerged from the Ford Tri-Motor plane to be greeted by a committee that included Mayor McFadden, Max Bickler, and Walter E. Long. Members of the Dallas and Waco chambers of commerce also accompanied the airline executives to Austin. Following the airport ceremony, Mayor McFadden entertained the visitors with a luncheon at the Stephen F. Austin Hotel. The following day, Long & Harmon six-place, single-engine Stinson "Detroiter" cabin planes began the regular Dallas–Waco–Austin–San Antonio service. Operating on a daily-except-Sunday schedule with a six-cents-per-mile fare, the southbound flight arrived at Austin at 11:05 A.M., while the northbound flight departed at 2:45 P.M.[3] There is no record of the traffic this airline generated.

The Austin market, bolstered by the University of Texas and state government economies, plus an expanding population, caught the attention of other airline investors. A city whose population had almost doubled within the last two decades contained the economic potential to support air transportation. Austin's 1910 population, 29,860, reached 53,120 by 1930. In less than three months a third scheduled air carrier began serving the Capital City, Bowen Air Lines.

Temple Bowen entered aviation with a varied background in transportation. After developing a thriving business hauling heavy equipment in the West Texas oil fields, he, with brother R. C. Bowen, formed Bowen Bus Lines in 1924. Aviation beckoned, and on November 12, 1927, he and his brother organized Texas Air Transport. Temple Bowen served as president of the company until he resigned October 31, 1928, selling controlling interest to A. P. Barrett. Ostensibly, the purpose of Bowen's resignation was to form a competitive airline that provided a more efficient service. Speed, he believed, was the key to success. "The only reason for air transportation is the saving of time through the use of high speed [aircraft], directness of route and frequency of schedule," he explained.[4] Therefore, high-speed schedules along the already heavily traveled routes would be his advantage over the larger carriers. On October 1, 1930, after acquiring a fleet of Lockheed "Vega" six-place aircraft, Bowen launched a new Fort Worth–Dallas–Houston service. The company's Lockheed "Vega" cruised at 150 miles per hour, some forty miles per hour faster that Texas Air Transport's Travelairs and Long & Harmon's Stinsons.[5]

Bowen Air Lines entered the Austin market on Sunday, May 17, 1931, the same day the company introduced its new high-speed Lockheed "Orion." This six-place, low-wing cabin monoplane with a retractable landing gear had a high speed of 240 miles per hour and cruised at 175 miles per hour, faster than any other type of aircraft then in scheduled airline service.[6] Bowen served Austin as an intermediate stop between Dallas and San Antonio. The inaugural northbound flight departed Austin at 7:37 A.M., while the southbound flight arrived at 6:25 P.M. The Austin-Dallas fare was seventeen dollars. Unlike its competitors, the Bowen company maintained its own ground transportation system and airfares included transportation between airports and the leading hotels. Passengers could purchase tickets at hotels and at airports served by the airline; reservations were made through any Western Union Telegraph company within two hundred miles of the Bowen service area. In addition to innovative accommodation of passengers, the company was unique in other ways. For example, Austin was listed as a "flag stop" on the Bowen air route. If the Stephen F. Austin Hotel sold a ticket after the incoming plane left its previous destination, the agent called the airport and an attendant would stretch a large "wagon sheet"— a tarpaulin—on the ground adjacent to the hangar. Since the Bowen airplanes were not radio equipped, the tarpaulin was the pilot's visual message to land and pick up the passenger.[7] Otherwise, the pilot continued to his next destination.

Responsibility for maintaining Robert Mueller Municipal Airport and servicing the three scheduled air carriers fell to John D. Miller, the airport's first manager. Miller received the unsolicited assignment mainly because he was the largest private user of the facility. Miller, founder of Miller Blue Print Company, operated the John D. Miller Aerial Service (which offered a free five-weeks ground school for people interested in learning to fly)[8] and served as treasurer of Southwestern Aerial Surveys, Inc., both based at Mueller. (Miller had initially operated from the Austin Air Service field on Cameron Road, as well as another landing field in the Del Valle area.) In March 1930, the United States District Engineers issued Southwestern Aerial Surveys a $50,000 contract to photograph some eight thousand square miles of the Mississippi and Red River valleys in a flood control project.[9]

Following a year as airport manager, Miller resigned, concluding his responsibilities far outnumbered the benefits. "The agreement [with the city] called for twenty-four hour service," he wrote later. "The only profit was an occasional sale of a tank of gas. After a year's time and a $2,000 loss I resigned as manager."[10]

The facility John D. Miller managed had a landing area bisected by a single gravel runway, a large beacon light, flood lights, and boundary lights that aided night operations. Service facilities at the all-weather airport included a gasoline pump situated near a small office-terminal building, located on the northeast side of the field. There was no hangar. Passengers arriving at the airport via a single dirt county road, found terminal amenities limited to a restroom and a telephone. The city's claim in 1930 that establishing Mueller represented "keeping pace with the inevitable march of progress," appeared more optimistic than accurate.[11]

Change, however, was in the offing, for aviation remained a viable industry. "Domestic production of commercial and military planes during the first six months of 1931 totaled 1,606, of which 1,069 were for civil use," reported the Aeronautics branch of the United States Department of Commerce.[12] Air carriers were also enjoying increased traffic. In July 1931, Transcontinental and Western Air reported an 867-passenger increase over the previous month.[13] As more people in the Austin market began choosing air travel, the carriers serving that city began switching to larger, faster, and more efficient aircraft. On September 4, 1931, American Airways, successor to Texas Air Transport, introduced its new 575-horsepower, nine-place, high-wing American "Pilgrim" monoplane. Cruising at a speed of 120 miles per hour, it was faster than the previous Travelairs, and possessed greater comfort and safety amenities. The "Pilgrim" featured increased insulation for noise reduction, outside ventilation, two-way voice radio for air-to-ground communication, and each passenger seat provided a radio for receiving broadcast entertainment. Baggage and mail was carried in a separate compartment located beneath the cabin."[14]

Competition bred competition. Bowen Air Lines, a regional carrier, resorted to a coordinated air and rail service to compete with the large trunk lines. Appealing especially to the passengers who objected to night flying, Bowen announced on November 1, 1931, that by flying during the day and traveling by train at night, Texas and Oklahoma passengers could enjoy the through ticket accommodations at the fastest possible speeds. While there is no record of what, if any, success the company achieved with the dual mode of travel plan, Bowen Air Lines was achieving a measure of success on its local routes. On October 1, 1931, the end of the first year's operation, the company announced it had carried a total of 12,086 passengers at an average speed of 158 miles per hour. Furthermore, during the month of August, Bowen carried 3 percent of all passengers transported in the United States. According to the company timetable, Bowen's service was the fastest in commercial aviation.[15] With increased competition, the air carriers serving Austin began exploring a new marketing technique, the telephone directory yellow pages. Listings for American Airways and Bowen Air Lines first appear in the 1931 Austin directory.

As economic indicators maintained a downward trend, the air transportation industry's growth pattern continued. In 1931, scheduled airlines flew 43,395,478 million miles, a 50.5 percent increase over the previous year, while during the first four months of 1932 the industry reported a 30.7 percent gain over that period in 1931. Part of that growth was due to increased public confidence in the safety of air travel. According to Col. Clarence M. Young, assistant secretary of commerce for aeronautics, the "nation's scheduled airlines flew 4,377,425 miles for each fatal accident occurring during the last six months of 1932."[16] Cognizant of the growing importance of air travel, the Austin City Council, with the firm support of the Chamber of Commerce Aviation Committee, continued to improve services at Robert Mueller Municipal Airport. To manage the airport following John D. Miller's departure, the city council entered into a contract with Gifford Flying Service of Beaumont, which designated Hal B. Naylor, a local pilot, as resident manager. In addition to servicing the scheduled air carriers landing at Mueller, the company launched a flight training program headed by Naylor.

A modern steel hangar, courtesy American Airways, Inc., became Mueller's next step toward modernization. On July 27, 1931, airline vice president C. R. Smith wrote Austin city manager Adam Johnson that "it will be necessary for the City of Austin to construct a hangar at [the] municipal airport before you can hope to secure a great amount of revenue therefrom or before the airport can be considered adequate." To facilitate that project, Smith offered to pay the City of Austin $6,460.96, in lieu of landing fees for a period of twenty years. However, he cited one condition: "the entire proceeds of this payment [will] be used for the construction of a hangar on the municipal airport." [17] The city accepted Smith's offer; in February 1932, Heierman-Tips Industries of Austin received the contract to construct a 80′ × 100′ all-metal hangar on the northeast side of the field, adjacent to the office-terminal building. Other improvements were forthcoming. In January 1932, the City Council appropriated $219 for weather bureau equipment and $2,217.60 to build a gravel runway connecting the new hangar and the present taxiway. [18] The improvements to Mueller did not go unnoticed. "Austin's well lighted airport has been frequently highly complimented and on stormy nights provides . . . a great boon to aviators," the Austin Chamber of Commerce reported. "The army planes are using the field more and more." [19]

On April 19, 1932, William J. Mackenzie, representing the Aeronautics Branch of the Department of Commerce, met with city officials, Chamber of Commerce representative Max Bickler, and airport manager Hal B. Naylor, to discuss changes necessary for Mueller to qualify for a Department of Commerce rating. In reporting his findings to the Chief, Aeronautics Branch, in Washington, D.C., Mackenzie recommended a number of changes at Mueller. Those included removing several trees that obstructed landing approaches to the field, adding obstruction lights on utility poles, additional lighting on the wind cone, and lowering a fence on the south side of the field. Considering the prospect of an aircraft accident, the inspector recommended acquiring emergency equipment, including a first aid kit, a crowbar, wire cutters, hack saw, ax, cloth-cutting shears, fire ex-tinguishers, two litters, and fire-fighting appliances. To ensure all-weather use of the field for scheduled air carrier operations, Mackenzie further ad-vised extending the present runway and adding an additional runway.[20] In order to expand the runway system, it would be necessary to extend the field to the south and west.

The City of Austin moved forward with Mackenzie's recommendations. The following year the city added the 146.51-acre Giles tract to the original Matthews farm, expanding the landing area to 337.09 acres. Subsequently, a second runway and additional field lighting were added.[21] Other changes at Mueller fell to the Gifford Flying Service employees. Jim Criswell, a high school student and part-time employee, drew the assignment to remove a wire fence. To facilitate the operation, Criswell and an associate tied the barbed wire strands to the bumper of an automobile and drove away, the fence following close behind. Their work, however, was less than complete; some two hundred feet of wire remained attached to the fence posts. Later, a student pilot, taking off, failed to gain sufficient altitude and caught the two hundred feet of wire with his tail skid, where it remained throughout the short training flight. Unaware he was dragging the barbed wire, the student pilot, on landing, made the usual approach. That approach, how-ever, differed from all previous approaches; the trailing barbed wire became entangled with electric utility lines, blacking out much of north Austin.[22]

That student pilot, like thousands of other young men who succumbed to the "Lindbergh Syndrome," was able to find both time and money to take flight instruction, even during the Depression Era. Another student pi-lot who patronized the Gifford Flying Service at Mueller was Sam Wilborn. But unlike many other aspiring student pilots, Wilborn had actually seen Charles Lindbergh, as well as his plane, the "Spirit of St. Louis." When Lindbergh visited Abilene, Texas, the Wilborn family was present as the fa-mous trans-Atlantic pilot landed at the Abilene airport. "I still remember the sound of the 'Spirit of St. Louis' engine," he recalled, "that [Wright] J-5 engine with short exhaust stacks." When Lindbergh later gave a public address in Abilene, "we were within a few feet of the rostrum where he was standing. And I don't think I have ever been so excited, or inspired, than I was that day. I was eleven years old. And so, from that day, *I simply had to fly.*"

When the family later moved to Austin, young Wilborn seized the op-portunity to fulfill his life's dream. At age sixteen, with money earned as a delivery boy, he began flight instruction with Gifford Flying Service. The cost was affordable, six dollars for thirty minutes, the equivalent of one week's pay. With neither parental knowledge nor consent, once a week Wilborn rode his bicycle to the airport for his flying lesson. Instruction continued, and on July 8, 1932, after a short flight, Wilborn's instructor gave him the order he had longed to hear, "Take it around the field— *by yourself.*" Momentarily startled by the prospect of a solo flight, young Wilborn taxied the aircraft into position, took off, and circled the field. The flight was routine until he turned on final approach. At that critical juncture the one thing happened that all pilots fear—*the engine quit!* With the runway less than two hundred yards away, Wilborn maintained his composure, gliding the small craft to a successful landing. "So my first landing was a "dead stick" landing," Wilborn recalled. "All of which was so exciting I could hardly stand it. I just had to tell somebody what I had done." When he arrived home, his mother was cooking breakfast. "I said, 'Guess what I did this morning?' and without even turning around, she replied, 'Well, I guess you must have flown by yourself today.' When she said that I was absolutely, completed deflated." [23]

Austin's pride in Robert Mueller Municipal Airport was an urban phenomenon shared by more than two thousand other towns and cities throughout the United States. By July 1, 1933, the number of airports and landing fields in the United States had grown to 2,136, an increase of ninety-nine since July 1, 1932. The increased availability of landing facilities brought airline service within the reach of a public that was turning more and more to air travel. In April 1933, Dallas-based Texas Airways inaugurated a new daily passenger service between Dallas and Longview, Texas. That service, which linked Dallas with the East Texas oil fields, was an extension of the line from Dallas to Tyler and Henderson. [24]

During the early 1930s, even with the growing confidence in air travel, tragedy seemed always to be lurking behind every takeoff and landing. On May 31, 1933, airport manager Hal Naylor was fatally injured on a training flight at Mueller. On July 1, Austin city manager Guiton Morgan appointed Webb Ruff to fulfill the remaining six months of Naylor's contract. Under the terms of this agreement Ruff was required to furnish the city "with regular schedules of raises and reports [and] pay the city 10 percent of the gross income from the sale of aviation gasoline and oils, hanger rent, repair fees, cross country flights, local sightseeing flights and student flying fees." [25] Ruff immediately began removing his equipment to Mueller from

University Airport, which he also operated. That equipment consisted of five aircraft, including a six-place cabin plane, and a repair department headed by mechanic Herman Newman.

The year 1933 drew to a close on another economic high note for the airlines serving Austin. Both American Airways and Bowen Air Lines reported satisfactory business throughout the year. Bowen, then operating a fleet of eight Lockheed "Vega" aircraft, extended its Dallas-Tulsa service to Chicago. And there was other good news. On December 11, Texas governor Miriam A. Ferguson issued a proclamation designating that day as National Aviation Day in Texas, which also marked the thirtieth anniversary of the Wright brothers' first flight. On December 15, C. R. Smith, vice president of American Airways, responded to the governor's proclamation as follows: "Although as yet we have not been successful in persuading you and Governor Jim to take a flight in one of our airplanes, we, nevertheless, very much appreciate the interest in aviation which prompted you to issue your proclamation of December 11. It was a very fine proclamation." [26]

With the new year came the news that shocked not only the airline industry, but the nation as well. The New Deal of the Roosevelt administration penetrated new and unexpected facets of the federal government. Post Office Department solicitor Karl Crowley discovered that the airlines had colluded to prevent competitive bidding for airmail contracts, that former Postmaster General Walter F. Brown "had illegally granted six-month contract extensions in 1929 and that the route extensions made under the Watres Act were of doubtful legality." [27] On Friday, February 9, 1934, faced with accusations of fraud and collusion in the granting of airmail contracts, Postmaster General James A. Farley cancelled all existing airmail contracts. President Franklin D. Roosevelt, in turn, ordered the Army Air Corps to carry the mail under the existing emergency. The president, however, had two other options: one, transport the mail by rail, as in years prior to air transportation; or two, since most airline pilots were also Air Corps Reserve officers, order them to active duty and benefit from their airline experience. He chose neither; the results were disastrous.

The genesis of the problem lay in terminology. The purpose of the Air Mail Act of 1925, as cited in the text, was to encourage commercial aviation by authorizing the postmaster general to contract for airmail service. [28] Former Postmaster General Brown, an appointee of the Hoover administration, interpreted the legislation literally. A man far ahead of his time in economic philosophy, Brown believed the airlines should be able to develop profitably without the help of airmail payments. He realized further that only large, well-financed, well-managed air transportation companies could achieve the objectives outlined in the legislation.[29] Brown, however, acted on good authority; the Amended Airmail Act granted the postmaster general the power to award contracts without competitive bidding.[30] Nevertheless, the complaints of small airlines not receiving airmail contracts, even though they were low bidders, enriched political debate during the 1932 presidential campaign. President Roosevelt, embarking on a crusade against government corruption and favoritism in the granting of contracts, was forced to act.[31] On February 19, 1934, after assembling 200 officers, 324 enlisted men, and 122 aircraft, the Army Air Corps was ready to embark on its new mission. The Army Air Corps, ill-prepared and poorly equipped, encountered problems from the outset. Three days before taking over the airmail routes, three pilots were killed en route to their new assignment.[32]

The impact of the new policy had already reached Austin. The departure of the northbound American Airways plane from Robert Mueller airport on February 18 at 5:52 P.M. marked the end of Austin's airmail service for some four months. Community leaders, nevertheless, expended every effort possible to regain the service, but to no avail. Congressman J. P. Buchanan reported to Austin business leaders on February 17 that he was unable to determine whether the army plane service would be extended from Dallas to Brownsville, a route which would include Austin. In the meantime, while the Air Corps flew the mail over a greatly reduced route mileage, the commercial air carriers maintained passenger service and Austin's mail moved by rail.

On March 27, 1934, President Roosevelt announced he was returning the airmail service to private carriers but with specific changes. For example, companies which formerly held airmail contracts must be reorganized to become eligible for the temporary certificates and, furthermore, "companies having any corporate connections or affiliations with operators of competitive routes or aircraft-part manufacturers should be prohibited from holding airmail contracts."[33] To qualify, the major carriers disguised themselves with slight name changes, American Airways became American Airlines, Eastern Air Transport became Eastern Airlines, and Trans-Continental & Western Air just added the suffix, Inc. However, in rebidding the airmail contracts, American Airlines lost the Dallas-Brownsville route to Long & Harmon, Inc., which previously served Austin only as a passenger carrier. That company's 1,125 route miles, bid at the rate of 19.75 cents per mile, extended from Amarillo to Brownsville and included Houston, Galveston, and Corpus Christi. Long & Harmon's flight equipment consisted of four Stinson "Reliant" cabin planes, with two aircraft in reserve.[34] On June 1, 1934, the first Long & Harmon Stinson landed at Robert Mueller airport. The northbound flight arrived at 10:20 A.M., the southbound flight at 6:05 P.M. After a four-month interruption, Austin again had daily airmail service.

The interruption of commercial airmail service had a far-reaching impact on the history of American aviation. The tragic record posted by the Air Corps—sixty-six crashes, twelve deaths, at a cost to the government of some $4 million—demonstrated the Air Corps' inadequacies, which led to increased congressional appropriations and drastic changes in aviation cadet training procedures. Furthermore, the subsequent passage of the Air Mail Act of 1934 mandated that the government award airmail contracts only by competitive bidding and further eliminated interlocking relationships between airline companies and aircraft manufacturers.[35] An indirect benefit of that episode was the airlines' recognition that the industry's future lay not in dependence on airmail contracts, but in the development of passenger traffic. That led to the major air lines establishing traffic and sales departments to develop passenger travel.

The ensuing fall-out from the 1934 airmail debacle left its mark on Austin aviation. On May 5, when American Airlines' northbound plane departed from Robert Mueller airport at 5:52 P.M., that marked the termination of the company's service to the Capital City for some four decades. American closed its Driskill Hotel office on May 18 and transferred its only remaining employee to El Paso. The company, however, continued to operate the Dallas–Los Angeles line. Long & Harmon Airlines, replacing American Airlines as Austin's new airmail carrier, envisioned increased passenger traffic developing along its recently acquired system. On September 19, that company introduced its ten-passenger Ford Tri-Motor aircraft to the Austin market. The radio-equipped Ford departed Austin daily southbound at 10:20 P.M. and northbound at 6:50 P.M. For the first time reservations were available on the Long & Harmon line; the company also announced a 10 percent reduction on round-trip fares.[36] Ford Tri-Motors had been used previously by other airlines, but the post-1934 trend was toward multiengine equipment. That was a sign of the times; multiengine aircraft afforded greater speed, greater carrying capacity, greater safety margin, plus additional passenger accommodations.

The year 1935 brought many changes to Robert Mueller airport and the services it provided to the aviation industry. First, the city appointed Harry Hammill to replace Webb Ruff as airport manager. Hammill's arrangement with the city was unique; under his lease agreement he operated the airport as a private enterprise. Since the City of Austin Engineering and Public Works Department maintained the facility's basic infrastructure, city budgets of that era contain no separate accounting of airport expenditures. However, beginning in 1932, the engineering department received a separate appropriation of $856.65, of which $489.65 was for runway repairs. The following year the department requested $210 for airport maintenance and the same the next year, which the city manager increased that year to $675 to cover $500 in building repairs. In 1935, from a total city budget of $2,249,545.49, the city council approved only $225 for the airport.[37] However, after some five years of virtual neglect, the city received a $45,000 Works Progress Administration grant to install a new 2,200-foot runway, resurface the existing runway, plus construct a taxiway leading to the passenger terminal.[38]

The addition of the 2,200-foot runway heralded a new era in Austin aviation; with the airfield's increased landing capacity, the city was about to enter the age of high-speed air transportation. On March 22, 1935, when Bowen Air Lines introduced its new, sleek, all-metal, low-wing Vultee V-1A transport, the company began providing the Austin market the fastest air service available. With a cruising speed of approximately 225 miles per hour, the Vultee, holder of two trans-continental speed records, reduced the Dallas-Brownsville flying time by one hour. The southbound flight arrived in Austin at 9:40 A.M., and the northbound at 4:05 P.M.[39] Bowen's dominance of the high-speed Austin market was, however, short lived. On January 1, 1935, Braniff Airways purchased Long & Harmon Airlines, which held airmail contracts for ten Texas cities, including Austin. Braniff immediately began serving the Capital City with its Lockheed "Vega" equipment, but on April 7 switched to its new ten-place Lockheed "Electra" aircraft. The twin-engine "Electra," which cruised at 190 miles per hour, represented a new dimension in air transportation. The trend toward greater speed, safety, and passenger comfort was reflected in the company's advertising campaign. Air travelers were encouraged to fly the Braniff "Electra" with its two engines, two pilots, two-tails (vertical rudders), and a two-way radio, which in the 1930s was considered an added safety factor. On March 21, 1935, William F. Salathe, Braniff director of public relations, wrote Max Bickler that the company was establishing a radio network of seventeen ground stations, six with 400-watt power and eleven with 50-watt power. With that equipment, Salathe explained, "We will be in contact with our planes en route all the time."[40] A licensed radio operator was on duty in Austin from 7:00 A.M. to 10:00 P.M.

Braniff's introduction of the "Electra" evolved into another gala event staged at Robert Mueller airport. The company mailed personalized invitations to all city and state officials, members of the legislature, and prominent business executives and their families, offering a free introductory flight over the city in the new "Electra." Company president T. E. Braniff and his wife were present to host the event.[41]

During the ensuing months, Bowen and Braniff, obviously realizing that future profits depended on developing passenger traffic, went "head-to-head" competing for the local air travel business. Both companies opened downtown ticket offices, Bowen in the Driskill Hotel and Braniff in the Stephen F. Austin Hotel. The competition carried over to newspaper coverage. On April 22, 1935, an *Austin Statesman* story bearing the headline "Braniff Speeds Its Schedule Up" described the new Lockheed "Electra" as "one of the most comfortable and reliable [aircraft] in service on the passenger lines today." Bowen responded the following day with a paid newspaper advertisement, inviting Austin citizens to "Ride the Luxurious Vultee, World's Fastest Transport; Only 60 Minutes to Dallas." Four days later, in obvious retaliation, Braniff announced a late-evening northbound schedule, urging its customers to "Ride the Better-Than-Three-Mile-A-Minute DE LUXE ELECTRA . . . Two Motors—Two Pilots—10 Passengers."[42] The Austin community apparently responded favorably to the two companies' promotions. During the last six months of 1935, deplaning airline passengers numbered 1,345, enplaning passengers 1,502.[43]

Temple Bowen eventually realized that, in the highly competitive short haul airline operation, an airmail contract was the difference between success and failure. Speed alone was not the answer. However, when the Post Office Department began using people to "Fly With Air Mail," Bowen believed that gave his competitors unfair advantage. He responded by displaying his slogan, Fly Past the Air Mail, on the side of his planes.[44] His company, however, faced problems that mere slogans could not resolve. While other major air carriers were turning to larger multiengine aircraft, Bowen invested heavily in a fleet of less efficient single-engine Vultees. Nevertheless, the company garnered a portion of the market; in May 1935, Bowen Air Lines reported its strongest showing in the company's five-year history, but to no avail. On February 15, 1936, Temple Bowen announced he was discontinuing his airline operation.[45] With Bowen's demise, Braniff became Austin's only air carrier.

Robert Mueller airport remained a source of civic pride and interest. Early in 1935, the Chamber of Commerce extended an invitation to Austin citizens to visit "your magnificent airport and view the activity going on there. . . . Frequently 200 or more cars are parked around the Municipal Building [airport terminal], usually on Sunday evenings." The airport was, indeed, the center of much activity. During the first six months of 1935, 347 Army Air Corps planes landed at Mueller, plus 190 transient aircraft, as well as the aircraft of fixed base operators carrying some 1,735 citizens on sightseeing flights over the city. Within that same time frame, the two commercial air carriers, Braniff and Bowen, enplaned 1,502 passengers and deplaned 1,345. Less visible, but also indicative of the community's growing dependence upon air transportation, were the 7,445 pounds of airmail and 820 pounds of air express that passed through Robert Mueller airport.[46]

Walter E. Long, Austin Chamber of Commerce manager, remained the city's premier aviation philosopher. A man far ahead of his time in predicting the lead time between aircraft development and the technical infrastructure necessary for its use, he urged the City of Austin to prepare for a new era in air transportation. He argued, "the heavier planes of today land with a striking weight of 28,000 to 30,000 pounds and the present runways cannot stand the force." Specifically, longer and better-constructed runways were needed to accommodate commercial air transports then in development. Long could also argue the future was here; the first six months of 1936 saw 567 commercial aircraft, 237 transport planes, and 180 Army Air Corps planes of various configuration land at Robert Mueller airport.[47] The improvements Long sought were not immediately forthcoming.

The ongoing dialogue between Braniff Airways and the City of Austin also focused on field conditions, a matter which for the most part went unheeded. On March 19, 1936, Braniff operations manager Donald C. Walbridge appealed to the president of the Austin Chamber of Commerce for assistance. "The airport is in very bad condition," he wrote. "To date, we have been unable to get any action [from the city] on the matter." He pointed out that the Works Progress Administration had allotted $36,947.50 for airport improvements and no work had begun.[48] Walbridge next wrote Max Bickler, chairman of the Aviation Committee, pointing out that unless the matter was expedited immediately, the WPA funds would be withdrawn by June 30. Bickler, in turn, appealed to City Manger Guiton Morgan, who explained that no action had been taken because relief labor was not available, and, furthermore, there was nothing the city could do to implement the project. Stuart Bailey, Braniff's assistant to the president, thought otherwise. Robert Burck, Braniff's Austin traffic manager, had previously contacted H. P. Drought, the local WPA administrator, who stated funds would be available if the city authorities would designate the airport project a priority matter. That was not to be; the Austin mayor remained steadfast in the matter. By the end of the year, a final appeal to Texas congressman James P. Buchanan had yielded no action.[49]

Obviously, the Austin city government accorded airport development a very low priority; the 1936 airport appropriation was only $325. The following year the airport manager requested $950 for a power mower, which the city manager rejected, reducing the airport appropriation to $285.[50] The city manager apparently based his fiscal conservatism on public perception of aviation during that era. "Airports did not play a major role in the lives of most Americans until very recently," wrote aviation historian Janet Bednarek.[51] To the average citizen, especially in the mid-1930s, flying was a rich man's indulgence or a daredevil's game and did not affect the lives of the urban taxpayer. The Austin city manager acted accordingly; adequate funding for the municipal airport still lay somewhere in the future. Other city governments, however, viewed commercial air transportation within a more positive context. That same year, 1937, the City of Houston purchased a 600-acre field known as Houston Municipal Airport (later William P. Hobby Airport), and expanded that facility to 1,240 acres. At that time Houston was being served by two air carriers, Braniff Airways and Eastern Air Lines.

Braniff Airways' introduction of its new, fourteen-passenger DC-2 [Douglas Commercial] air transport to the Austin market on June 10, 1937, partially fulfilled Walter Long's projection of the coming air age. The DC-2 carried a maximum takeoff weight of 18,560 pounds, only 1,440 pounds less than the minimum weight Long previously cited. Compared to two predecessor aircraft, the DC-2 outweighed Bowen's Lockheed "Orion" by 13,360 pounds and Braniff's Lockheed "Electra" by 8,260 pounds.[52] The arrival of the new airliner attracted a wide audience of state officials, Austin businessmen, and aviation enthusiasts; Bob Burch, Braniff's long-time city traffic manager, hosted the event. The new aircraft carried a

three-person crew—two pilots and an attractive, uniformed "hostess"—
and cruised at 190 miles per hour. The introduction of the DC-2 by the nation's air carriers represented a major milestone in the history of commercial aviation. Essentially it was the fulfillment of former Postmaster General
Walter Brown's belief that the airlines should be able to operate profitably
without airmail dependency by focusing instead on developing passenger traffic. The Douglas DC-2's in-flight passenger accommodations—
food and beverage service and passengers addressed by name—represented
a major step in achieving that goal. According to aviation historians Robert M. Kane and Allan D. Voss, "by the end of 1936, the [airlines'] income
from passengers exceeded the income from airmail profits."[53]

Despite the limited appropriations, construction at Mueller continued
during 1937. With a combination of municipal and Public Works Administration funding—$17,794.79 from the city and $40,000 from the
PWA—the Public Works Department completed a 2,100-foot northwest-
southeast runway, with a balanced topping of asphalt and crushed stone.[54]
The benefits were almost immediate. In late October the Army Air Corps
staged a two-week maneuver at Mueller with some thirty-six aircraft participating. At the conclusion of the maneuver, the Air Corps held a public
reception, where some three thousand people inspected the military aircraft
display.[55]

Even in the late 1930s, aviation and aviators continued to stimulate great
public interest. On July 24, 1937, San Angelo native and trans-Atlantic flyer
Jimmie Mattern landed his Lockheed "Vega" monoplane at Robert
Mueller airport seeking Governor James V. Allred's blessing for a proposed
San Diego–Moscow nonstop flight. His arrival evoked all the pomp and
pageantry of a state ceremony; National Guard planes escorted Mattern
into Austin, while other private aircraft bearing public officials from around
the state landed at Mueller for the ceremony. The governor cooperated to
his fullest. As a host of state government officials, oil company executives
sponsoring the flight, and hundreds of townspeople stood in reverent si-
lence, the governor, after making a short speech, swung a bottle of Lake
Buchanan water across the wing of Mattern's plane, naming it officially
"The Texan." Despite the official nature of the occasion, all was for naught;
Secretary of Commerce Daniel C. Roper refused approval of the 6,400-
mile flight over the North Pole to Russia.

Austin's greatest celebration for a famous flyer was yet to come. Douglas
Corrigan remains American aviation's most notable anomaly. After being

denied permission to fly his Curtiss "Robin," a three-place light aircraft, to Ireland, he filed a New York City to Los Angeles flight plan; however, instead of flying west, he flew east across the Atlantic Ocean to Ireland, winning the sobriquet "Wrong Way" Corrigan. The likelihood of his surviving a trans-Atlantic flight in a small plane was so remote, the achievement further stimulated public interest in the man; all America wanted to see "Wrong Way" Corrigan. Invitations from Texas governor Allred and American Airlines president C. R. Smith led to the Galveston-born flyer's visit to Austin on August 25, 1938. A forty-eight-member committee developed reception plans commensurate with the importance of the event.

The celebration began at noon at Robert Mueller airport. When Corrigan landed and taxied to a stop on the airport runway, he became the focus of a pushing, pulling, and shouting crowd assembled to see the famous flyer. Corrigan later joined Austin mayor Tom Miller and Texas governor James V. Allred in the mayor's car, which embarked for downtown Austin led by a police escort with sirens screaming. Arriving at Eleventh Street and Congress Avenue, the official entourage parked in front of a flatbed truck on which was mounted an airplane, *headed backward.* Taking his position astride the symbolic aircraft, Corrigan rode down Congress Avenue waving and smiling at some 15,000 spectators who lined the street. Following a Lions Club luncheon at the Driskill Hotel attended by some 214 Austin citizens, Corrigan left for San Antonio to attend another reception.

Against a background of increased world tension, the good times in Austin continued to roll. Five days after British prime minister Neville Chamberlain returned from Munich, claiming there would be peace in our time, the Austin Aviation Club sponsored a free air show at Robert Mueller airport. Held in observance of National Air Week, the Sunday, October 2, 1938, event opened with a grand parade of planes over the Capital City. The aerial spectacle lured some 5,000 of Austin's 80,968 citizens to the airport to see pilots from Austin, San Antonio, Dallas, Fort Worth, and Houston participate in events that included balloon bursting, bomb-dropping (actually sacks of flour), acrobatic flying, a free-turkey parachute drop, and air races. Austin pilot and flight instructor F. R. "Doc" Haile won first place in the heavy plane race.[56]

Some of those who attended the air show on that autumn afternoon recalled the late 1930s as a happy time in Austin. The Depression appeared to be loosening its hold on the economy, employment was on the upswing, mass entertainment was either free or inexpensive, and the University of

Texas had fielded what appeared to be a winning football team. But change was in the offing; the warning signs were beginning to appear on the distant horizon. And although few people seemed to realize it, one period in the broad scope of American culture was nearing an end; another was about to begin.

World War II Civilian Pilot Training Program two-place Taylorcraft trainers at Ragsdale Flying Service, Robert Mueller Municipal Airport. The University of Texas administered the college/university–level program in cooperation with local fixed base operators.

Second graduating class of the Non-College Civilian Pilot Training Program, sponsored by the Austin Public Schools, at Browning Aerial Service. Standing, left of propeller, Emma Carter Browning, school executives N. H. Wittner and T. B. Barnett, Superintendent of Schools A. N. McCallum, and Chamber of Commerce Aviation Committee chairman Max Bickler. Others unidentified.

Mary Aletha Miller, member of the first Non-College Civilian Pilot Training Program class, spins the propeller on a training aircraft. One woman from each class of ten was accepted for flight training.

Robert L. (Bobby) Ragsdale began flight instruction at Robert Mueller Municipal Airport in September 1941, operating a Civilian Pilot Training Program. Ragsdale Flying Service, developed jointly with his wife, Pearle, became one of the major fixed base operators in Texas. Photo by Neal Douglas.

Some of the Navy N3N-3 intermediate trainers used at Ragsdale Flying Service. By January 1, 1943, the company employed seven mechanics and eight instructors for twenty students.

Browning Aerial Service instructors with the War Training Service program at University Airport. On December 19, 1942, the Civilian Pilot Training Program was renamed the War Training Service, which accelerated flight instruction.

The former schoolhouse that became Austin's second airport terminal in 1942. More than twice the size of the original terminal, this facility also housed the United States Weather Bureau, the CAA office, and the Braniff ticket counter. A restaurant was added later.

Source: Austin History Center, Austin Public Library, PICA 26439.

In December 1939, Braniff Airways began DC-3 service to Austin. The twenty-one-passenger DC-3, which replaced the fourteen-passenger DC-2, cruised at 165 mph and carried a three-person crew—two pilots and a "hostess."

Source: Austin History Center, Austin Public Library, PICA 19730.

On September 19, 1942, the arrival of fifty-two Douglas C-47 transports of the 316th Troop Carrier Group marked the opening of Del Valle Army Air Base, located southeast of Austin on some 2,900 acres along State Highway 71. Later designated Bergstrom Air Force Base, that facility, later acquired by the City of Austin, became Austin-Bergstrom International Airport in 1999.

Source: Austin History Center, Austin Public Library, PICA 30712.

The Douglas C-47, military version of the commercial DC-3, became the military's primary transport during World War II. One of the world's most successful aircraft, by 1991 the DC-3/C-47 had been in continuous use some fifty-five years.

Source: Austin History Center, Austin Public Library, PICA 19593.

Following World War II, a number of new air transport models began serving Austin. The Martin 202, introduced in the Austin market by Pioneer Air Lines, carried forty passengers and a three-person crew, at a maximum speed of 312 mph.

CHAPTER 5

WAR TRAINING RETURNS TO THE UNIVERSITY

A S the decade of the 1930s drew to a close, the national psychology was in transition. In the wake of Munich, policy makers began to view the American nation within a broader world context, their perspective colored by a growing awareness of military weakness. By 1937, among world powers, the United States had dropped to sixth place in combat military strength, a fact of which President Roosevelt took note.[1] On December 27, 1938, at a White House news conference, he announced he had approved a Civil Aeronautics Authority (CAA) plan to annually teach twenty thousand college students to fly. In early 1939, with $100,000 funding from the National Youth Administration (NYA), the CAA launched the experimental program in thirteen institutions. Although the program was presented within a civilian context, the military benefit appeared obvious.[2] Success was soon forthcoming. By the twelfth of April, 325 student pilots had logged 3,386 hours flying time, while 199 had soloed and 4 had received their private pilot's license.[3] North Texas Agricultural College was the only participating Texas institution.

The success of the initial program led to the passage of the Civilian Pilot Training Act of 1939 on June 27 of that year. It was not an easy victory for the Roosevelt administration; opposition to the measure formed along partisan lines. Some Republicans denounced the Civilian Pilot Training Program (CPTP) "as a fraud and the CAA as just a war-mongering government agency."[4] Those who recognized the program's potential prevailed, however. The act authorized the CAA "to train civilian pilots or to conduct programs for such training, including studies and researches as to the most desirable qualifications for aircraft pilots."[5] No person would be denied the benefits of the program on account of "race, creed, or color," and at least 5 percent of the persons selected for training would be noncollege students. Local aviation, educational, or civic institutions would conduct the training programs under contract with the CAA. Austin citizens first learned of the program on December 5, 1939, when Hugh Herndon, CAA private flying specialist, presented plans for ground school and flight training to the directors of the Austin Chamber of Commerce. Chamber manager Walter E. Long responded positively, informing Herndon on December 7 that the organization was willing to cooperate in the establishment of a noncollege pilots' training school in Austin. Long's only provision was that the chamber be relieved of any financial or legal liability that may be incurred in the operation of the school.[6]

That same day the CAA issued a local press release, outlining the scope of the program. Aviation ground school instruction would be open to all noncollege citizens between the ages of eighteen and twenty-five as of January 1. Local authorities would choose the students to participate in the seventy-two-hour ground school course, to be conducted by instructors fulfilling requirements for a CAA instructor's rating. Each instructor would be assigned fifty students who attended class six hours a week for twelve weeks. The required ten-dollar registration fee included textbooks. The top ten students from each class would be eligible for flight training. Although women would be admitted to the ground courses without restriction, only one woman from each class of top-ten students would be accepted for flight instruction, the same proportion allowed in the college-level course. Since the Austin program was the only one in Texas, students from other sections of the state were eligible to apply for admission.

Locating a teaching facility to offer the instruction became Walter Long's next objective. Dr. Homer Price Rainey, president of the University of Texas, refused participation. He explained that "the University would not operate such a school unless they were requested by the government."[7] The Austin Independent School District, however, was more responsive. On February 9, 1940, Superintendent A. N. McCallum signed a contract with the Civil Aeronautics Authority to conduct the Civilian Pilot Training Program (CPTP) ground school at Austin High School. The ground school opened on February 22, with seventy enrollees; classes met from 7:30 to 9:30 P.M., three times a week for twelve weeks. C. Julian Baldwin represented the Chamber of Commerce in the project; Superintendent McCallum appointed Thomas B. Barnette to direct the school, with Norbert H. Wittner as his assistant. Neither had flight training; however, both had mathematics and physics backgrounds and qualified as CAA ground school instructors.

In his new assignment, Wittner recalled he was challenged by the lack of instructional equipment. In teaching a course in aircraft instruments, he relied solely on an aneroid barometer; the CAA provided no actual aircraft instruments for the classroom. In teaching meteorology, Wittner improvised further. He used the school's darkroom to produce 3" × 4" lantern slides of the various cloud formations pilots should be able to recognize. In spite of the lack of teaching aids, the instructional staff achieved a level of success; on March 5, Hugh Herndon inspected the school and filed a favorable report with the Fort Worth CAA office. Wittner believed student motivation accounted largely for his success as a CPTP instructor. For some students, the goal was to earn their private pilot's license; for others, facing the draft, it was a way to avoid the infantry and enhance their chance of being accepted by the Air Corps.[8]

Lloyd Fry Jr. was typical of many of the students attending the Austin CPTP ground school. A 1936 Marble Falls [Texas] High School graduate, he moved to Austin the following year to work as a reserve brakeman on the Southern Pacific railroad. Fry learned of the ground school through a newspaper announcement and recognized an opportunity to fulfill his childhood dream of learning to fly. He applied for the school and was admitted. Although Fry's railroad work schedule sometimes conflicted with ground school, he studied hard and scored high on all the tests. And while the students shared a common objective, there was no camaraderie: Fry explained they were all competing for the scholarships. The ground school ended on May 14. Hugh Herndon supervised the final test where forty-six of the seventy students competed for the ten flight-training scholarships. Fry survived, just barely; he was number nine among the ten scholarship winners.[9]

The Chamber of Commerce Aviation Committee faced a major decision in selecting a school for the flight training. At the January 27, 1940, meeting, Committee Chairman C. Julian Baldwin Sr., director of Flight Training, submitted the applications of four Austin fixed base operators for CAA approval. They were Harry A. Hammill, Lt. C. Dibrell Fator, Robert M. Browning, and F. R. (Doc) Haile. They, in turn, submitted individual applications to Ralph R. DeVore, Federal Aviation Authority (FAA) senior private flying specialist at Fort Worth. Although Hammill was then offering flight instruction at Robert Mueller airport, no record of his application exists. Lt. Fator, a graduate of the Army Air Corps Flight Instructors School at Kelly Field, operated Austin Flying Club, Inc. at Penn Field, the former World War I Air Service Field. The lieutenant submitted a summary of his military career with a list of six character references; however, his flight equipment, two Taylorcraft trainers, was "on order."[10]

Robert M. Browning, a former Abilene, Texas, fixed base operator, learned of the forthcoming Austin CPTP school from his old barnstorming friend Hugh Herndon, then associated with the FAA. Herndon encouraged Browning to consider relocating his operation in the Austin area. In early September 1939, Browning, his wife, son, and a University of Texas student flew to Austin in Browning's four-place Stinson cabin plane, NC-416-Y. Aware that Harry Hammill was well established at Mueller, Browning landed at University Airport, where he met Webb Ruff, who owned that facility. Ruff, reportedly in poor health, had turned that operation over to his cousin, F. R. (Doc) Haile. Browning leased the airport from Ruff, and Haile moved his base to a site at 5600 Avenue F, located some two miles south of University Airport.

Haile's new base of operations, which consisted of ninety-eight acres leased from Ella Campbell, was some four miles north of downtown Austin, then at the outer fringe of city occupancy. Hoping to provide flight instruction for the CPTP ground school graduates, both Browning and Haile filed formal applications with the FAA. Browning listed his flight equipment as one Taylorcraft training aircraft and the Stinson cabin plane, to be housed in a 60' × 120' steel hangar. By that time, Browning had a contract with the University of Texas Aeronautical Society and some thirty-five members were receiving flight instruction at University Airport. He noted the airport was located about three-and-one-half miles from Austin High School; transportation to the field was available via either taxi or Greyhound bus. Haile's training fleet included two Aeroncas and a Pitcairn biplane, in which some thirty students were then receiving instruction. His other facilities included a 50' × 100' steel hangar, plus fuel and aircraft repair services. Neither field had hard-surface runways; all applicants reported having the required two parachutes.[11]

Occurring in the final months of the Great Depression, all fixed base operators regarded the CPT program as a great financial windfall and made every attempt to strengthen their applications by including personal endorsements with them. At a meeting of the Aviation Committee on January 27, 1940, Austin businessman Howard Bull, representing the University of Texas Aeronautical Society, stated that the society favored the appointment of Robert M. Browning. Bull pointed out that there was little air traffic at University Airport, plus Browning was also a licensed aircraft mechanic. When it appeared the flight school assignment might go to an out-of-town firm, Austin attorney William Carssow intervened in Haile's behalf. In a letter to United States Senator Morris Sheppard, Carssow described Haile as a licensed flight instructor who owned his airport and a fleet of five airplanes, with three more on order.[12] When Ralph R. DeVore made a final choice for an Austin flight school, he disqualified Haile because his landing field was less than three miles from the nearest airport. Browning received the appointment; instruction began in May 1940.

Lloyd Fry, continuing his railroad employment, rode a bus twice a week to University Airport for flight instruction. His first impression of Browning Aerial Service proved valid; Robert Browning was a well-organized, fair but demanding instructor. He expected promptness, uniformity (everyone had to purchase white coveralls with "Browning Aerial Service" printed on the back), and total concentration in the air. Fry's instruction began at half-past three on the afternoon of May 27, 1940, in a side-by-side Taylorcraft trainer, powered by a sixty-five horsepower Continental engine. Following his initial thirty-minute flight, Browning's log book entry indicated Fry was "Calm—easy on controls." Subsequent entries document Fry's increasing airmanship: "More confidence," "Reaction good; progress good," "Relaxed—smoothing out maneuvers," and "Improved coordination in turns."[13] During the initial instruction, Browning taught Fry basic flight skills, emphasizing air safety. With a limited instrument package in the Taylorcraft, Fry learned to concentrate on what was occurring outside of the aircraft. "He wanted you to keep your head moving all the time," looking out for position orientation and other aircraft. "Stiff neck pilots do not live long," Browning explained. Browning was equally demanding when Fry began performing the basic flight maneuvers. "If you made a skidding turn [an uncoordinated turn that lost altitude]," Fry explained, "he would chew on that cigar and make all kinds of mean remarks, like 'If I had a parachute, I would jump out of this airplane!'"[14]

Apparently Fry never gave Browning sufficient justification to bail out. Some eight weeks later, following a short instructional flight, Fry heard the words he had been longing to hear: "Alright, take it up." Browning ordered him to "Go around the pattern, bring it in and land it. And if I wave you on, make another landing," Fry recalled. "So he gave me the 'go ahead' and I made a second landing. It was very exciting—very, very exciting." On August 2, following a 1 hour, 22 minute instructional flight, Fry achieved the next level of pilot proficiency. Browning's log book entry reads, "Good time—solo X-country." Fry's first solo cross-country flight was another memorable experience. His instructions were to fly to San Marcos municipal airport, land, and return to University Airport. Arriving at the San Marcos field, Fry entered the traffic pattern, and while on final approach, he saw something he had never seen before—a concrete runway. "I was afraid of that runway," he recalled. "I looked at that concrete and I looked at the grass. Needless to say, I landed on the grass."[15]

Lloyd Fry and seven other graduates of the Non-College Civilian Pilot Training Program received their private pilots' licenses at University Airport. Fry passed his flight test on August 15, 1940, and FAA Inspector Frank J. Miller issued him Private Pilot Certificate No. 49115-40. With licenses in hand, the graduates' next objective became cadet training in the Army Air Corps. News from Europe forecast a growing need for their services; by June 23, 1940, German troops had swept through The Netherlands and Belgium and occupied most of France, including Paris. With the forces of Hitler poised along the English Channel, his threatened invasion of England appeared imminent. The possibility of the United States becoming involved in the conflict prompted many political leaders, previously reluctant to address the issue, to reevaluate their positions. By July 29, when seventy-seven new students entered the second Non-College CPTP ground school at Austin High School, University of Texas president Homer Rainey had assumed a more positive view of the University's role in military preparedness.

Dr. Rainey's initial reluctance stemmed from three factors: a limited budget, an overly committed teaching faculty, and the below-college-level courses required by the CAA. However, Dean W. R. Woolrich, dean of the Engineering School, viewed the University's role in aeronautics within a much broader context. Foreseeing the increased demand for aeronautical engineers, he argued the University should assume a leadership role in providing men, research, and design to keep pace with the aviation industry's burgeoning growth.[16] Dr. Rainey was hesitant, but no doubt the massive bombing raids Germany launched against Great Britain during the summer of 1940 prompted him to alter his stance. Writing to the University Board of Regents on September 6, Dr. Rainey requested a "mail vote" approving an application to the Civil Aeronautics Authority to offer the Civilian Pilot Training course at the University of Texas. That step was the first on the way to a three-point program he hoped to establish, which would include inauguration of a primary training unit for fifty persons by October 1, 1940; provision of an advanced class following their graduation in February 1941; and, in obvious response to Dean Woolrich's recommendation, development of both undergraduate and graduate programs in aeronautical engineering in the School of Engineering. Dr. Rainey concluded, "I believe we can inaugurate this program without any additional cost to the University." The returning "mail vote" unanimously supported the proposal.[17]

The FAA, under the Department of Transportation, quickly expedited the matter. On September 14, 1940, only four days after Dr. Rainey filed the University's application, he signed a contract launching the University's Civilian Pilot Training Program for forty students. The contract provided that each student purchase insurance coverage in the amount of three thousand dollars, plus five hundred dollars for hospital and medical care, while the University would furnish transportation from the campus to the airport where the students received flight instruction. For financial compensation, the government agreed to pay the University twenty dollars for each student completing the course. The initial contract was to be completed by January 31, with an option for extensions.[18]

The announcement of the impending opening of the CPT program attracted wide interest on campus; some two hundred students applied for the fifty class openings. (Following the signing of the contract, the University's class allotment was increased to fifty.) Instruction began on Monday, October 14, in the Mechanical Engineering Department. The four-month, seventy-two-hour ground school included civil air regulations, navigation, meteorology, aircraft servicing, and 35 to 45 hours of flight instruction in light aircraft, such as Taylorcraft, Aeroncas, and Piper "Cubs." Upon completion of the course, the trainees received a private pilot's certificate. The secondary course included 108 hours of ground school instruction in navigation, power plants, and aerodynamics, plus 35 to 45 hours of flight instruction in larger Waco UPF-7 aircraft. Hours completed in the secondary course could be applied toward a commercial pilot's license. Ten percent of the initial enrollment was available to women; nine enrolled and eight completed the course.[19]

University President Rainey appointed Vice-President J. Alton Burdine administrator of the Civilian Pilot Training Program. Initially, Professor Harry L. Kent coordinated the primary program, while Professor Venton L. Doughtie coordinated the secondary program. However, in the fall of 1941, Professor Doughtie became coordinator of all aviation classes. R. V. Vittucci, W. J. Carter, and J. H. McLendon also served on the instructional staff. W. E. Sjoberg operated the airport bus. Launching the program, however, was not the financial burden Dr. Rainey anticipated. The University added only one staff member as a replacement for one reassigned to the new program. H. G. Johnson, a graduate of the University of California, joined the faculty on November 1, 1940, at a salary of two hundred dollars per month. His appointment expired on June 15, 1941.[20]

When the forty initial CPTP students entered the Engineering Building that October morning, they embarked on a new adventure, the extent of which no one could possibly foretell. The daily news conveyed a mixed metaphor. While foreign headlines reported battlefield disaster ("Nazis Heavy Air-Blitz Over London's Historic Buildings"), campus activities followed traditional themes. The same day students in formal dress danced to the music of Ozzie Nelson's Orchestra at the Pledge Night German in Gregory Gymnasium and Col. George Hurt announced openings for three twirling drum majors for the Longhorn Band. Although both the war and the local items attracted considerable campus interest, there was evidence of change: of the forty students accepted for CPTP flight training, four were women. Evelyn Eckert, Rebecca Henry, Pauline Strickland, and Lorraine Alice Stutzman joined their thirty-six male classmates as they boarded the bus for the airfields. Thirty disembarked at the municipal airport, where contractor Harry Hammill helped them launch their aviation careers, while ten continued on to University Airport, where flight instructor Robert Browning awaited their arrival.[21]

Richard Bloomer, a graduate student in geology, well remembered his first CPTP training flight at Browning Aerial Service. Never having flown before, he had no idea of what to expect, but once he felt the controls of that little Taylorcraft, he knew he had made a wise choice. "I'll never forget the sensation of my first flight," he recalled. "When we got up and made turns, I felt like I was just pivoting in the air. You don't see the land go by like you used to [on the ground]. I'll never forget that sensation, that first day in that Taylorcraft; my first flight in an airplane. I thoroughly enjoyed it." With his graduate studies in geology, his teaching fellowship, plus the CPT program, Bloomer led a hectic life on campus. He would rush out to the field—his girlfriend had an automobile—get in his hour of flying, and rush back to campus. Although there was little time for socializing at University Airport, Mr. and Mrs. Browning created a family atmosphere. "The Brownings were just excellent," Bloomer explained. "Everybody thought so much of them. It was kinda like mom and pop." It was not until Bloomer entered the Air Corps cadet program that he fully realized the benefits of the CPTP training. "I sailed through cadets," he recalled. "I was the first one to solo in [the Air Corps] primary school. And at that time, they were washing out sixty percent in primary."[22]

Like most University students entering the CPT program, Ray Keenan viewed flight training from a twofold perspective: the fulfillment of a teenager's dream to fly and in the event of military service, the choice of the Air Corps over the infantry. Keenan's flight instruction began on October 1, 1941, at University Airport, and especially for him, time was a factor. He hoped to learn to fly before his twenty-sixth birthday, the age limit for entering the Army Air Corps cadet program. Eagerly responding to Max Logsdon's instruction in the 65-horsepower Taylorcraft, Keenan soloed on October 28, just two days before his birthday. After the United States entered the war, and hearing nothing from his draft board, Keenan enrolled for the secondary CPTP course, which began on February 22, 1942.[23] The secondary students received instruction in a Waco UPF-7 open cockpit biplane. In that aircraft, powered with a 220-horsepower Continental engine, they developed a broad complex of aerobatic skills, including loops, snap rolls, and figure eights.

The skills Keenan and his classmates acquired during the CPT program hastened the end of their university careers, leading the way to a new mission in life. The task of fighting a three-continent war, especially following the recent fall of Corregidor, prompted a reevaluation of the nation's military policy. When Keenan's class graduated on May 10, 1942, they had the choice of entering either the army or navy air service. Keenan chose the Army Air Corps cadet program.[24] Based on the completion rates of students entering the CPT program, Keenan and his classmates compiled an enviable record. The first five classes—from the fall of 1940 through the spring of 1942—enrolled 272 students, 225 of whom completed the course, yielding a completion record of 82 percent.[25]

While the CAA was launching the CPT programs in Austin, many changes were occurring at Robert Mueller airport. With passenger traffic increasing, Braniff introduced its new Douglas DC-3 aircraft in the Austin market in December 1939. The twenty-one-passenger DC-3, which replaced the fourteen-passenger DC-2, carried a gross weight of 25,200 pounds, 6,640 pounds greater than its predecessor.[26] The increased use of the airfield by heavier and faster aircraft, both commercial and military, necessitated the acquisition of more land for extending the runways. Between May 29, 1939, and January 8, 1940, the City of Austin acquired 161.73 additional acres for airport expansion.[27] With limited local resources—as in 1939 when the Aviation Department requested $1,235 but the city manager recommended $285—the City of Austin turned to the federal government, which appropriated $321,000 for paving and extending the existing runways, building connecting taxiways, and improving drainage.[28] To further facilitate all-weather operation at the airport, the Department of Commerce installed a radio range station roughly two-and-one-half miles northwest of the airport. That electronic guidance system enabled aircraft to land and take off from the airport in weather conditions that otherwise would not have been possible. That appropriation was part of a government program to create a national airport system, as well as to expand airport facilities under a program of national defense. At the time the grant was approved, the CAA reported 2,374 airports in the nation, including 791 municipal facilities.[29]

With the expansion of military flight training, Harry Hammill, operator of the CPT program at Robert Mueller airport, relinquished his contract and embarked for Ballinger, Texas, where he established an Army Air Corps primary flight school. With Hammill's departure, the CAA, with the approval of the University of Texas, assigned that portion of the program to Robert L. Ragsdale. After learning to fly while attending Texas Technological College (later Texas Tech University), Ragsdale qualified for an instructor's rating, and later operated CPTP schools at Las Cruces, Silver City, and Socorro, New Mexico. With student enrollment declining in New Mexico, Ragsdale requested another school and, with Hammill vacating the University of Texas program, he accepted that assignment. Ragsdale acquired some of Hammill's equipment, which included two Taylor "Cubs," some spare parts, plus a disassembled Wiley Post biplane, which Hammill had used for student instruction. For his headquarters, Ragsdale leased the East Fifty-first Street steel hangar and the airport terminal building from the city for two hundred dollars per month. At that time he was the only occupant on the east side of the airport.[30]

That transaction occurred in late August 1941. With the University of Texas fall semester scheduled to begin in less than three weeks, time was of the essence. Still based in Socorro, Ragsdale departed immediately for Socorro to begin the move to Austin. It was a perilous journey. In violation of most basic rules of safe flight operations, Ragsdale took off from Austin after dark in a single-engine Culver "Cadet" that had no radio and no flight instruments. He followed the airway beacons to Big Springs, Texas, where he refueled, and continued on to El Paso Municipal Airport, where he had to wake the attendant for more fuel. He took off from El Paso around midnight, cleared the Organ Mountains at just under 8,000 feet, and pointed the nose of the little Culver "Cadet" northwestward toward the San Andres range and some of the most remote and hazardous sections of New Mexico. After about forty-five minutes he identified the Rio Grande, which he followed northward toward Socorro. When the streetlights came into view, Ragsdale circled the town, "buzzed" his residence, awakening his wife, Pearle, who drove to the airport to meet him.

Together Robert and Pearle launched the Ragsdale Flying Service, operating five light two-place training aircraft with four instructors, including Ragsdale himself. Pearle served as office manager. By the time the 1941 fall semester at the University of Texas began, Ragsdale Flying Service was ready to accept its quota of the thirty CPTP students entering the primary course. The ultimate growth and expansion of their business far exceeded their expectations. The December 7, 1941, Japanese attack on Pearl Harbor helped deem it so. In less than three months after their arrival in Austin, the nation was at war, and the product of their enterprise—trained pilots— suddenly was in great demand.

The war touched all aspects of American life, and Ragsdale, now deeply committed to the war effort, had to adjust to a new and unfamiliar environment. Immediately following December 7, amid reports of unidentified planes, the CAA (now the Civil Aeronautics Administration) grounded all private aircraft, including those engaged in the CPT programs, and temporarily cancelled all private pilots' licenses, a measure that startled the entire aviation industry. Four days later, on Thursday, December 11, CAA inspector Frank J. Miller met with local pilots whose planes had been grounded since Sunday to discuss the emergency. Miller offered sympathy and professional concern but little else; the grounding was a wartime emergency measure, the final decision awaited action from Washington. The matter remained in limbo until January 2, 1942, when the CAA announced that all CPTP trainees and instructors would be required to have new pilot identification cards by January 8.

In the meantime, some two hundred local pilots (including student pilots) converged on the municipal building and county courthouse to secure personal data necessary to renew their licenses. On January 6 and 7, a CAA inspector again appeared at the municipal airport to accept pilot applications. Relief, however, was slow in coming; by February 18, 1942, little had changed. More than thirty Austin airplanes, most of them engaged in pilot training, had been grounded since Saturday midnight, February 4, and activity at all airports in the city, with the exception of Mueller, had come to a standstill due to the CAA order.[31] Reports from Browning Aerial Service and Haile Flying Service indicate they had complied with all CAA requirements, but the inspectors had not had time to check their applications and reissue their permits to operate.

Ragsdale, however, received approval to continue flight training but was confronted with other wartime restrictions. In the wake of the Pearl Harbor attack, fear of sabotage swept the nation, and Robert Mueller airport, because of its current military importance and rural location, was considered vulnerable to clandestine attack. Since the city made no provision for an airport guard, and with the CAA requiring twenty-four-hour security, Ragsdale took the initiative. Travis County Sheriff Rip Collins deputized Ragsdale, issued him a badge, and after borrowing a .32-caliber automatic pistol from his father, he became the airport's first police officer. Lacking specific instructions from either Sheriff Collins or the CAA, Ragsdale assumed that "if any Jap planes come over, I was to shoot them down."[32] Although he sighted no Japanese planes, Ragsdale's tenure as airport guard was short-lived. On March 12, the City Council appointed Austin businessman-pilot C. G. (Red) Cross airport manager, and by early April he had organized a security force to protect the facility.[33] Only persons wearing properly signed identification cards were permitted to enter the hangar area. Cross explained that the large number of army and navy planes using the municipal airport as a practice base mandated the increased security.[34]

Before the United States entered the war, Air Corps officials began surveying airfield sites throughout the Southwest for both training and operational bases. Recent developments in the European conflict, plus the deteriorating relations with Japan, hastened the process. On November 2, 1941, four Air Corps officials visited Austin to evaluate possible landing field sites in that area. Aided by both Chamber of Commerce and city officials, the officers selected a three-thousand-acre site in the Del Valle community, located some seven miles southeast of downtown Austin.[35] Tenth District congressman Lyndon B. Johnson supported the project; however, fearing another Texas congressman might intercede in behalf of his own district, "the city and the Chamber of Commerce . . . kept the projected field hush-hushed for several months under the guise of military information."[36] The city council, in secret negotiations, agreed to purchase the three-thousand-acre tract for the airbase with a projected $600,000 bond issue. It was further agreed that, when the present emergency passed, the land and improvements would revert to the city. On February 16, 1942, the city council, meeting in executive session, adopted a formal resolution to submit to the voters a $600,000 bond issue for the purchase of land "to be used, maintained, and operated as an airport." Significantly, the resolution fails to state that the airport is to be used as a military installation. The formal resolution concludes with the words, "and declaring an emergency."[37]

After the matter was made public, City Manager Guiton Morgan addressed the immediate benefits to the city: some three hundred families of military personnel with an estimated $120,000 monthly payroll. In the long term, the prospects were even more appealing: acquiring a new cost-free landing field, substantially larger and better equipped than the present Robert Mueller Municipal Airport. In the March 5, 1942, election, the bond issue passed by an overwhelming majority—2,488 to 338. Ten days later Congressman Johnson's office reported to Mayor Tom Miller that the War Department had given final approval of the site.[38] Establishing the base was a race against time. Surveyors and land appraisers were already in the field preparing to acquire the property, while army engineers, given temporary quarters in the basement of the city hall, were busily drawing plans for the new military airfield.

The acquisition of the military base suddenly forced the city council to address a long-smoldering issue—the inadequacies of the present airport terminal—that suddenly had taken on new meaning. Erected in 1930, the 900-square-foot multiple service building housed Ragsdale Flying Service, Braniff Airways ticket office, the CAA office, two restrooms, a parachute storage area, a counter, plus a small area for passengers awaiting their flights. Robert L. Ragsdale remembered "the quarters were so cramped that, if more than four or five people came in, somebody had to move out." [39] When weather permitted, most passengers awaited their flights on benches placed outside the building. This situation did not go unnoticed. In December 1939, CAA inspector H. D. Cline inspected the building and declared the quarters assigned to that agency as too cramped for efficient work. Aware of the problem, the city had previously applied for federal funds to construct a new terminal building, but no action had been taken in the matter.

While negotiations were still underway for the Army Air Corps base, City Manager Morgan announced that the present terminal would be moved to the southwest corner of the field. In that new location, the city planned to enlarge the structure by some 250 square feet, to partially alleviate the present crowded conditions. Since that section of the municipal airport had no street access, Morgan added that the city engineering department was planning to extend a yet-unnamed street to the new location. However, as plans to establish the new airbase progressed, the city council began to reassess its immediate plans for the municipal field. With prospects of acquiring the larger military field after the war, Morgan believed spending $100,000 for a terminal building on the present municipal airport site was not advisable. He added that since the new field would eventually serve as Austin's major air terminal, the city planned to maintain the present municipal field for general aviation and flight instruction. The journalist reporting the story, apparently expressing the feelings of most Austin citizens, concluded, "Until these plans come about, however, air travelers alighting at the Municipal airport will have to continue to sneer at the meager accommodations." [40]

The city's airport policy was in obvious transition. Two days later, City Engineer James E. Motheral announced that the present terminal building would not be moved but would remain in its present location for the use of student pilots. Instead, the city had purchased a school building from Harry Hammill, which he had erected just north of the airport.[41] That structure, which would require little alteration, would provide 1,800 square feet of floor space, about twice that of the present terminal. Motheral, addressing the emergency, added in jest, "Something just had to be done. Every time [an airliner] lands and passengers go inside you can see the walls bulge." The added space meant further aviation services would be available at the airport. Adding those services included moving the United States Weather Bureau from the present downtown location to the airport and providing new space for the CAA to install teletype machines and other essential communication equipment. In the matter of access to the new location, Motheral pointed out that city engineers were creating a new street to the new terminal site. Later, the Texas Highway Department planned to construct a cutoff highway between the highway to Dallas (now North Lamar Boulevard) and Montopolis bridge.[42] That cutoff would become known as Airport Boulevard.

While city workers were busily grading the right-of-way for the extension of Forty-first Street from Red River Street to Wilshire Boulevard, another crew began mounting the Hammill schoolhouse on construction skids for removal to the unoccupied southwest corner of the airport. By late April, workmen were renovating the new terminal building, providing more space for the Braniff ticket office, the CAA office, and the United States Weather Bureau. Other Texas cities, however, were according air travel a much higher priority. A year before city workmen began moving the former schoolhouse in position to serve as Austin's temporary airport terminal, the City of San Antonio, already looking ahead to expanded postwar air travel, had purchased twelve hundred acres of undeveloped land north of the city on which to establish that city's next municipal airport.[43] However, by late summer, with street access complete, Austin's new terminal was ready for occupancy. While there were noticeable changes—more space for the federal agencies, the air carriers, and especially passenger accommodations—the structure still looked like what it was originally, a rural schoolhouse. However, from a service standpoint, it was, nevertheless, a marked improvement over the previous facility, and airline employees could exhibit a measure of pride when Braniff's DC-3 airliners began serving its customers at the new facility.

That was, however, an ironic celebration. Prior to the war, Braniff, as the city's only airline, had been expanding its Austin service. On March 1, 1940, while operating ten daily Austin schedules, the company inaugurated a new Houston-Austin service, and one week later a Houston-Waco operation. At that time the industry was enjoying a 72 percent traffic increase over the first two months of 1939. Although the ensuing emergency further stimulated air travel, the airlines' contribution to the war effort would ultimately constrain their domestic operations. In May 1942, Braniff sold a number of aircraft to the government for military cargo operations, which forced the company to reduce its daily scheduled mileage from over seventeen thousand miles to about ten thousand miles per day.[44] That change was soon reflected in the company's Austin service. On June 2, 1942, Braniff announced it was cancelling six daily Austin flights because of the wartime emergency; ten daily schedules were reduced to four.[45] Despite the reduced airline operations, air traffic at Robert Mueller airport remained brisk, and with increasing military training, it was destined to grow.

Meanwhile, some seven miles southeast of the airport, another crew of workmen was changing the face of the once-placid Del Valle countryside. Working under the pressure of wartime emergency, Project Manager H. E. Wassell moved with dispatch. When property owners hesitated to accept the appraised value of their property, the federal government filed petitions in federal court to obtain immediate possession. Documents filed in the name of Secretary of War Henry Stimson requested condemnation of 1,919.5 acres of the proposed 2,700-acre tract. After May 9, 1942, when Judge W. A. Keeling granted the government immediate possession of the property designated for the airbase, teams of workmen began their first major task—removing existing structures.[46] In addition to houses, barns, and windmills, they dismantled and moved a cotton gin, a telephone exchange, two churches, and five miles of power lines, and new locations were being sought for the then-segregated black and Mexican-American schools located on the government tract.[47]

By the end of May, with the land cleared, a fleet of graders and bulldozers moved in and began reshaping the contour of the land. Next came the construction workers. On June 29, the War Department began awarding contracts for buildings, utilities, streets, and drainage systems. Austin-based Montgomery-Page-Hemphill-Page received the general contract, estimated at more than $1 million. To expedite the project, the contractors initiated the process of "build first and negotiate later." The five-mile railroad spur from the Missouri Pacific main line, over which much of the building materials would be transported, was nearing completion, even though negotiations with landowners were still underway. The City of Austin, in agreeing to supply construction water to the site, also responded to the wartime emergency. By the time the contract for the pipeline from the Colorado River to the base was finally approved, the entire line was in operation.[48] And if wartime shortages threatened work stoppage, the city, if possible, came to the rescue. When an electrical contractor was unable to purchase the necessary copper wire, the city engineer arranged a loan of seventy thousand pounds of the high-priority material from the city's inventory.

With the airbase scheduled to open in mid-September, the Air Corps faced another critical shortage—people. Representatives from Randolph Field visited Austin in mid-August recruiting some 280 civilian personnel to staff the new base. Of the roughly 300 applicants, about half were women just entering the wartime workforce. Interviewing at Austin High School between August 31 and September 2, the Air Corps accepted 106 for both technical and staff positions. During the sixty-day salaried training period at Randolph Field, the women quickly realized that equality in the workforce was a vision of the future; male employees were housed in base dormitories at Randolph, while the women were told they could find accommodations in nearby San Antonio.[49]

By September 1, with the scheduled opening of the then-designated Del Valle Support Command Base less than three weeks away, the tempo of preparation quickened. The civilian workforce, then totaling some sixteen hundred, had either finished or started most of the proposed 175 buildings and next directed their efforts to the landing area, pouring the final asphalt topping on the main 6,500-foot-long northwest-southeast runway. Although concrete for the 6,500-square-foot aircraft parking ramp had been poured, the other two runways were still under construction. The railroad spur from the International, Great Northern main line was complete, with freight cars standing at the base loaded with construction materials. However, the train crews soon discovered "the Bergstrom spur" would not be a typical railroad operation, especially since farmers, from whom the city had purchased the fifty-foot right-of-way, had erected wire gates across the railroad to keep their stock from wandering on the tracks.[50] One of the construction crew's final assignments addressed airbase security. A greatly reduced staff erected a five-strand wire fence around the entire 2,800-acre facility, punctuated periodically by "No Trespassing" signs.

In the final cost assessment, J. M. Patterson Jr., acting city attorney for the City of Austin, reported to Mayor Tom Miller that the city had acquired thirty-three tracts of land, totaling 2,899.749 acres, at a cost of $413,890. That figure was $52,710 less than the $466,600 originally made available to the federal government for the acquisition of the airbase property. The Austin City Council approved the final settlement on April 10, 1943. Throughout the negotiations it was understood, though not stated, that following the emergency the airbase property would revert to the City of Austin. City Attorney Patterson concluded his report with a statement destined to confound city leaders for years to come: "the conveyance of the property by the Federal Government to the City of Austin will have to be considered after the war."[51]

Unquestionably, what occurred during the summer of 1942 in the Del Valle community was another wartime miracle. In less than three months some sixteen hundred civilian workers had converted the almost 2,900 acres of cotton fields into an operational airbase. By September 19, the then-designated Del Valle Army Air Base was ready for dedication, which fifty-two Douglas C-47 transports of the 316th Troop Carrier Group did in spectacular fashion. Lt. Lee Arbon, who flew in the third plane to land at the new base, recalled there were several Texans in the squadron "who wanted a show, so we came in mass formation right over the top of the Capitol, about as low as you could go without taking the top off." Landing at Del Valle, Lieutenant Arbon recognized the base had all the earmarks of a new facility: acres of black sticky mud, runways still under construction, no permanent buildings, tarpaper barracks, and an unfinished church.[52]

Once established at the new base, Lt. Col. Jerome B. McCauley embarked on the 316th's primary mission, troop carrier training. The constant rotation of young lieutenants practice landing C-47 transports on the airbase's main runway quickly exceeded the capacity of the Del Valle air traffic pattern. With air safety a primary concern, many of those young military pilots were directed to practice their "touch-and-goes" at the nearby Robert Mueller airport, which they began sharing with other military trainees, private pilots, Braniff DC-3s, and the University of Texas CPTP student pilots.[53] Thus, in the autumn of 1942, the skies over Austin became crowded with hundreds of young pilots, many training for the great air battles that lay ahead.

The same factors that led to the establishment of the Del Valle Army Air Base—fighting a three-continent war—also prompted a revision of the University of Texas CPT program. The Civilian Pilot Training Program, conceived originally as part of the New Deal economic recovery program, was reshaped to comply with changing military requirements. The age limit was reduced from nineteen to eighteen, married men were accepted if their dependents had other means of support, and all signed affidavits that, at the end of primary pilot training, they would enlist in one of the military services. University students entering the July 1942 class were fulltime trainees and received room, board, and transportation, but no pay. The navy trainees, however, were V-5 Cadets on inactive duty. During the summer of 1942, campus ambiance began to reflect the presence of the military; trainees, working under strict military supervision, observed taps and reveille, took meals together at a specific time, and participated in military drills. Their course of study, lacking academics, included 240 hours of ground school given entirely at the University, plus thirty-five to forty-five hours of flight training conducted by either Browning Aerial Service or Ragsdale Flying Service. The first class under the accelerated program consisted of forty army pilot trainees and thirty-five from the navy. On December 15, the name of the program was changed from Civilian Pilot Training Program to War Training Service (WTS).[54]

The following January 15, 1943, the navy took over the entire pilot training program at the University of Texas. The cadets, on active duty, were quartered in Brackenridge Hall, received pay, and were issued uniforms. Those military trainees took two courses, elementary and secondary, which consisted of 240 hours of ground school, and thirty-five to forty-five hours of flight training. The cadets received elementary flight training in light aircraft at either the Browning or Ragsdale flight schools, while only Browning Aerial Service offered the secondary-training Waco UPF-7 aircraft. In May 1943, an intermediate flight course replaced the secondary course, which was given by both contract schools in navy two-place N3N "Canary" biplane trainers.[55]

The magnitude of the University's accelerated flight program was soon reflected in staff and equipment requirements of the two contract flight schools. Between July 1, 1943, and June 30, 1944, Ragsdale Flying Service employed two mechanics, five helpers, and eight instructors, operated seven navy N3N aircraft, and instructed twenty students. At that same time Browning Aerial Service employed two mechanics, two helpers, and seven instructors, operated eight light aircraft, plus seven N3Ns, and instructed nine students. During the course of the wartime emergency, those figures changed frequently. In December 1943, for example, Browning operated twenty-one aircraft—sixteen light planes and five N3Ns—and employed ten instructors, who taught twenty-eight students, while Ragsdale reported a twenty-aircraft inventory and employed twelve instructors, who were responsible for twenty-eight students.[56]

The Browning operation, conducted at University Airport, was relatively traffic-free. Such was not the case for Ragsdale at Mueller. According to Reuben Rountree, Austin director of Public Works, by 1942 Robert Mueller airport had become "one of the busiest civil airports in the United States. . . . Air traffic . . . increased to approximately 12,000 aircraft landings and 120,000 passengers per year."[57] During periods of peak activity, Ragsdale's instructors worked a dawn-to-dusk schedule, and when the C-47 pilots from Del Valle began practicing "touch-and-goes," air traffic at Mueller became almost chaotic. Without the aid of an airport control tower, the participants averted disaster through mutual agreement. They designated five traffic lanes for takeoffs and landings (most municipal airports use two). The military used the long runway and the grass on one side, while the University flight students and private pilots used the short northeast runway and the grass on both sides. And when the student traffic pattern became too congested, some landed on the grass area behind the parked aircraft near the East Fifty-first Street hangar. The airspace was also carefully allocated; student pilots flew a 600-foot traffic pattern, whereas the military pilots flew at 1,200 feet. Since all takeoffs and landings are determined by wind direction, when the wind changed at Mueller, it was Ragsdale's responsibility to telephone the Del Valle control tower and tell them the proper runway to use. "We weren't about to buck their pattern," Ragsdale recalled. "When they changed, we changed." Ragsdale credited pilot vigilance for avoiding disaster: "At times there would be three [C-47s] on the runway at one time, one landing, one in the middle of the runway, and one at the end taking off. And no control tower; they had to do their own spacing."[58]

The absence of a control tower was subsequently remedied. Commercial airliners operating in such congested and uncontrolled airspace prompted the Civil Aviation Administration to act. Sometime in late 1942 (the exact date could not be confirmed), the city erected what was facetiously described as the "dog house control tower" on top of the new terminal building.[59] Cathryn Batson, one of the first controllers assigned to the new tower, recalled the difficult access to the facility. After climbing a ladder at the rear of the terminal building, she walked across the roof to "this little shack" no larger than 8′ × 10′ and equipped with a "big black radio." With that device Cathryn and her two coworkers attempted to bring order out of the Mueller chaos. Braniff pilots, accustomed to being given preference when approaching the field, were the least cooperative. "They were used to coming straight in," she recalled, "[and] didn't want to have to get in the traffic pattern with all these other airplanes." Cathryn's feminine persuasion, however, prevailed, and air traffic at Mueller began to flow in an orderly manner. Despite the heat in the summer and the cold in the winter, Cathryn and her two associates could, at times, enjoy a rare sight from their rooftop position. "I grew up in Northwest Texas, and I had never seen bluebonnets is such great quantities," she remembered. "That particular spring of '43, the field was just covered with them. All you could see were bluebonnets and the runways. It was so pretty, I wrote all my family and friends." [60]

The "dog house" control tower was short-lived. In 1943, the city erected a separate control tower some fifty yards east of the airport terminal. Standing on fifty-foot utility poles, the facility both was better equipped and provided a superior view of the air traffic pattern. There were, however, two major disadvantages: a five-story climb up an open-air stairway and, during high winds, especially thunderstorms, the controllers had to abandon the swaying tower to ensure their personal safety. The establishment of this control tower, and a second airplane hangar located near the airport terminal building, was part of the city's plan to develop the west side of the airport, that area offering the most convenient access to the city. And there was another reason for the city council's renewed interest in aviation; with increased activity at Mueller, both commercial and military, the Municipal Airport Division had begun to turn a profit. Following a $13,184 loss in 1941, the division reported a $14,986 profit in 1942, from $19,663 in gross receipts.[61] However, in preparing the 1943 budget, the head of the Municipal Airport Division requested only $29,189.36, which the city manager, with the council's approval, increased to $44,189.36. The largest item, $26,000 for capital expenditures, earmarked $23,000 for buildings, including the new hangar.[62] On August 20, 1942, the city council appropriated $17,000 for the construction of the hangar, and on November 9 awarded the contract to J. M. Odom Construction Company, the lowest bidder at $19,987. The project was to be completed by June 10, 1943.[63]

Construction of the 130′ × 75′ hangar, referred to as the Quonset hangar (and later the Browning hangar), also reflected the wartime limitations of building materials. Lacking steel for the superstructure, the contractor used glue-laminated wooden trusses, which workmen fabricated at the construction site. The half trusses were secured in place by 2″ × 6″ joists, over which the builders placed half-inch decking for the asbestos roofing. The steel tracks on which the eight hangar doors were opened and closed constituted the only metal used in the hangar.[64]

The completion of the new hangar added more than 9,000 square feet of much needed civilian hangar space. Although private flying was greatly restricted during the war—the government purchased practically all civilian aircraft with over 150-horsepower for training purposes—a number of Austin private pilots remained active at Mueller.[65] Those pilots, who had been leasing hangar space from Ragsdale Flying Service, moved their aircraft to the new facility, releasing that space for Ragsdale's CPTP-WTS training aircraft. "I had more airplanes than I could put in that [old 51st Street] hangar," Ragsdale explained. "Before the end of the war we were completely out of space. We had a lot of airplanes tied down adjacent to our hangar."[66]

Other civilians flying at Mueller included young infantry soldiers attempting to gain flight proficiency to strengthen their applications for Air Corps cadet training. Since Ragsdale Flying Service owned its aircraft—the government provided training aircraft for some CPTP schools—that company was free to train civilian students on weekends. Even at wartime prices, the cost appeared minimal—six dollars per hour for aircraft rental, plus one dollar for the instructor. Ragsdale explained many of the weekend students were Army Ski Troopers from Camp Swift, near Bastrop, Texas. Although they were eager to learn to fly, their socioeconomic backgrounds—growing up in New York or Boston—retarded their progress. Many, never having learned to drive an automobile, had difficulty in responding to right-turn and left-turn directions. Ragsdale's instructors also had problems with students taking the flight instructor's course, which required the use of aircraft radio in communicating with airport control towers. Although everyone had listened to commercial radio, few had ever spoken into a microphone, and many students succumbed to "mike fright." The solution was to park the aircraft in view of the flight school radio operator; seeing the person to whom they were talking seemed to ease the anxiety. That was all part of the daily regimen of a wartime emergency flight training school. In addition to the University of Texas program, Ragsdale explained, "we had good business on weekends. We flew seven days a week."[67]

Seven-day workweeks were part of the wartime effort. The same was true for their Air Corps colleagues at Del Valle, where change was an integral part of their assignment. In November 1942, the 89th Troop Carrier Group, whose mission was also troop carrier training, replaced the 316th Troop Carrier Group, which was reassigned to the North African campaign. On March 3, 1943, the Del Valle base was renamed Bergstrom Army Air Base in honor of Capt. John August Bergstrom, believed to be the first war casualty from Austin. On November 11, 1943, the designation was shortened to Bergstrom Field.[68] The growing demand for the skills of those being trained at Bergstrom continued. In July 1943, using North Africa as a springboard, the Allies seized Sicily, invaded mainland Italy, and pushed northward into Germany. On June 6, 1944, Supreme Commander Gen. Dwight D. Eisenhower launched the Normandy invasion, secured a beachhead, and began forcing the Germans back across France. News from the Pacific front was also encouraging. The island-hopping strategy led to the seizure of the Marshalls, the Mariannas, and the Carolines, and by October 1944 the Philippine campaign was underway.

Success on the battlefronts prompted a revision in military training. The current pilot inventory appeared sufficient to bring the conflict to a successful conclusion. The last War Training Service class at the University of Texas, officially designated "44-N Intermediate," completed flight training on July 19, 1944, and ground school training ended on July 29, 1944. In making his final report, Professor Venton L. Doughtie, who coordinated both the CPT and WTS programs, stated that 1,020 trainees, registered for 1,426 courses, had flown a total of 53,659.25 hours, with only one student injury. He lost four teeth in a forced landing and later became a commissioned naval officer.[69] The achievement at Bergstrom Field was equally remarkable. Between December 20, 1942, and September 1, 1943, the base graduated 3,176 pilots, and from September 1, 1943, to February 1944, another 1,346 graduated.[70]

The prospect of victory and an ensuing peace were greatly welcomed, yet there was a touch of sadness as the runways at Mueller grew quieter with each passing day. It fell to bus driver W. E. Sjoberg to witness the symbolic end of an era that left an indelible imprint on the memories of all who had banded together to help win the war. As he stood by the open door of the schoolbus he had driven for some four years, the last six trainees entered the yellow vehicle for the final trip to Bergstrom Field, where they boarded a plane for reassignment at Memphis, Tennessee. And all that was left to do was counting the money. On July 2, 1943, University comptroller C. D. Simmons directed to acting president Dr. Theophilus S. Painter a contract supplement from the Bureau of Naval Personnel, providing for the final payment of $30,982. He wrote, "I recommend that the Board of Regents approve the proposed settlement and authorize the Chairman to sign the instrument."[71] That signature closed another chapter in the University of Texas' contribution to the nation's war effort.

CHAPTER 6

AN ERA OF PEACE AND THE GROWTH OF PRIVATE FLYING

THE war, however, was far from over. Fighting would continue for more than a year and more than a million people, both military and civilian, would die. Yet victory appeared inevitable; Germany was being attacked on three fronts, while the Japanese were confined to their homeland and a receding perimeter of island fortresses. And as the victory clock continued to tick, all thoughts focused on the coming era of peace. America and the industrialized nations were about to enter a period of exceptional change. There would be continuity, but beyond continuity it was the unknown that fascinated, challenged, and intrigued. From this milieu of philosophical ponderings emerged one dominant question: What would life be like in postwar America?

Two key dates document the progression toward peace: Germany surrendered on May 8, 1945, the war with Japan concluded on September 2, 1945. During the next five months, the American nation experienced a welcome but transforming social phenomenon as "three-quarters of a million persons were separated from the armed forces." By June 1946, "demobilization had been virtually completed."[1] Some 12,807,000 veterans of World War II had returned to civilian life. Those young men and women, who went off to war in the twilight years of the Great Depression, came home to a vastly different country. "By war's end unemployment was negligible," wrote historian David M. Kennedy. "In the ensuing quarter century the American economy would create some twenty million new jobs . . . By 1960 the middle class included almost two-thirds of all Americans, most of whom owned their own homes . . . Small wonder that Americans choose to think of [World War II] as the good war." For the millions of Americans who remained on the home front and avoided "the staggering sacrifices and unspeakable anguish" suffered by millions of other people around the world, it was indeed a good war.[2] But that was the past; the future was now.

The vision of postwar America varied with the individual. Those in aviation (especially those in general aviation, who viewed the future with unbridled optimism), looked to the past for precedent. World War I had given aviation a new identity, and in the years that followed airlines spanned the nation, municipal airports proliferated, private flying became almost commonplace, and World War II flight training helped establish the fixed base operator (FBO) on a sound business foundation. The future never looked brighter. "We thought all those [some 200,000] military pilots trained during the war would want to come home and buy an airplane," recalled Austin FBO Robert L. Ragsdale. Bruce K. Hallock, former navy pilot and later an FBO, was even more emphatic. "We thought everybody was going to have an airplane in their garage," he explained. "Or you owned an airplane just like you owned a boat or a motorcycle. We were all going to end up flying around everywhere."[3]

The airplane manufacturers, who also shared that vision, were already tooling up for the anticipated postwar civilian market. Republic Aviation Corporation, builder of the World War II P-47 "Thunderbolt," was already testing the prototype of its "Seabee," a four-place amphibian designed for the private pilot, while North American Aviation was busily developing its "Navion," a four-place private craft employing many of the design concepts found in its World War II P-51 "Mustang" fighter. Although those two air-

craft were to be priced in the $6,000 range, there were a host of other man-
ufacturing firms being formed to produce more affordable two-place trainers for the mass market, priced in the $2,000–$3,000 range. By war's end
the aviation industry was also promoting the idea of a "roadable airplane,"
a multipurpose vehicle that could be flown, and upon landing, with wings
folded, could be driven on streets and highways. In his article "An Airplane
in Every Garage," author David R. Zuck predicted this vehicle "will enable
the businessman and the wage earner alike to find in the airplane an economic justification for ownership."[4]

The roadable airplane was merely a vision that never materialized. There
was, however, a postwar demand for affordable aircraft, which the United
States government supplied from a seemingly inexhaustible inventory—
World War II surplus. Following the surrender of Germany, as military pilot training bases began closing, the first surplus aircraft became available to
civilian purchasers. By January 1, 1945, the Reconstruction Finance Corporation had declared 32,462 military aircraft surplus and available for private
purchase on a price-tag basis. Bid and auction sales had been discontinued.
The list included 14,607 single-engine trainers—primary, basic, and advanced. The civilian aircraft types available included 2,949 liaison, 5,399 War
Training Service trainers (N3N-3s, for example), and 190 utility cargo aircraft. Large aircraft types included 2,012 light, medium, and heavy twin-
engine transports, plus a wide range of fighters, bombers, rotary wing aircraft, and gliders. The purchasers accepted their surplus aircraft "as is" and,
if it was airworthy, were allowed to fly it to their home base for modification
and licensing. The cost of complying with factory bulletin specifications
and making alterations required by the Civil Aeronautics Authority usually
averaged less than $150.[5]

In the Austin area, Ragsdale Flying Service became the major purchaser
of surplus military aircraft. Buying, converting, and reselling them provided
a much needed economic cushion following the termination of the Civilian Pilot Training Program. The bargains were many; primary and basic
trainers—Fairchild PT-19s and Vultee BT-13s—had the greatest public appeal. Originally, BT-13s were available for around $600; the price later
dropped to three for $1,000. Some government-owned Aeroncas, Taylor-
craft, and J-3 "Cubs" used in CPTP schools were priced as low as $200 or
$300. "Seems like every weekend we would get three people [pilots] and
go buy three of 'em," Ragsdale recalled. Airlines, and FBOs specializing
in air charter work, preferred the twin-engine transports. Douglas C-47s

(DC-3s) first appeared on the surplus lists at about $25,000; some later sold for as little as $5,000. The Cessna UC-78 "Bamboo Bomber" was the first twin-engine aircraft declared surplus by the government. Ragsdale remembered he was flying a converted UC-78 on a charter operation to New York when the first bomb was dropped on Hiroshima.[6]

The actual cost of converting and licensing primary and basic trainers ran from $300 to $500; twin-engine utility transports conversions, which required new paint and upholstery, cost around $3,000. Converting and reselling surplus military aircraft proved highly beneficial to FBOs; Ragsdale estimated his company marketed at least fifty surplus military airplanes. In July 1944, when the War Department began phasing out the War Training Program, participating FBOs began releasing their staff of flight instructors. Consequently, their training fleets remained idle for some eighteen months until the Veterans Administration launched a new program of unprecedented magnitude. Enacted by Congress as the Serviceman's Readjustment Act of 1944, commonly referred to as the G.I. Bill of Rights, that legislation provided unemployment benefits, hospitalization, funding for schooling and technical training, and low-interest loans to purchase homes, farms, and small businesses.[7] The bill's educational provisions were sufficiently broad to include most fields of endeavor, including aviation. The Veterans Administration, in cooperation with the Federal Aviation Administration, designed a flight training program to enable returning servicemen, both with or without previous flight training, to earn a living in aviation. The G.I. Bill proved to be another major economic boost for aviation, especially for the FBOs.

Participating FBOs negotiated individual contracts with the Veterans Administration, outlining specific courses of study, with the relative cost of each. The approved curriculum included four flight courses: Private Pilot, Commercial Pilot, Flight Instructor, and Instrument Rating. The Certificate of Charges included 65-horsepower aircraft, dual instruction at $10 per hour; solo practice, $8 per hour; aircraft over 145-horsephower, dual instruction, $18 per hour, solo practice, $15 per hour; ground school instruction for all courses, $0.70 per hour. Each course had a minimum and maximum completion time allowable. The minimum time for the Commercial Pilot Course was 288 hours; the maximum, 308 hours. The maximum cost could not exceed $1,781.10.[8] When the government launched the G.I. flight training program in 1946, it appeared to reconfirm what most people in aviation already believed—in postwar America, practically everyone would own an airplane. And furthermore, the financial benefits available to the FBOs spelled opportunity for many young pilots hoping to enter the aviation business. It was, however, the established Austin FBOs—Ragsdale Flying Service, Browning Aerial Service, and the Haile Airport—that first began flight instruction under the new G.I. program. Others would follow.

William D. Pfeil, a former flight instructor at Ragsdale Flying Service, was the first local pilot to embark on that new venture; he simply moved across the airport and set up business as Austin Flying Service in the new west side hangar. His advertising campaign addressed what many perceived as the new era of aviation: "Never Too Young to Fly. Don't Wait. Learn to Fly Now. Be Ready to Take Advantage of the Many Opportunities that will be Afforded Both the Commercial and Sportsman Pilot After the War."[9] Pfeil's promotion apparently reached a receptive audience; on December 31, 1945, he reported income for five part-time employees. However, the success Pfeil anticipated was not immediately forthcoming. By March 31, 1946, his staff had dwindled to two; Mary Waurine "Ziggy" Hunter, his flight instructor, was top earner at $576.58.[10]

Pfeil realized if he was to remain in the aviation business he needed two things—an infusion of cash and experienced business management. He found both in James B. Cain. Cain had learned to fly in the CPT program at Schreiner Junior College in Kerrville, Texas. After graduating from Southern Methodist University in 1942, with a major in engineering and a minor in business administration, he joined Ragsdale Flying Service as a flight instructor in the navy V-5 program. Later Cain transferred to active duty, became a navy educational officer, retired in March 1946, and returned to Austin hoping for a career in aviation. On learning that Pfeil was an operating Austin FBO, he discussed the business with Pfeil, and they foresaw how, with their combined resources, Austin Flying Service would prosper under their joint guidance. The benefits appeared obvious. Both had commercial instructor's ratings and wide experience in flight training, and both came from fairly affluent backgrounds.[11] And so, in April 1946, with high expectations, Cain and Pfeil joined forces in the Austin Flying Service.

They made immediate changes. First, they renegotiated their lease, which afforded the company more space for ground school classes. After surveying the company's refurbished facility, they made another executive decision. "We looked at each other and decided, 'Gee, you gotta have airplanes to fly,'" Cain recalled, "and we didn't have any airplanes." In order to purchase the flight training equipment, the partners established a loan at The Fidelity State Bank of Austin, committing Cain's stock as security. With that loan—and there would be others—they purchased two tandem Interstate "Cadets" for flight training. "We had good business, and surprisingly, we got some students," Cain added. "And we kept getting more students." [12]

Next, the partners began expanding their services. They added a ground school, began offering complete aircraft and engine repair service, and developed an aircraft sales program. The Houston-area Ercoupe distributor agreed to "floor plan" his aircraft with Austin Flying Service. As the first Ercoupe dealer in Central Texas, Cain launched an innovative sales program for an equally innovative aircraft. The all-metal, twin-tail Ercoupe was one of the first commercial aircraft to employ a tricycle landing gear and the first (and only) plane controlled by a single wheel, similar to the steering wheel on an automobile. Training time averaged about five hours, but it was the safety factor that made the craft most appealing: the Ercoupe was certified "incapable of spinning" by the Civil Aeronautics Administration. With the standard model selling for less than three thousand dollars, Cain envisioned the University of Texas student body as a potentially fertile and unexploited sales target. To showcase the new craft, he leased a vacant lot one block west of the University campus, which he enhanced with flood lights, recorded music, and a pretty coed seated in the silver metal Ercoupe. Although the display attracted a lot of attention, there was no student rush to purchase airplanes. The company did, however, sell some Ercoupes, which prompted them to negotiate for the Bellanca and Luscombe dealerships to compete with Ragsdale Flying Service's Cessnas. But success had its downside; the city continued to raise the rent on the hangar at Mueller. [13]

At that point the partners made another critical decision; they abandoned Mueller and established their own airport. On May 21, 1946, they purchased fifty-four acres on Burnet Road (now Research Boulevard) northwest of Austin, for $500 per acre. They made a small down payment with manageable monthly payments. And in order to provide adequate space for two 2,000-foot runways, the company leased an additional one hundred acres north of the original tract. [14] Their site possessed a distinct advantage; it was located beyond development, well north of the Austin city limits.

Cain and Pfeil also changed the name of the firm; Aero-Tel reflected

Cain's vision of the future. Cain foresaw aviation assuming a greater role in business and industry in postwar America. He envisioned the postwar business executive traveling in his personal aircraft and landing at private airports that provided on-site hotel accommodations, conference facilities, automobile rentals, plus aircraft service.

Construction on the site began on July 1, 1946. The company erected two hangars, a small office building, and a classroom for ground school instruction, but slated a hotel facility for future development. The partners financed the major construction with bank loans, although they did much of the work themselves. Accounts for services they could not provide themselves they resolved by offering flying lessons as compensation. Cost cutting became a way of life. Needing metal for hangar construction, Cain ordered 39,100 pounds of corrugated sheet metal from the War Assets Administration, and to further reduce costs, Cain learned to weld.[15] In February 1947, the company engaged E. B. Sneed, owner of Special Equipment Company, to grade two runways, which were surfaced with gravel and caliche. The cost, $1,755.51, cited in a promissory note, was subsequently covered by teaching Sneed to fly.[16] To house their original flight equipment, the partners purchased a 40' × 28' Quonset hut for $4,133.68, with $2,668 as down payment and $1,465.68 due upon completion. In maximizing use of the restricted quarters, they parked the airplanes tilted nose-down on a five-gallon can covered with a cushion to prevent propeller damage.

By September 1946, Aero-Tel Airport was fully operative, offering government-approved flight instruction, complete aircraft and engine repair service, plus airplane storage. The company was soon doing good business; with the Ercoupe and Luscombe dealerships they competed with Ragsdale's Cessnas, and with the Bellancas they developed a charter service. "We also had a sub-dealership with Aeronca, and were buying, renovating, and reselling military surplus airplanes," Cain said. "We were selling airplanes all around the country."[17] And a growing number of students were finding their way to the Burnet Road airport for flight instruction. The company's training fleet consisted of ten aircraft, which included a Piper J-5 "Cub," Aeronca "Champion," Luscombe "Silvaire," plus a war surplus Stearman PT-17 and a Vultee BT-13A. Only three of the aircraft were of pre–World War II design.[18] And things were going to get better.

On October 3, 1946, the partners received an Amended Approval of Veterans Administration authorization, changing the location of the operation from Austin Mueller airport to Aero-Tel Airport. In December, the company expanded its sales department to include a Culver dealership; CIT financed the purchase of the first demonstrator. Before year's end the Aeronautical Engineering Department of the University of Texas launched a flight training program and contracted with Aero-Tel to provide the instruction. The University subsequently purchased five new Piper J3-C Cubs for the program, which were also based at Aero-Tel. The company had definitely entered the success mode; January 1, 1947, assets totaled $76,257.13. One month later that figure reached $170,982.47.[19] With assets came a larger staff; the company engaged a receptionist and an accountant, paying the latter with flying lessons.

A large portion of the company's income came from dealing in surplus military aircraft, an operation in which Pfeil exhibited special interest. It was that special interest that eventually forged a change in company ownership. When Pfeil's expenditures exceeded what Cain considered sound business judgment, he offered to purchase Pfeil's interest in the company. On February 4, 1947, both partners signed the document terminating the partnership, which provided Pfeil "a certain sum of money."[20]

Continuing alone at the helm of Aero-Tel, Cain looked forward to an optimistic future. On March 24, 1947, the company reported twenty-five G.I. students, who had flown 216:10 hours, yielding $1,875.67.[21] That income was destined to continue. On May 9, the Veterans Administration informed Cain his contract would be extended through June 30, 1948. The following month the War Department designated Aero-Tel as the training site for Officers Reserve Corps liaison pilots to maintain proficiency. The contract authorized six pilots to fly four hours per month at eight dollars per hour at government expense. That income helped replenish the company's coffers. On August 11, Aero-Tel received $960 from the War Department for 120 hours of solo flying. The G.I. veterans, however, remained the company's more constant income source. Between April 1 and September 30, 1947, Aero-Tel received $21,181.83, "for tuition, supplies, equipment, etc., furnished beneficiaries of the Veterans Administration." VA payments, however, constituted less than half of Aero-Tel's income. During the year the company's deposits totaled $47,270.82. There were, however, major expenses. For the period April 2, 1947, through February 20, 1948, the company borrowed $20,685 from The Fidelity State Bank of Austin, which was repaid on schedule.[22] Attempting to further broaden his income base, Cain leased the Taylor, Texas, airport, assigned an employee there, and launched a satellite FBO operation. After some six months, difficulties encountered with the city government prompted him to abandon that project. He then leased the Smithville airport, which he operated successfully for about a year.

By the end of 1947, G.I. enrollment had begun to decline, with only nine students enrolled in the commercial pilot course. The downward trend continued. The following year bank deposits dropped almost 50 percent, from $47,270.82 to $27,440.28. Note payments also declined. With Veterans Administration vouchers no longer available as loan security, Cain was forced to turn to his personal resources to keep the company solvent. On March 24, 1948, he gave The Fidelity State Bank five hundred shares of West Ohio Gas Company stock as loan collateral, valued at $5,000.[23] Cain was also preoccupied with other matters, an airplane crash, in particular. While instructing a student in a Stearman PT-17, the engine lost power on takeoff. As the aircraft approached the southern boundary of the field, Cain faced a critical decision: should he attempt to fly over or under the utility lines. He made the wrong choice; the wheels of the aircraft became entangled in the power lines, dragging down two utility poles, and thrusting the ailing craft nose first into the middle of Burnet Road. In the final seconds before the crash, Cain cut the ignition switch, avoiding a fire. It was, however, Cain's previous handiwork that actually saved the two pilots. A few days before the crash, he had installed a thick layer of foam across the instrument panel. "If I hadn't done that it probably would have killed us both," Cain explained. "I hit that thing so hard [in the crash] that my fingers went through the aluminum panel." Employing a military training practice, Cain encouraged his student to get in another aircraft immediately and fly a short while to regain his confidence. "He flew for about thirty minutes, landed, got out, and said, 'I'll see you tomorrow.'" There was, however, no tomorrow; the student never returned. For Cain, the crash represented a double tragedy; he had lost both an airplane and a student at a time he could ill afford to lose either.[24]

After some two years as an FBO, Cain began to reassess his role in aviation; Aero-Tel was not fulfilling his hopes for the future. He had achieved a measure of success, but a portion of that success came from temporary institutional sources. And by early 1948, when it appeared the G.I. funding for flight training was nearing an end, Cain's great uncle and surrogate father, C. H. Coleman, wrote him on February 25, inquiring about "the 200-Million cut in G.I. 'Training-For-Fun.'" Coleman, suggesting that Cain abandon the project, added further, "If you could sell the land with all of your equipment of approximately $60,000, it would be a good thing; the value of the land itself would help sell the equipment."[25] Although Cain had created substantial indebtedness in establishing the business, he was not ready to abandon the project. He did, however, sell some unneeded training craft to meet his immediate obligations; by April 15, he had reduced his inventory to only four aircraft valued at $8,780.86.[26] With both student traffic and airplane sales declining, Cain began to reassess his economic position. On June 2, 1948, he negotiated a one-year lease with the University of Texas to operate the University's Flight Training Program. The rent was three hundred dollars per month.[27] Cain still had the use of the facility, plus a guaranteed income. Change, however, was in the offing; following the death of his uncle in April 1949, Cain began commuting almost weekly to Athens, Texas, to help settle his uncle's estate. In view of his ongoing responsibilities in Athens, he accepted a year's extension on the University's lease. However, after evaluating his responsibilities, Cain liquidated his remaining inventory, and in January 1950 established permanent residence in Athens. After August 1949, Aero-Tel Airport was no longer listed in the classified section of the Austin telephone directory.[28]

James B. Cain's determination to carve a niche for himself in aviation's future was shared by many other young pilots leaving military service. At approximately the same time Cain purchased the Burnet Road property to establish Aero-Tel, Charles Quist, a recently discharged Air Force pilot, launched a similar operation some ten miles south, near St. Edward's University. The two had much in common. Long before Quist was discharged from the Air Force in January 1946, he also had decided to continue in aviation. The G.I. Bill seemed to offer that opportunity, not as a student, but as a contracting FBO. But first he needed a base of operations. With Ragsdale well established at Mueller, and Browning and Haile operating from their individual fields, Quist examined several sites in South Austin and decided on a sixty-seven-acre tract owned by St. Edward's University. The rent, one dollar per acre per month, seemed reasonable. Construction began immediately; Quist graded two sod runways (the longest was 2,000 feet), built a hangar, and on May 26, 1946, acquired his first airplane, a two-place Interstate "Cadet."[29] Austin Aero Service, Inc. began as a family endeavor. Mary Catherine Quist, Charles' sister and a former World War II WASP pilot, joined her brother in the operation; she contributed five hundred dollars, as did their parents. With a three-thousand-dollar investment, the company began operations with two war surplus PT-23s.[30]

The Quist family business subsequently grew into a partnership. Shortly after establishment of the field, popular Austin aviatrix Mary Waurine (Ziggy) Hunter joined the firm. She contributed no funding but had wide experience in aviation, especially as a flight instructor. They were soon joined by another returning veteran, Bruce Hallock, a former navy PBY pilot who also wanted to be in "the flying business." Hallock contributed some funding, plus two airplanes. With an abundance of students, Austin Aero Service prospered from the beginning. In addition to the G.I. trainees, Quist developed a cooperative student-training program with St. Edward's University, in which students received university credit for flight training. The individual students paid for the instruction: six dollars per hour solo and eight dollars dual. That was in addition to the ten dollars per hour the company received for the G.I. instruction. And as the student body grew, so did the training fleet. At one time the company owned or operated fifteen airplanes. Quist later acquired dealerships for both Aeronca and Luscombe airplanes. In addition, Hallock developed a charter business with his two Stinsons—Dallas and back, for fifty dollars. The future looked bright. "We were receiving $8 per hour training G.I.s," Hallock recalled. "With gasoline at twenty cents a gallon, we were making money."[31]

There were, however, blemishes on Austin Aero Service's record of operation. Mary Catherine lost one student, a G.I. who violated a cardinal rule in flight training—"You don't buzz." On his first solo flight, he, unfortunately, violated that rule. He "buzzed" his mother's house, lost control of the airplane, and crashed and burned in the street in front of her house.[32] The company also lost another airplane in Mexico. Bruce Hallock developed a profitable import business, flying fresh lobster from Belize, British Honduras, to San Antonio, Texas, where the Gunter Hotel purchased five hundred pounds each week at sixty cents per pound. On one return flight, while using Charles Quist's Aeronca "Sedan," the airplane developed engine trouble and Hallock made an emergency landing on a private airport in Tampico, Mexico. With Hallock unable to continue the flight to Austin, Quist and a mechanic flew down to Tampico in another airplane, a Stinson, to replace a damaged piston. After making the necessary repairs, Quist elected to fly the Aeronca back to Austin himself. However, taking off from Tampico, the engine quit, and he crash-landed into a building belonging to a railroad company. Quist sustained serious injuries, including a broken leg, facial lacerations, and a severely scarred left hand. But that's when his troubles really began.

Admitted first to a PEMEX hospital, Quist was refused treatment, other than first aid, because it was a company hospital. The main hospital in Tampico also refused treatment since the accident occurred outside its service area. When taken to another hospital, an inept attendant placed his broken leg in a cast without setting it, bandaged his face, and sutured his lacerated hand. And the worst was yet to come. Quist discovered he was in deep trouble with both the Mexican government and the railroad company, and was placed under house arrest in a Tampico hotel. Learning that "they wanted a lot of money," he hastened his exit from Mexico by first bribing the hotel manager, and later the airport guard placed on his Stinson. Accompanied by his mechanic, Quist quickly took off, headed for Brownsville, Texas, refueled, and later that day landed at St. Edward's Airport. He abandoned the crashed Aeronca "Sedan" in Mexico, and never returned.[33]

In retrospect, the Mexico crash appears as a harbinger of change. Mary Catherine had married and left the company. Charles purchased Hunter's interest in 1947 and, shortly after the Tampico crash, acquired Hallock's interest. The company, nevertheless, enjoyed some four years of profitable operation, with income generated from two primary sources—the G.I. Bill and St. Edward's University students. "When the G.I. Bill ran out, we finally ran out of qualified students," Hallock remembered. "The business just kinda dried up in the late 1940s.[34] Charles Quist was more specific: "I shut it down, liquidated the business, and sold the training fleet, some airplanes for as little as $400. Had a lot of assets but no money." He, nevertheless, maintained a positive assessment of his four-year tenure at St. Edward's Airport. "We taught a lot of students to fly," Quist recalled, "helped others to launch a career in aviation, and for a while made some money."[35]

But most important of all, in addition to creating Austin Aero Service, he and Hallock were able to fulfill their post–World War II ambitions— they remained in aviation. Quist later joined the Air National Guard, advanced to the rank of colonel, and became commander of the 149th Fighter Group at Kelly Air Force Base. Hallock joined the Chance-Vought Corporation as a flight test engineer and later became staff pilot for the University of Texas Applied Research Laboratory, flying a Douglas DC-3 in the research and development of missile guidance systems. Nothing remains today of St. Edward's Airport or the Austin Aero Service. Construction of Interstate Highway 35 in the 1950s bisected the landing field; the parking lot of the Internal Revenue Service now occupies what was once a portion of the north-south runway.

The closure of two privately owned and operated airports within the span of two years, while individually significant, was also symbolic of even greater changes that were occurring in postwar Austin. The city had entered an aggressive growth pattern. The decade of the 1940s brought 44,529 new citizens into the city; by 1950, more than 5,000 were arriving annually. That influx of humanity created a demand for new middle-class housing. As developers began searching for building sites north and northeast of the city, they were drawn instinctively to the unoccupied expanses of other private airports. On March 12, 1948, Ella Campbell conveyed to L. L. McCandless, president of McCandless Homes, Inc., 29.15 acres, thereby creating the Skyview Addition, an area then occupied by the Haile Airport.[36] By the end of 1950, Doc Haile had sold his remaining aircraft and terminated operations. Haile's tenure at 5600 Avenue F, however, was predetermined long before Ella Campbell sold the property to McCandless. In November 1947, when the author purchased his first Austin home at 5414 Avenue F, two blocks south of the Haile Airport, he inquired about the noise factor. His realtor, Glen E. Lewis, reassured him, "Don't worry. Doc's gotta go. *That land's too valuable to land airplanes on.*" Lewis, unknowingly, had articulated the metaphor for Austin airport controversy for the next half-century.

Appreciating land values were indeed changing the face of Austin. As the city spread steadily northward, University Airport became the next target for development. The Brownings' move to Mueller in September 1946 marked the last permanent occupancy at University Airport. On July 21, 1952, Webb Ruff and Myrtle N. Ruff deeded 22.98 acres to the Northway Crest Development Company, Inc., creating the Northway Crest subdivision.[37] Thus, within the scope of some two years, all four of Austin's original private airports had closed, leaving the city with a single, municipally owned landing facility. It would be there the two surviving FBOs, Ragsdale Flying Service and Browning Aerial Service, would continue their role as regional leaders in the field of general aviation.

The economics of these transactions appeared to invalidate most people's vision of the postwar aviation boom. Returning servicemen accorded higher priority to owning a home, getting an education, raising a family, and earning a livelihood within the traditional job markets. The airplane manufacturers were also forced to recognize the realities of the aviation marketplace. The January 1947 issue of *Aero Digest* lists fifty-six types of new light personal aircraft that had been test flown "and are expected to be in productions during 1947." There were nine additional models listed as "not quite ready for the market." In the same issue, William T. Piper, president of Piper Aircraft Corporation, warned of the dangers of overestimating the light plane market. "For the vast majority of Americans," he wrote, "there is not now—nor will there be in the very near future—much need for personal planes. It is inevitable that the personal-aircraft industry will boil down to a handful of substantial manufacturers."[38] History proved him correct. Ten years later, of the original forty-three manufacturing firms listed, only sixteen were still producing airplanes, and all sixteen were in business prior to World War II. As the 1940s gave way to the 1950s, both Austin FBOs were forced to heed Piper's warning of a postwar light plane market that would never reach fruition. Peacetime seemed to tarnish the wartime luster of the "wild blue yonder."

The dismal light plane market bore no relevance to urban growth; new citizens continued to take up residence in the Capital City. While some came by automobile and train (the Missouri Pacific and Houston and Central Texas railroads), others chose air transportation. Although Austin emerged from World War II with a single carrier, Braniff Airways, that was destined to change; federal regulations had revamped the structure of the industry. The Civil Aeronautics Act of 1938 transferred regulatory control from the Bureau of Air Commerce to the new Civil Aeronautics Authority. That freed the airlines of Post Office Department control and accorded them permanent rights to their routes. In essence, they became common carriers.[39] Under the reorganization plan of 1940, the Civil Aeronautics Board (CAB) became the airlines' primary regulatory agency, which oversaw safety and economic regulations. In terms of the latter, the Board's role in establishing interstate routes and issuing airline "certificates of convenience and necessity, stabilized commercial aviation and encouraged increased investment in new planes and equipment."[40] Long before VJ Day, airlines, anticipating postwar expansion, had begun ordering new equipment and filing new route applications before the CAB. Throughout the war years, however, the Austin Chamber of Commerce continued to play an active role in bringing increased airline service to the Capital City. In 1942, University of Texas professor Dr. John H. Frederick, representing the Chamber, appeared before the CAB in behalf of Braniff Airways' application to extend service from Amarillo to Denver, which the Board approved in July 1943.[41] The Chamber also presented briefs to the CAB supporting Braniff's Austin-Houston extension, as well as Eastern Airlines' application to serve Austin as an intermediate stop between Houston and San Antonio.

With a strong postwar economy and increased air travel, the Chamber's effort continued to yield results. Essair, an early "feeder" airline owned by Maj. William F. Long of Dallas, entered the Austin market on August 1, 1945, flying ten-place, twin-engine, Lockheed 10 "Electra" aircraft. That company served Austin as an intermediate stop between Amarillo and Houston. On June 17, 1946, new management changed the name to Pioneer Air Lines and replaced the Lockheed "Electras" with twenty-one passenger Douglass DC-3s.[42] Two additional feeder carriers, Dal-Air and Mercury Airlines, began Austin service in 1947. Mercury's tenure was short-lived; in early 1949, East Texas Air Lines, another feeder line, occupied Mercury's space at Mueller. The following year, East Texas Air Lines ceased operation, leaving only two carriers, Braniff and Pioneer, to provide Austin's air service.

While the majority of travelers still choose ground transportation, others in business and industry began exploring the use of private aircraft for its advantages of frequency and flexibility in business travel. Also, there was the added opportunity of extending their markets into areas not presently served by scheduled airlines.[43] That new era of personal air travel was made possible through the design and performance characteristics of postwar civil aircraft. Those included all-metal construction, retractable landing gear, electric starter, constant speed propeller, electrically controlled landing flaps, complete instrumentation, including two-way radio and automatic pilot, cabin soundproofing, expanded baggage compartments, plus extended cruising ranges at speeds in excess of 150 miles per hour. Time-proven Lycoming and Continental engines powered most new models. While some of the design features appeared in prewar aircraft, the development of more efficient, high-performance World War II military aircraft opened new opportunities for the postwar private flyer. And for the business executive needing long-distance, high-performance service, there were also the new twin-engine models: the Cessna 310, Aero-Commander, and Piper "Apache," as well as the World War II military conversions.

Madge Janes was one of the first Austin pilots to use personal aircraft for business purposes. The R. E. Janes family owned the Bar-Nothing Ranch, located some seven miles south of Austin. Before World War II, the family developed a thriving business marketing turkey poults (young turkeys) and turkey eggs throughout Central Texas. Madge learned to fly during World

War II, purchased a two-place Taylorcraft, and joined an active circle of women pilots, many of whom were members of local Civil Air Patrol squadrons.[44] With the experience gained during the war years, Madge foresaw the advantages of using aircraft to deliver turkey poults. In 1946, the Janes family purchased one of the first postwar Stinson 150 "Station Wagons." The four-place cabin aircraft cruised at 125 miles per hour with a 500-mile cruising range and could easily be converted for cargo use. With the new Stinson, Madge began delivering the farm's turkey poults throughout Central Texas, landing at airports where available, other times in pastures and open fields. Using the Stinson not only saved time, but was also a great sales promotion technique. No other Texas turkey farmer delivered its product by air.[45]

With the expansion of the R. E. Janes construction and building materials company, Ralph E. Janes Jr., a World War II pilot, followed his stepmother's example, purchasing a Cessna 180 to serve company clients throughout Texas and the Southwest. With greater dependence on personal air travel, the company added a twin-engine Cessna 310 in 1964. And some five decades after Madge Janes first soloed in her Taylorcraft, her grandson Ralph E. Janes III was still flying a twenty-year-old Cessna 180 on company business.[46]

In the early 1950s, Herman Heep, an Austin-based rancher, dairyman, independent oil operator, and philanthropist, also entered the business air age. In 1953, he purchased a new six-place twin-engine Beechcraft D-18 to more closely supervise his drilling crews in Texas, Louisiana, and Mississippi.[47] In addition to its utilitarian purpose, the Beechcraft was also a symbol of personal pride. Heep engaged a porter, whose primary responsibility was to maintain the cosmetic appearance of both the exterior and interior of the silver and green aircraft.[48] While an aircraft owner, Heep engaged several different pilots, including Dabney Cauley, who served him briefly in 1957. For his $500 monthly salary, Cauley remembered he was on call twenty-four hours a day but seldom made more than one or two flights weekly, either on business or on behalf of Heep's alma mater, Texas A&M University.[49] Later, needing more passenger space, speed, and range, Heep purchased a Lockheed 18 "Lodestar," which he used for business, as well as pleasure. Kenneth Cox, who once served as copilot on the "Lodestar," remembered a trip to Tucson, Arizona, to pickup actor James Arness for an appearance at the Austin Headliners Club.[50]

Former governor Allan Shivers was another Lockheed "Lodestar" owner. In 1957, at the completion of his second term in office, he assumed the presidency of Western Pipeline Company, Inc. To service construction sites in both United States and Canada, the company first purchased a Beechcraft D-18, which they later replaced with a Beechcraft "Twin Bonanza." The latter aircraft, equipped with a tricycle landing gear, was better adapted for small-field operations, especially when delivering supervisory personnel to remote construction sites. As the company grew, so did the need for larger and more efficient aircraft. To meet those needs, the company next acquired a Lockheed "Lodestar," and then moved up to a "Learstar," thence to the pure jet Hawker-Siddeley DH 125, and finally the larger, long-range turbo-prop Grumman "Gulfstream." When the original investors sold Western Pipeline in 1965, Gov. Shivers purchased the "Lodestar" for his personal use and retained the services of his longtime pilot, Leonard Smith. With wide-ranging personal business interests—banking, ranching, citrus farming, plus memberships of several boards of directors—he relied almost entirely on the "Lodestar" for personal transportation. And following Gov. Shivers' death on January 14, 1985, members of the Shivers family continued using the aircraft in the family businesses.[51]

About the same time Madge Janes began delivering turkey poults in the family's Stinson "Station Wagon," several state agencies also began exploring the use of aircraft in government business. In 1946, the Texas Game, Fish and Oyster Commission (after August 23, 1963, Texas Parks and Wildlife Department) purchased a Cessna 140 from Browning Aerial Service to monitor shrimping along the Gulf Coast, and later added a second Cessna 140 to facilitate wild game assessment in the Trans-Pecos area.[52] Although the aircraft purchase date and price could not be verified, the agency's annual report documents a growing reliance upon aerial surveillance. For the 1946–1947 fiscal year, airplane expense totaled only $264.74, which increased to $883.05 the following biennium. After 1947, aircraft use increased substantially: 1948–1949 expenses were $3,197.35; 1949–1950 expenses, $3,139.82; and 1950–1951 expenses, $4,629.35.[53] The same year the recently formed Texas Aeronautics Commission purchased a Luscombe "Silvaire," which was assigned to popular Austin aviatrix Ziggy Hunter, then the agency's statewide airport inspector.[54]

Realizing the State of Texas was an untapped aircraft market, Robert L. Ragsdale, owner of Ragsdale Flying Service, began soliciting the Department of Public Safety (DPS). Ragsdale arranged a demonstration flight in a new four-place North American "Navion" with DPS director Col. Homer

Garrison, at the department's base at Camp Mabry. The director appeared interested. He was, however, already aware of the use of aircraft in law enforcement. Several DPS employees owned personal aircraft, which they used frequently in departmental business, but at their own expense. In 1946, Joe Thompson, a Texas Ranger based in Waco, acquired a World War II surplus Vultee BT-13, and in 1948 Jim Boutwell, an Austin-based DPS radio operator-technician, rented a surplus Ryan PT-22 to assist in apprehending an arsonist who was setting brush fires in the hills west of Austin. The following year Boutwell and Kenneth Martin, another DPS employee, acquired a used Luscombe 8-A. Based at Camp Mabry, they used the aircraft primarily to service department radio transmitters in Corpus Christi, Harlingen, and Boerne, where they usually landed in open fields near the transmitters. "It beat driving," Boutwell wrote, "and not only attracted the attention of the Director, Col. [Homer] Garrison and Ass't. Dtr., Chief Joe Fletcher; it also attracted the attention of a lot of single girls working at DPS." [55]

Another event also attracted the director's attention and had profound impact on the future of law enforcement in Texas. In early 1949, the DPS headquarters in Austin received an urgent message that a convicted felon had escaped from the Jourdanton, Texas, jail and was believed to be headed toward Mexico. Col. Garrison ordered a detachment of Texas Rangers to Jourdanton to aid in the search. Ragsdale, who learned of the matter from Boutwell, offered use of a North American "Navion" in the operation. He landed at Camp Mabry, picked up Boutwell, and departed for Jourdanton. Some fifty minutes later they landed in a field near where the escapee was hiding in a heavily wooded area. Ragsdale and Boutwell received their assignment: once airborne and they sighted the fugitive, Ragsdale was to circle the area while Boutwell directed the ground forces with a walkietalkie. The plan worked, and according to Boutwell, "we got to witness a pretty dandy gun battle, with the subject and the officers shooting at each other with pistols. The battle ended pretty quick when the subject ran out of ammunition and surrendered." [56] When Ragsdale landed the "Navion" in a field near the capture site, he noted the subject was "cussing the airplane more than he was the people [Texas Rangers] and the dogs." [57]

Ragsdale's volunteer service to law enforcement had immediate as well as unexpected results. The publicity generated by the use of aircraft in apprehending an escaped prisoner gave Col. Garrison the necessary political clout to garner an aircraft appropriation from the state legislature. With

$10,000 designated to purchase a "new motor vehicle," the DPS ordered a $9,746.03 Ryan "Navion" from Ragsdale Flying Service, plus $244.00 in "supplementary equipment."[58] Col. Garrison based the aircraft at Camp Mabry and appointed Patrolman Max Westerman, a World War II Air Force veteran, as the DPS's first pilot. The aviation department, however, was destined to grow. By 1953, when requests for statewide aerial support exceeded the service of a single pilot, Westerman added Patrolman George Burnup to the pilot staff. From 1953 to 1957, the pilot staff remained unchanged, although the aircraft fleet had been upgraded from one single-engine "Navion" to three twin-engine Cessna 310s.[59] Years later, when assessing the ultimate impact of the Jourdanton operation, Col. Garrison acknowledged it was the media coverage of the event that helped elevate the Department of Public Safety to a new level of law enforcement. Through the use of aircraft, the Department reduced its response time from days to hours, multiplying its services manifold.

Change was also occurring in commercial air transportation; more people were flying in bigger and faster airliners. The World War II emergency, plus postwar business expansion, bred a new generation of air travelers, many of whom chose Austin, Texas, as their destination. Some arrived in the Capital City aboard Braniff International Airways' new, four-engine Douglas DC-4, which the company introduced in 1947. That airliner bore scant resemblance to its immediate predecessor, the venerable twin-engine DC-3. With carrying capacity increased from twenty-one to eighty-six passengers and cruising speed from 165 to 227 miles per hour, fewer aircraft were carrying more passengers at greater speeds.[60] That change is reflected in the Robert Mueller Municipal Airport annual traffic statistics. During the 1948–1952 period, 1,935 fewer scheduled flights departed Mueller, but they carried 10,778 more passengers.[61] Such technical advancements in aircraft performance were destined to affect airport design. Already in 1936, Austin Chamber of Commerce manager Walter Long had foreseen problems when he pointed out that runways could not stand the force of planes then landing with a striking weight of 28,000 to 30,000 pounds.[62] The correctness of Long's observation far exceeded his imagination. Compared with the DC-3's 29,200-pound striking force, the new Douglas DC-4, with maximum load, touched down at more than 73,000 pounds.[63] Increased weight and relative landing speed also required greater runway length, a matter which Braniff representatives pointed out repeatedly to the Austin city administration. While a DC-3 pilot felt comfortable approaching Mueller's 4,612-foot main runway at around sixty-five miles per hour, the DC-4 pilot, traveling at more than one hundred miles per hour, viewed the same strip with cautious apprehension. With Braniff's larger and faster DC-6s then on order, runway length at Mueller was a matter the Austin city council would be forced to address.

Acknowledging there was a problem at Mueller, Austin city manager Walter Seaholm proposed on June 30, 1950, a comprehensive plan for airport modernization, which included extending the runways and constructing a new administration building. "Top priority will go to a new administration building," Seaholm emphasized. "The city is embarrassed about the present relic. When speaking mildly, officials say it is totally inadequate . . . they call it a disgrace to the entire city. Even the old building's toilet facilities are embarrassing." [64] However, the lack of federal grant money postponed any immediate airport renovation. Airline complaints continued unabated. On December 10, 1951, Braniff International Airways filed a complaint with the Aviation Committee of the Austin Chamber of Commerce, reemphasizing the airport's inadequacies. R. H. Burck Jr., Braniff's Southern Region traffic manager, focused primarily on two areas: runway length and runway lighting. He noted that the airport's main ILS [Instrument Landing System] runway was too short to accommodate the company's new DC-6s, and while the company still operated six DC-4 daily flights at Austin, frequently, in bad weather, the runway lights were so dim the pilots were authorized to bypass Austin as a safety precaution. The complaint also addressed the approaches to the main runway: "There are deep ditches at the north end of two runways—including the instrument strip—which constitute mental and physical hazards and have the effect of further shortening the runways." [65] City Manager Walter Seaholm acknowledged the problem but postponed any action pending federal funding. Although Seaholm failed to address Mueller's obvious shortcomings, he no doubt was aware of concurrent airport developments in other Texas cities. In 1953, Amon Carter Field (later Greater Southwest International Airport) opened midway between Dallas and Fort Worth, and the new San Antonio International Airport, situated on that city's near north side, also opened that year.

The problems at Mueller, however, remained an issue before the Austin City Council for some five years. Finally on May 16, 1955, in its fifth special session of the week, the council voted to embark on the long-studied plan for airport expansion. [66] The availability of a $392,000 federal airport grant prompted council action. By adding $376,000 to grant funding, the city had $768,000 to launch the first phase of a two-step airport improvement project.[67] That grant, however, provided no funds for terminal construction. Phase I, costing $187,300, begun in September 1955 and completed in August 1956, added 1,100 feet and new lighting to the main ILS runway. Additional land for that extension cost $137,300.[68] Phase II, begun in March 1957, and completed in September 1958, included rerouting a portion of Manor Road to add an additional 2,050 feet to the main runway, extending that strip to 6,400 feet. That project included additional runway lighting, plus pavement overlays on runways and taxi strips to accommodate heavier aircraft.

Whatever the shortcomings Mueller may have possessed in the mid-1950s, air traffic to the Capital City continued to multiply annually. By 1953, when Trans-Texas Airlines began serving Austin, three carriers scheduled 7,300 annual departures, enplaning 47,080 passengers, 563 more than the previous year. Two years later, after Continental Airlines acquired Pioneer Air Lines, a total of 61,789 passengers departed Austin, bringing the two-year increase to 14,709.[69] In addition to expanding air service, population growth also contributed to the increased passenger traffic; between 1951 and 1955, twenty thousand new citizens arrived in Austin.

Incoming airline passengers, plus those arriving in private aircraft, are not included in the above totals. During the first eight months of 1955, according to airport officials, 33,267 planes, a record number, landed at Mueller, carrying "a total of 40,345 passengers—22 percent more than were landed here in the same period of last year."[70] And all the while, scheduled airline service continued to improve. On February 15, 1957, some ten years after the Austin Chamber of Commerce filed briefs before the CAB supporting Braniff's East Coast extension, the company dispatched its first Washington nonstop flight from Mueller. That gave Austin its first one-carrier service to Washington and New York City. And on April 1, Continental Airlines began operating its new pressurized forty-four passenger Super Convairs between Midland-Odessa, San Angelo, Austin, and Houston. Increased passenger traffic, however, had its downside; more and more people were forced to tread the corridors of Austin's civic embarrassment, the former schoolhouse that continued to serve as the airport terminal. But that was about to change.

On May 11, 1956, Austin citizens approved a $26,750,000 bond issue that included $1,200,000 for airport expansion, including a new terminal building.[71] Following extensive consultation with other city departments, commercial airlines, and the Civil Aeronautics Administration, City Manager W. T. Williams Jr. announced on September 9, 1957, that Austin would have "an airport terminal so big that people won't be running over each other."[72] The initial $887,000 budget included $600,000 in municipal bond money, plus a $287,000 federal grant. Austin architects Arthur Fehr and Charles Granger developed plans for a 33,000-square-foot functional structure that was three times the size of the present terminal and included space for the United States Weather Bureau, the Civil Aeronautics Administration, a restaurant, a coffee shop, and a newsstand, plus offices for the two fixed base operators. (Final plans called for more than 45,000 square feet.) The city council specified a facility sufficiently large to meet the city's needs until 1970, as well as one adaptable for future growth. In fulfilling those requirements, Fehr and Granger achieved national recognition, winning the 1958 *Progressive Architecture Magazine* award. The magazine cited the Austin terminal design as "Best in the Nation."[73] Contracts were awarded in October 1959; construction began immediately.

Col. Vance Murphy, director of the recently formed Department of Aviation, supervised the project.[74] His first major decision was choosing a site for the new terminal. Faced with a recent FAA advisory requiring the passenger terminal to be located further from the centerline of the runway, Murphy had two choices. One, keep the present site on the west side of the airport, which meant rerouting a section of Airport Boulevard and locating the new terminal some two hundred yards south on city-owned acreage occupied by Patterson Park. His other option was to choose another location. The city council, on the advice of Colonel Murphy, elected to locate the new terminal on the south side of the field, with access off Manor Road. As construction progressed, curious citizens were intrigued with the flared central superstructure, the eighty-six-foot-high control tower that dominated the new complex. When winter gave way to spring, the crowds of spectators along Manor Road grew larger, watching the profile of the modernistic design gradually assume form. Finally, on April 30, 1961, construction complete, the first airline passengers began proceeding through the corridors of the steel, glass, and aluminum structure to the new departure lounges that projected from the main building. At last the vision became reality, Austin's $1.3 million "golden dream," a civic edifice in which all citizens could at long last take pride.

The two-day airport dedication, held May 27–28, followed a traditional pattern, attracting some fifty thousand visitors. There were the ever-visible political figures: Vice President Lyndon Baines Johnson, Secretary of the Navy John Connally, Congressman Homer Thornberry, Austin mayor Lester Palmer, Austin aviation director Colonel Vance Murphy, and FAA regional administrator Archie W. League. And the visitors thrilled to the aerial acrobatics of the Air Force Thunderbirds, the massed fly-over by planes from the Texas National Guard, and thirty-minute scenic flights over Austin in either Braniff's new sixty-eight passenger, 400 miles-per-hour Lockheed "Electra II," Continental's new Vickers "Viscount," or Trans-Texas Airlines' Super Convair, all powered by turbo-jet engines.[75]

As the visitors left the airport that Sunday afternoon, no doubt remained in anyone's mind that Austin, Texas, had indeed entered the modern jet age. And while few people attending the airport dedication may have realized it, the same forces of change that brought Mueller to fruition were also reverberating throughout other growing American cities. That same year, 1961, a group of far-sighted Houston business men and civic leaders purchased almost three thousand acres of land some sixteen miles northeast of downtown Houston on which to build that city's airport of the future. That event represented a sign of changing times; suburban airports were the wave of the future, a matter which Austin citizens would ultimately be forced to address.

CHAPTER 7

MUELLER, MARFA, AND THE GATHERING STORM

T HE dedication of the new Robert Mueller Municipal Airport Terminal on May 27–28, 1961, marked the beginning of a major watershed era in the history of Austin aviation. Changes were occurring in all sectors of the industry—commercial air carriers, private flying, executive aviation, state government aviation, military aviation, and fixed base operations. During the past decade, traffic at Mueller increased some 200 percent; commercial air travel, especially, was expanding with unprecedented rapidity. Vance E. Murphy, director of aviation, predicted that by 1964, passenger traffic at Robert Mueller Municipal Airport would reach approximately 750,000 passengers annually. While Murphy was overly optimistic in his prediction, growth, nevertheless, continued. He later reported that

January 1964 records show an increase of 2,731 airline passengers over January 1963; February 1964, an increase of 2,132 over February 1963; March of this year [1964] increased 2,000 over the same month last year, and April figures reveal an increase of 2,850 airline passengers over April 1963. April 1964 saw the establishment of a new all-time high record for individuals processed in one month, when a total of 20,323 airline passengers arrived at or departed from Municipal Airport.

Murphy added that more than half the travelers using the Austin facility were "traveling on business or pleasure in privately owned or executive type aircraft." By the mid-1960s, some 160 corporate or privately owned airplanes were based at Mueller.[1]

This growth of general aviation, especially during the past decade, ultimately gained the attention of the Austin City Council. During the recent debate over airport expansion, Chamber of Commerce representatives reiterated the need for more hangar facilities for private aircraft. Airport Committee chairman M. J. Thompson told the council at least forty to fifty hangars were needed.[2] The council, a reluctant supporter of general aviation, allocated some $120,000 to erect forty T-hangars to be assigned equally between Ragsdale Flying Service and Browning Aerial Service.[3] Although the decision to erect the new hangars was singularly important, it also symbolized major changes that were occurring in general aviation.

The economic slump that followed World War II, plus the availability of surplus military aircraft, greatly depressed general aviation, forcing many manufacturers into bankruptcy, while others curtailed production. Cessna Aircraft Company, for example, which produced 6,114 military-type aircraft between 1941 and 1943, produced only 551 light commercial models in 1951.[4] That was destined to change; by 1951 the nation had entered a new economic mode. Texas, especially, responded to the upward trend, reporting "a roaring volume of production and trade that exceeded any level ever reached by the economy of the state." In Austin, the housing boom reflected the new economy. In 1950, the city issued $39,404,052 in building permits, up 30 percent from 1949.[5] That general economic vitality stimulated all facets of aviation, including general aviation; major manufacturers began producing executive, as well as training and recreational aircraft. By 1952, for example, Cessna's production of private, single-engine training and recreational models had more than doubled. Those relatively inexpensive new training aircraft, combined with the great backlog of G.I.-trained pilots, provided the foundation for the private flying industry that would gain momentum in the mid-1950s. Piper Aircraft Corporation's introduction of the "Tri-Pacer" in 1951 helped accelerate that process.

The four-place, single-engine "Tri-Pacer" was the first commercially produced light aircraft to employ a tricycle landing gear. The tricycle gear concept—two main wheels and nose wheel—proved to be a great improvement over the traditional "tail dragger" design. Tricycle gear aircraft not only made taking off, landing, and maintaining ground control safer through better vision but, most important, made it easier to teach students to fly. And therein lay the harbinger of change. The "Tri-Pacer" was a hit with private pilots. The company sold 353 of them, priced at $5,355, in the first year of production.[6] The "Tri-Pacer" also had an immediate impact on the Austin market. Browning Aerial Service, the Austin Piper dealer, far outsold all other light aircraft models in the Austin area. Robert M. "Bobby" Browning III, son of Robert M. Browning, remembered it was his assignment as a seventeen-year-old to fly on commercial airlines to the Piper factory in Lock Haven, Pennsylvania, and ferry "Tri-Pacers" back to Austin—solo—for waiting customers.[7]

To compete with the Piper "Tri-Pacer," Cessna entered the tricycle gear–light plane market in 1955, with the introduction of the four-place 172 "Skyhawk." In one year production jumped from 173 to 1,419 units. That same year, 1956, Piper marketed 1,072 "Tri-Pacers."[8] With flight training a substantial portion of the income of FBOs, they recognized the need for a small, two-place, tricycle gear training aircraft. Cessna, nevertheless, remained reluctant to expand its model lines, until that 1956 landmark sales meeting in Wichita, Kansas. Regional Cessna dealers argued that the only way to generate aircraft sales was to expand the pilot base by teaching more people to fly. The obvious solution, they believed, was for the company to produce a small, relatively inexpensive two-place trainer with a tricycle landing gear. Wayne Champney, an El Paso Cessna distributor, was one of the more outspoken persons at the meeting. He argued that simply putting a nose wheel on the present two-place Cessna Model 140 would fill that market void. Company officials finally agreed, and in 1957 Cessna produced the first prototype; the following year the company distributed 122 of the new Model 150. Its popularity was immediate; in 1959 Cessna sold 648 Model 150s. Production continued to multiply; during the ensuing decade, some 11,920 units of the popular two-place trainer found their way into private hands.[9] In the early 1960s, Robert Ragsdale remembered placing one order for 110 Cessna 150s for distribution in the Central Texas market.[10]

By the mid-1950s, both fixed base operators at Robert Mueller Airport were enjoying the benefits of a strengthening economy, plus the growing popularity of private flying. While the sales appeal of the Piper line attracted many new plane buyers, the Browning company nevertheless began focusing primarily on flight training, service, maintenance, aircraft storage, and charter operations. Ragsdale Flying Service, on the other hand, while expanding its service divisions, embarked on a broad-based sales program.

Prior to 1951, the FBO aircraft dealers and the manufacturers maintained a rather casual relationship; dealers could usually sell any aircraft, regardless of make, either in cooperation with another dealer or direct with the factory. However, by the early 1950s, with the marked growth of private flying, the manufacturers began assigning franchised territories to specific dealers and distributors. Authorized Austin dealers included Aero-Tel, offering Ercoupe and Bellanca aircraft; Austin Aero Service, Aeronca and Luscombe; Haile Airport, Globe "Swift"; Browning Aerial Service, Piper; and Ragsdale Flying Service, Cessna. Also, the manufacturers began developing cooperative marketing campaigns with the aircraft dealers to stimulate sales in local areas. Cessna's "Who Me, Fly?" newspaper campaign, for example, profiled various local professionals—doctors, attorneys, stock brokers, bankers, insurance executives, and so forth—with a brief account of how easily they learned to fly ("as easy as driving a car") and are now using their personal aircraft for both business and pleasure. Austin doctors comprised one of the more active pilot groups.[11]

Although there is no supporting documentation, most contemporary observers agree that Ragsdale Flying Service emerged as the major private aircraft dealer in the Central Texas region.[12] The popularity of the Cessna models was one factor; another was the marketing programs the company developed. "Breakfast in Bandera" introduced many Austin citizens to the pleasures of private flying. The company would invite a group of potential customers to fly to Bandera, Texas, on Sunday mornings for a Western breakfast at the Flying-L Ranch. This not only acquainted the guests with the fun of private flying, but introduced the potential of weekend pleasure flights to the many Hill Country resorts equipped with landing strips. Another productive sales technique was offering free flight instruction if a person purchased an aircraft from Ragsdale Flying Service.[13]

Although fear of flying remained one of the major obstacles to aircraft sales, Ragsdale found a solution. Often, when given a demonstration flight in the Austin area, the potential customer would pose that often asked question, "What would happen if the engine quit now?" Ragsdale would respond, "I'll show you." He would then turn off the ignition switch, and knowing the wind direction, velocity, and the distance from the airport, he would simply glide the aircraft back to the airport. And after a moment of quiet reflection, Ragsdale added, "Sure sold a lot of airplanes that way." [14]

And Ragsdale's customers sometimes came from unexpected sources. During the 1956 spring semester, a group of University of Texas students, under the leadership of Morris S. Johnston, formed the Longhorn Flying Club.[15] Their objective was to "provide low cost flying and flight instruction and [to further] its members' knowledge of flying techniques, navigation and other general aeronautical subjects." Membership was available to anyone affiliated with the University—faculty, students, and staff—and was affordable for most. The initiation fee was $30, with $6 monthly dues that covered aircraft insurance, maintenance, cost of equipment, and general overhead expenses. With the initial cash on hand, the club acquired two used aircraft, a Cessna 140 and a Piper J-5 "Cub" trainer, for around $1200 each, and based them at Ragsdale Flying Service. Aircraft rental was also nominal: flight time in the Piper cost $3.60 per hour, in the Cessna $4.20 per hour, and the instructor's fee added $4 per hour. Membership grew from the beginning. By the summer of 1957, forty-five members had flown over two thousand accident-free hours, while sixteen students had received their private pilot's licenses.[16]

The Longhorn Flying Club's initial success stemmed primarily from the students' personal commitment to the organization. They wrote their own operational rules and contractual terms, which as a nonprofit organization they filed with the secretary of state. The students also established their membership dues and the hourly aircraft rental rates based solely on the actual operating costs; there were no salaries and no profit. "If it had not been for the enthusiasm and devotion of our group of would-be-flyers, and the tolerance and guidance of the Ragsdales," Morris S. Johnston wrote later, "I fear the club would not have survived its first 100 hour inspection." [17]

Success bred success, and as the Longhorn Flying Club grew in size and popularity, the prospect of profit did not go unnoticed. Sometime in the mid-1960s, physics professor Robert Crutchfield reorganized the club as the Longhorn Flying Club, Inc., which had no relationship with the University of Texas. According to a former club member, Crutchfield had "grandiose ideas." And grandiose they were; the organization literally mushroomed. By 1967 Crutchfield was operating "what without question is the largest flying operation in the world," wrote Austin journalist Dave Shanks. "[He] supervises purchase of more airplane units than any person in general aviation. Longhorn now has 2,000 members in 15 cities, all but one in Texas (Albuquerque, N.M., is an outpost)." Two years later the affiliated clubs had increased to twenty, with Southeastern State College of Durant, Oklahoma, sponsoring a second out-of-state flying club. According to Shanks, the largest club in the system remained the one in Austin, where "700 members pilot 23 airplanes from Austin Municipal Airport." System-wide, club utilization was three hours per day per airplane; club billings for dues and flight time amounted to more than $80,000 per month.[18]

The Longhorn Flying Club, Inc. unquestionably made private flying affordable to many persons who otherwise would have been denied the opportunity. And, in addition, club members had access to a wide range of new aircraft, all well maintained and serviced by local FBOs. Crutch field purchased Cessna aircraft exclusively; Ragsdale Aviation and its regional affiliates provided most of the flight equipment. The club's investment, however, was substantial; purchase prices ranged from $10,195 for a Cessna 150 to $44,000 for a Cessna 210 turbo. To make flying even more affordable, the club offered members discounted hourly rental rates: a Cessna 150 rented for $7.60 per hour; a Cessna 172s for $9.90; a Cessna 177 for $11.10; a Cessna 182 for $17.60; and a Cessna 210 for $24.80.[19] With the club's graduated fleet of aircraft, members had access to every type of aircraft from the Cessna 150 two-place trainer to the six-place, pressurized, 221-miles-per-hour 210 "Centurion." Thus, club members could learn to fly, build up flight time, acquire an instrument rating, and graduate to a high-performance, executive-type aircraft, all of these being within the economic range of most middle-class individuals. And therein lay the problem.

With some two thousand members representing twenty clubs in three states, administrative control remained an ongoing problem, especially in terms of flight safety. Repeated warnings that safety rules must be observed apparently went unheeded. On August 26, 1968, the board of directors reported "insurance rates have risen 100% in the last 30 days," while posting the following deductibles: in-flight damage, $1,000; taxiing damage, $1,000; and ground damage, $50. The board warned further, "If a member is in violation of Club rules, or FAA regulations, or is found to be careless or negligent by the FAA, the member pays the deductible portion."[20] According to a report on aircraft damage, club members were guilty of all of the above.

> October 22, 1966. Cessna 150. Rough engine caused landing in a pasture near pilot's girl friend's house. After eating lunch, engine rechecked and no longer rough. Pilot attempted to take off and was unable to leave the ground due to 24" grass. Plane was totaled. Probable cause: Pilot judgment and carelessness.

> June 15, 1967. Cessna 172. Pilot attempted flight from Austin to New Orleans nonstop. Ran out of fuel 10 miles from New Orleans airport. Landed in field. Nose gear damaged. Probably cause: Judgment and negligence in preflight planning.

> October 25, 1967. Cessna 210. On landing, pilot failed to extend landing gear. Damage slight. Probable cause: Pilot negligence.

> May 26, 1968. Cessna 177. On a flight from El Paso to Truth or Consequences, New Mexico, pilot changed plan and landed at unattended [2,000 ft. long] ranch strip having 7800 ft. elevation. On takeoff failed to clear trees. According to the operator's manual . . . the runway was not long enough for take off with the temperature and wind conditions . . . Plane was totaled. Probable cause: Judgment.

Amazingly, the report concludes, "in all of the above accidents [sixteen entries], there have been no fatalities or serious injuries."[21]

While negligence at member level greatly affected the club's day-to-day operation, negligence at the administrative level caused even greater concern. In August 1968, the board of directors advised club members the crux of the expense problem was low aircraft utilization from December 1967 through May 1968. Poor flying weather during the winter months kept the airplanes grounded. Because, in essence, airplanes earn no revenue while parked in a hangar, Crutchfield faced a growing financial crisis. He approached the problem in a manner less than likely to succeed. In addition to leasing aircraft at below-market fees, he placed the club in further financial jeopardy by purchasing new and expensive aircraft for each new club before that club established a viable membership base. And there was also credit card abuse—or misuse; club members flying cross-county carried a club credit card to purchase fuel and other ground services. Apparently the policy for credit card accounting and personal refunds was never clearly articulated; most issues of *Propwash,* the club's newsletter, contain repeated instructions covering these matters. In October 1968, in an attempt to bring fiscal order to the club's operation, the board of directors engaged retired banker Arch Adams as club manager.[22] Adams soon learned the extent of the club's financial dilemma: some $80,000 in unpaid fuel bills and a monthly income far short of the debt service. Sometime in the early 1970s (the date could not be confirmed) the board accepted the inevitable—bankruptcy. The airplanes were sold, thus bringing to an end what had been the world's largest flying club.

For almost a decade, Robert Mueller Municipal Airport had served Austin's expanding aviation community as the area's only landing facility. That was destined to change. On January 16, 1956, when Theodore R. Timmerman Sr. purchased 250 acres of prime farm land on Dessau Road, some five miles north of Mueller, his purpose was agriculture, not aviation. That also was destined to change. Shortly after acquiring the property, Jim Boutwell, the former Department of Public Safety pilot and later sheriff of Williamson County, offered to purchase a portion of Timmerman's land to establish a private airport. At first Timmerman refused, but later reconsidered and leased Boutwell some twenty acres for an airport. Timmerman, however, continued improving the landing field. He paved the original 2,800-foot runway, installed runway lights, erected a maintenance shop and several T-hangars, and expanded the aircraft tie-down facilities.[23] Attempting to keep his investment to a minimum, he purchased a small residence scheduled for demolition, which he moved to the field for an operations office. Boutwell's tenure, however, was brief. When he left to join Champion Aircraft Corporation, Theodore R. Timmerman Jr. took over the operation temporarily. The firm's name, Tim's Airpark, reflected the change in management.[24]

Hoping to establish Tim's Airpark as a viable aviation center, young Timmerman sold a small acreage adjacent to Dessau Road to Donald R. Castleberry, where Castleberry established his aviation electronics business. Timmerman, however, continued to operate the flying school, acquired a small training fleet, and engaged Bruce Linn and Jim Armstrong as instructors. As the student population grew, so did Timmerman's fixed base operations. His Mooney dealership, hangar and tie-down rentals, line service, and aircraft maintenance and repairs comprised Timmerman's other sources of income. Business activity at Tim's Airpark caught the attention of Bobby Stanton. In January 1968 Bobby, in partnership with his father, Leo, purchased Jim Boutwell's interest in Aviation Training Centers, Inc., the original flight operation, and negotiated a three-year lease with Timmerman. Operating a fleet of some twenty training aircraft, Stanton's firm was also an authorized G.I. flight training center, offering a complete instructional curriculum that included the transport pilot's course.

To offer that instruction, Stanton, with a $20,000 loan from the Austin National Bank, purchased a Douglas DC-3 airliner from Denver-based Aspen Airways.[25]

Stanton's reference to his bank loan marks another major milestone in the field of Austin private flying. Prior to the 1960s, ownership of private aircraft was limited mainly to those with sufficient resources to negotiate a personal loan, or pay cash for an airplane.[26] In 1961, however, that all changed in the Austin market, when R. A. Lewis invited ballroom dance instructor Bob Wilson to accompany him on a weekend flight to New Orleans in a Piper "Comanche." That was Wilson's first flight in a private aircraft, and he was "hooked." Returning to Austin, he went immediately to Browning Aerial Service and explained that, although he was not a pilot, he wanted to buy an airplane. Robert Browning, in turn, referred Wilson to an individual who wanted to sell his Piper "Tri-Pacer" for $4,500. Wilson saw the plane, liked it, and agreed to buy it but was greatly disappointed to learn that banks did not finance airplanes—at least not at that time.[27]

A man of persistence and imagination, Wilson remembered he had a dance student, Walter Chamberlain, who was a loan officer at Austin National Bank. When Wilson approached Chamberlain for an aircraft loan, Chamberlain explained that banks did not make aircraft loans. He agreed, however, to present the matter to bank vice president Buck Fitzgerald, fully expecting Fitzgerald's emphatic response: "I'd sooner make a loan on a hive of bees!"[28] Chamberlain, however, was persistent. He explained to Fitzgerald that financing personal aircraft was no longer a speculative venture; a new breed of private pilot had replaced the barnstorming, accident-prone thrill-seekers of the 1930s. In addition, financing general aviation aircraft represented a promising field for the lending institutions, plus serving a community need.[29] Fitzgerald pondered Chamberlain's advice, reversed his position, and approved Wilson's loan. The vice president's precedent-setting decision benefited not only Wilson, but a host of other private pilots in the Austin area. According to Chamberlain, the Austin National Bank ultimately financed hundreds of private aircraft purchases, and for several years carried some $10 million in "aircraft paper." That included financing dealer aircraft inventory—"floor planning."[30] Aided by the new lending policies of Austin banks, Bobby Stanton, in partnership with his wife, Dawana, continued to prosper at Tim's Airpark. As his business expanded, so did his staff; he hired former navy pilot John T. Baker as general manager, and later engaged Robert White as part-time instructor. Stanton, subsequently recognizing other business opportunities, sold the flight school to John T. Baker in 1973.[31]

The scheduled air carriers, unlike private flying, enjoyed the ongoing stewardship of the Austin city government. From February 6, 1928, when the first airmail plane landed in Austin, to the dedication of the new Mueller passenger terminal, city sponsorship through bond issues, federal grants, and cash appropriations provided the necessary facilities for air carriers to serve Austin. The city also occupied the investor role; airline landing fees, property leasing, and aircraft fuel sales yielded the city a steady income. From 1944 to 1960 (with the exception of 1957), the Department of Aviation reported annual profits, varying from $9,329 to $30,228.[32] General aviation, however, lacking the profit potential of airline operations, received scant support from the city government. In addition, the city's closing of the old west side terminal building in 1961 dealt the two Mueller FBOs, Ragsdale Aviation and Browning Aerial Service, a severe blow.

Previously, executive aircraft arriving in Austin chose the west side FBO service facilities adjacent to the old terminal. While their aircraft were being serviced, passengers and crews could avail themselves of the terminal's facilities—food, beverages, restrooms, telephones, cab service, and the like—before continuing their journey. Without those facilities, the visitors—many times CEOs of major corporations—had the choice of waiting in the Browning hangar or standing on the service ramp. And the Texas weather was not always conducive to visitor comfort. Consequently, the FBOs were forced to take action. Ragsdale based his initiative on previous dealings with the city government: "The main thing I learned, if I needed anything I had to build it."[33]

In February 1962, after acquiring a long-term lease for the original Mueller terminal site, Ragsdale began construction on the city's first transient aircraft terminal. Following a design complementary to the new municipal terminal building, the steel, glass, and concrete structure was ready for occupancy by May 12, 1962. The 2,500-square-foot terminal contained the necessary amenities to accommodate passengers and crews of the growing fleet of executive aircraft. Those included a pilot's briefing room with navigational charts and the latest weather information, a pilots' lounge, a private executive conference room, catering service from the Driskill Airport Restaurant, automobile rental service, and direct telephone lines to all major hotels and motels. Some eight thousand people attended the two-day dedication.[34]

While the Ragsdale terminal was still under construction, Robert M. Browning III was already working with Austin architect Pat Riley on plans for that company's transient terminal. Browning erected his two-story glass and masonry structure on thirty-five acres leased from the city and located some two hundred yards east of the Ragsdale terminal. Planned with the corporate executive in mind, the spacious 44,000-square-foot facility contained lounge areas and briefing rooms, plus facilities for business conferences and corporate meetings. Company president Emma Browning viewed the terminal as the gateway to the city for visiting dignitaries arriving in private aircraft, and she wanted their first impression of Austin to be positive.[35]

In retrospect, building the transient terminals appeared to launch a mini-construction boom at Mueller; other flight service structures were in the offing. On October 28, 1967, Austin mayor Harry Akin dedicated the new Flight Training Center, a one-story, brick structure built by the city and located on the east side of the airport. The mayor explained the structure contained facilities for flight training and flight services for general aviation in the Austin area. Describing the city's new relationship with the FBOs, Colonel Vance Murphy, director of aviation, added, "The new facility is another of those on the airport in which the city participates with private aviation firms."[36] Although the city constructed the facility, it was leased to Ragsdale Aviation, a private firm, for that company's flight training program. Ragsdale vice president Kenneth Cox explained further the city's new posture regarding general aviation: "Col. Murphy, with a life-long career in aviation, added a degree of professionalism in airport management. He made it possible for the city and the fixed base operator to cooperate for the general development of aviation." And in addition, Murphy foresaw the benefits of "reinvesting some of the city's income into ramps, hangars, and other airport facilities" that benefited the FBOs.[37]

The city also extended its cooperation to the military. On September 1, 1970, three units of Texas National Guard Aviation were transferred from Camp Mabry to new permanent quarters located at 2001 East Fifty-first Street, on the northeast side of Mueller.[38] Established on 18.08 acres leased from the City of Austin for one dollar a year, a permanent contingent of 115 officers and men operated and maintained twenty-seven rotary-wing aircraft at that location. In retrospect, the transfer to Mueller remains a historic milestone; the adjutant general's order marked the end of more than a half-century of civilian and military aviation activity on the Camp Mabry parade ground.

Development of landing fields in other areas of the city during the 1930s eventually switched the focus from Camp Mabry, once the hope for Austin's aviation future. The immediate post–World War II era, however, brought renewed aviation activity to the former cavalry post. In 1947, the Department of Defense assigned an L-17, a North American "Navion," to Texas National Guard Adj. Gen. K. L. Berry, which he based at Camp Mabry.[39] Lt. Grady M. Roberts, General Berry's personal pilot, quickly recognized the limitations of operating modern aircraft from that restricted parade ground. On one occasion, taking off north on the grass runway with General Berry aboard, the aircraft barely cleared the top of a ten-foot chain-link fence, which General Berry subsequently ordered removed. After that, Lieutenant Roberts planned his takeoffs with a veteran pilot's care. Taking off north, he could, if necessary, fly between the buildings along Mabry Drive before gaining altitude; taking off south, he chose the "slot" in a grove of oak trees.[40] Because of obvious safety concerns, the field was ordered closed on January 6, 1950; however, the order was rescinded on April 20, and small fixed-wing aircraft continued using the facility for another decade.[41]

On March 16, 1959, Camp Mabry entered a new era of military aircraft operations; the United States Army ordered two new Texas National Guard air units stationed there. Those were the 136th and 112th Transportation Companies, manned by 293 officers and enlisted men who operated and maintained twelve rotor-wing military aircraft.[42] It eventually became apparent those unit operations greatly overtaxed the field's facilities. By 1966, forty-six pilots, in maintaining minimum proficiency, flew 5,074 hours and initiated 10,016 takeoffs and landings.[43] Negotiations, however, were already underway with the City of Austin for a long-term lease to establish the maintenance shop and armory at Robert Mueller airport. Benefits to the city were apparent: an additional payroll in excess of one-quarter-million dollars in return for the use of the 18.08 acres located on the northeastern perimeter of the field.

When a budgetary freeze delayed the project's funding, Texas National Guard Adj. Gen. Thomas S. Bishop appealed to the Chief, National Guard Bureau, to expedite the matter. He cited a recent report by the National Guard Aircraft Accident Prevention Survey identifying "the extremely hazardous conditions associated with the conduct of flight activities at Camp Mabry." General Bishop argued, "This project is required, not only for the pilots and passengers, but also to safeguard the lives of the residents, hospital patients and school children in the surrounding Camp Mabry." If the project is authorized prior to December 31, 1966, he explained, a fifty-year lease will become effective immediately for a consideration of only one dollar."[44] The deadline passed, but not the $532,499.75 appropriation. The city, however, extended the lease, with federal funding eventually forthcoming. On September 1, 1970, the three aviation units departed Camp Mabry for new facilities at Mueller. Thus, the City of Austin, through the Department of Aviation, was gradually broadening the tenant base at the municipal airport. There would be others.

Bergstrom Air Force Base, however, remained the area's primary center of military aviation activity. By January 1958, the base had a population of some 10,000 people, including about 5,000 airmen and their dependents. The concomitant funding also further enriched the area economy: $25 million in annual maintenance costs, $15 million in annual salaries paid to the 5,000 airmen and 335 civilian workers (with at least 90 percent spent in Austin), plus another $10 million invested locally for equipment and maintenance.[45] The combat units based at Bergstrom fluctuated in accordance with changing world conditions. In 1958, during the height of the Cold War, Strategic Air Command B-52 "Stratafortresses," supported by KC-135 "Stratatankers," flew daily trans-Arctic surveillance missions from Bergstrom. In 1966, when the base reverted to the Tactical Air Command, the 12th Air Force's RF-4C "Phantom" jet fighters replaced the heavy bombers, and in November 1967, the 75th Tactical Reconnaissance Wing departed Bergstrom for temporary service in Vietnam. The following year the 12th Air Force occupied its circular headquarters building, referred to locally as "The Doughnut," the base's most distinctive structure.[46]

Technical changes occurring in commercial airliners serving Mueller were equally advanced. On May 31, 1971, the last propeller-driven aircraft of a trunk line carrier, a Texas International Airlines Convair 600, departed Austin for Houston, marking the beginning of complete jet service for the Capital City.[47] The Boeing 727s, BAC 111s, and McDonald-Douglas DC-9s operated by Braniff International Airways, Continental Airlines, and Texas International Airlines represented a new breed of jet transports. The Boeing 727, the larger and faster of the three aircraft, for example, carried up to 189 passengers at 621 miles per hour, a decided advancement over its predecessor, the 52-passenger, 300 miles-per-hour Convair 600. The new jet transports were being rushed into service during the mid-1960s, a period of rapid growth in air travel, when "potential passengers were multiplying at a higher rate than aircraft seats to carry them."[48] Austin's air traffic statistics also reflected that change. During the decade of the 1960s, airline enplanements increased from 77,034 to 260,761, a growth of 238.5 percent. For the same period, a 33 percent increase in Austin population, from 186,545 to 251,808, further stimulated local air travel.[49] The increased air activity at Mueller soon began taking its toll on the facility's basic infrastructure; the Boeing 727s, with a runway striking force of more than 200,000 pounds, were, according to one journalist, "destroying the runways, and an extensive repaving program was initiated."[50] That was the harbinger of things to come.

The private aviation sector was also experiencing substantial growth. In 1967, Browning Aerial Service launched one of the region's more unique charter operations. It all began with a conversation between Charles E. Jenkins, a project manager with the University of Texas Department of Astronomy, and Robert M. Browning III. Jenkins, who was taking flying lessons with Browning, had assignments at both the Austin campus and the department's McDonald Observatory on Mount Locke, located in Jeff Davis County in Far West Texas. Commuting between those two locations was an ongoing problem; train and automobile travel were fatiguing and time-consuming. However, from his flying experience, Jenkins recognized the potential of using aircraft to shuttle staff personnel between Austin and the observatory. Observatory director Harlan J. Smith, who claimed he "wore out a VW Bug" in six years of commuting to the McDonald facility, approved Jenkins' suggestion.[51] In late 1967, using a four-place Piper "Comanche," Browning began the charter service on a standby basis, landing at the Marfa airport. Staff members traveled the remaining thirty-five miles to the observatory in a University vehicle. The shuttle operation became an immediate success. With increased demand for space, Browning switched to the larger, six-place, 200 miles-per-hour, twin-engine Piper "Aztec" and began scheduling regular twice-a-week flights.[52]

Following a year's successful operation, Jenkins wrote to University of Texas business manager E. D. Walker, explaining that "a leased airplane was the only practical solution for the rapid transportation of engineers and consultants required to meet project schedules." Walker accordingly included use of a leased airplane in the 1970 budget. To support Jenkins' recommendation, Browning submitted proposals for four different types of aircraft, from the fifteen-seat Beechcraft "King Air" (monthly rental, $27,000; hourly rate, $60) to the four-seat Piper "Twin Comanche" (monthly rental, $1,300; hourly rate, $25). Thomas G. Barnes, who later replaced Jenkins as the McDonald director, also supported the shuttle operation; he believed twice-weekly flights to Marfa were the most effective way to transport astronomers and staff to and from the observatory.[53] The flights departed Austin on Monday and Friday mornings, landed in Marfa for service and to pick up the returning passengers, and then headed back to Austin immediately. Cruising at around 200 miles per hour below 10,000 feet, the west-bound flight required about two hours and thirty minutes; the return flight was somewhat faster. The pilot on most flights was Ingvar (Jake) Jacobsen, who is remembered most favorably by all who flew the Austin-Marfa shuttle. Jacobsen, who made his first flight on June 11, 1971, remained with the Browning organization about thirteen years.

Most veteran members of the Astronomy Department have a favorite shuttle story, and although the operation was accident free, there were times when circumstances prompted them to consider the advantage of automobile travel. Observatory director Harlan J. Smith remembered encountering a thunderstorm during which the turbulence was so violent "none of the three of us, I think, really believed we were going to survive." Also, there was "light hail, which was as frightening as all get out [and] the rain was practically solid, and the lightening, of course, was more or less continuous all around . . . But we obviously got through it."[54]

Some of the thrills of flying the Marfa shuttle stemmed from lapses in good judgment. Charles Jenkins, who held a private pilot's license, was also working on an instrument rating and took advantage of the Marfa flights to practice his blind-flying skills. Thomas G. Barnes recalled on occasion Jenkins would take over the controls to hone his instrument flight skills. To simulate instrument conditions, Jenkins used an instructional hood that blocked out all vision except the instrument panel. Although the regular pilot was always present, Barnes found it disconcerting to see Jenkins quickly remove the mask just before the aircraft touched the runway. Barnes, however, was one of the shuttle regulars who developed absolute confidence in Jacobsen's skill as a pilot. On one occasion, when approaching Marfa, the fog was so dense he was not sure they would be able to land. However, there was one option. Lacking an instrument landing system, Jacobsen took a bearing on the Marfa VOR (very high frequency omni-range) station, oriented his position, located the highway, which he followed to the Marfa airport, and landed. Barnes came to realize that Jacobsen never took unnecessary chances. He remembered that, sitting in the copilot's seat adjacent to Jacobsen, he had just finished reading *The Daily Texan* and "offered it to Jake," who "was just sitting there with the autopilot on. We were in the middle of nowhere, but he said no, *he had to watch for other airplanes!* Watch for other airplanes! In hundreds of flights out there with him, *I never saw another airplane!*"[55]

The Marfa shuttle's sixteen-year longevity attests to the operation's success. The increasing demand for the charter flights is documented in the University of Texas Accounting Office records. Although there are no financial records prior to fiscal year 1969–1970, that year the University paid Browning Aerial Service $29,727.78 for the shuttle operation. Payments increased annually to fiscal year 1976–1977, when they reach a maximum of $87,824.73. Although financial records for the fiscal years 1977–1978 through 1979–1980 are not available, the demand for the charter service remained strong. Payments of $64,915.72 were posted in 1980–1981 and $69,988.58 in the following year. In 1982–1983, Browning's Marfa shuttle income reached a fourteen-year low, $12,096.85.[56] The operation's success was hastening its demise.

During the period of the Marfa operation, other state agencies discovered the advantages of operating private and charter aircraft. The practice quickly gained wide acceptance. In 1964, five state agencies and one state university system owned a total of ten aircraft; ten years later, eleven agencies, plus the governor, the attorney general, and two university systems owned or leased a total of thirty airplanes, valued at $1,206,113.[57] The general underutilization of individual aircraft financed through state appropriations ultimately gained the lawmaker's attention. In 1979, the state legislature passed the State Aircraft Pooling Board Act, empowering the state to establish and operate a fleet of state-owned aircraft for the benefit of state officials and employees on official business. Although not funded until 1981, the Pooling Board ultimately acquired a fleet of aircraft available to all state agencies.[58] The Astronomy Department, in compliance with the new directive, began using a Pooling Board Cessna 421 aircraft for the twice-weekly Marfa shuttle. However, Harlan J. Smith soon discovered the Pooling Board operation cost almost twice what the department had been paying Browning.[59] Ultimately, staff member Bob Tull found in Southwest Airlines a less expensive alternative; the overall cost of using commercial flights to Midland and rental cars to cover the remaining 175 miles to Mount Locke was lower than using the Pooling Board service.[60]

Thus, within the legislative framework of departmental efficiency, the era of the Browning shuttle operation unfortunately came to an end. Jake Jacobsen made his final logbook entry on August 18, 1983. In appreciation for his many years of service, the Astronomy Department staff staged a farewell party, but it fell to astronomy professor Dr. David Evans to pay final tribute to the colorful shuttle pilot.

> "We flew out to Marfa through thunder and gale,
> All the visiting firemen were shaken and pale.
> But the rest of us knew, with no chance of mistake,
> With our special pilot, it would all be just Jake.[61]

In 1983, the State Aircraft Pooling Board became Mueller's next occupant. The agency established a flight center on seventeen acres located on the northeast perimeter of the municipal airport, just east of the National Guard hangar. On June of that year, the agency staff moved into the new facility, which consisted of a storage hangar, a fuel farm, and a portable structure that served as an office and passenger lounge. As demand for the Pooling Board's services increased, the state legislature responded with additional funding. The Seventieth Legislature appropriated an additional $1,080,000 and authorized the sale of $2,787,000 in revenue bonds to expand the Mueller facility. Construction began in March 1988, and a year later the Pooling Board staff of some forty employees, including administrative staff, pilots, mechanics, and line service employees, moved into the new quarters. Eventually, more than twenty aircraft were based and serviced at that site. Those included the Pooling Board fleet, plus independently operated aircraft of other state agencies: the Department of Public Safety, Texas Department of Corrections (Texas Board of Criminal Justice), Texas Highway Department, Texas Parks and Wildlife Department, and the University of Texas System.[62] The increased availability of landing facilities fostered the rapid growth of both private and institutional aircraft usage. In 1975, the Texas Aeronautics Commission reported 663 public and private airports in Texas.[63] In 1931, the year Mueller opened, there were only 131. In the meantime, two of the nation's largest and busiest airports opened in Texas. On June 8, 1969, Houston International Airport began operation, followed by Dallas–Fort Worth International Airport on January 13, 1974.

The increased airline traffic being generated by Austin's three trunk line carriers—Braniff, Continental, and Texas International—was again taxing

Mueller's capacity. By 1973, annual enplanements reached 328,717, a three-year 22-percent gain over 1970. During that same period airline freight traffic registered a 46 percent gain, with Austin industries dispatching 838.31 tons of high priority material.[64] And with a daily average of some thirty scheduled departures, airport crowding was destined to increase. On June 7, 1974, Texas International Airlines inaugurated Austin's first daily, one-carrier round-trip service to Mexico City, and the following September Braniff announced plans for direct one-plane service to Chicago, Denver, and New York. The Austin City Council took note of the Mueller situation, and on December 27 the mayor appointed a ten-member Citizens' Aviation Advisory Committee, supported by a seven-member technical committee, to assess the city's future aviation needs.[65]

To further complicate the issue, an article appearing in the April 1975 issue of *Texas Monthly* cited Mueller as one of the most dangerous airports in Texas. Of the ten airports evaluated, Austin ranked fifth in the "high risk" category. Based on an interview with Braniff International Airways captain William Alford, chairman of the Airline Pilots Association Airport Evaluation Committee, the article concluded: "Austin possesses one of the state's real air travel problems, a cramped, dangerous airport that has no business being where it is." Being completely surrounded by business and residential development and having takeoff and landing approaches to runways too short to accommodate modern jet airliners earned the airport its "high risk" rating. Given the shorter north-south runway, "a plane landing short or faltering on takeoff could come down squarely in the middle of the Capital Plaza shopping center."[66] The article, appearing at that critical time of policy assessment, addressed three issues that would dominate the airport debate for months to come: neighborhood safety, enlargement or relocation of the airport, and joint use of Bergstrom Air Force Base for military and commercial airline operations.

There was justification for neighborhood concern. On April 22, 1970, eight people died when a Beechcraft "Twin Bonanza" piloted by Austin neurosurgeon Robert G. Farris crashed into the residence of Freddie Anthony Bobbitt at 916 East Forty-eighth Street while attempting to land. Farris, his wife, two daughters, his office partner Dr. Ben Edward Becker Jr., and medical student Jimmy Doyle Dickens were all occupants of the aircraft. Bobbitt died instantly when the plane plunged into his bedroom; his wife, Peggy, died the following day at Brackenridge Hospital. The Bobbitts' four-month-old baby survived.

Farris, returning to Austin from a neurosurgeon's convention in Washington, D.C., received a late-night clearance to land on runway 16-Right (southeast). However, instead of continuing on that heading, the aircraft suddenly turned west and, for reasons unknown, crashed about one-half mile west of the airport. The cause of the crash was never clearly determined. And there would be others. On August 18, 1975, a twin-engine Cessna 401 crashed in the front yard of a residence at 912 East Fifty-fifth Street, killing all persons on board: the pilot, Willie L. Masterson, Stanley J. Schepps, owner of Schepps Grocery Supply of Dallas, and his seventeen-year-old daughter, Cynthia. In the immediate aftermath of that crash, it appeared the pilot made a too-steep turn on final approach, the aircraft stalled, and, according to witnesses, plunged straight down. Fire erupted; the building's only occupant escaped injury through a back door of the residence.[67]

The following day the *Austin American-Statesman* expressed alarm over the neighborhood carnage. "Six times in five years airplanes have gone down within a mile and a half of the city's Mueller Municipal Airport," wrote journalist Mike Cox. "Two of those crashes claimed eleven lives." City officials responded verbally to the ongoing tragedy. City Planning Director Dick Lillie, addressing the concerns of some twenty thousand people who lived within a half-mile of Mueller, recommend creating "clear zones" west and south of the airport. Mayor Jeff Friedman, referring to the current work of the Citizen's Aviation Advisory Committee, indicated a possible solution to the problem "could be a change in flight patterns over the airport or 'a newer and isolated airport.'" That, unfortunately, was not to be, and certainly not in the near future. The problems at Mueller—congestion, fear, and noise—were matters the surrounding neighborhoods would have to tolerate. "City officials have said before," Cox concluded, "there are no plans to relocate the airport in the immediate future."[68]

Against a background of neighborhood complaints and official platitudes, the Advisory Committee nevertheless moved forward with its assignment. On June 5, 1975, after reviewing the proposals of three engineering consulting firms, Chairman Dick Hodgkins recommended the City Council retain R. Dixon Speas Associates of Los Angeles, California, to develop a comprehensive twenty-year airport master plan study. The firm's recent work with the City of San Antonio appeared the deciding factor. Speas, according to Hodgkins, had developed a program for the Alamo City that had great consideration of environmental issues and broad citizen input. The council accepted unanimously Hodgkins' recommendation.[69] Citizen input, especially relating to environmental issues, was destined to color the Austin airport issue for the next quarter-century.

Some six months later, in December 1975, Speas Associates filed its initial report with the city council. "The object of this study," the report stated, "has been to project growth in aeronautical activities at Robert Mueller Municipal Airport for a twenty year planning period, identify alternatives for meeting this growth, and evaluate in detail the most feasible alternatives." In forecasting the twenty-year overall traffic growth at Mueller, the report projected airline enplanements would increase from 378,037 in 1974 to 1,330,800 in 1995, or an annual average growth rate of 6.8 percent. And for that same period, general aviation aircraft based at Mueller would increase from 183 to 305. In addressing the conflicting airspaces between Mueller and Bergstrom Air Force Base, especially with regard to runway alignments, the report concluded: "A hazardous airspace environment . . . still exists." Mueller's future was further challenged by Speas' analysis of runway length. The current "jumbo" jet airliners—the Boeing 747 and Douglas DC-10—both requiring a minimum 9,000-foot runway, exceeded the growth potential of Mueller. Given the projected increases in air traffic over the next twenty years, the airport would begin to run out of runway capacity sometime in the 1980s.[70]

Speas Associates cited four alternatives for fulfilling Austin's future aviation needs:

1. Accommodate continued general aviation and commercial aviation growth at Robert Mueller and develop an east-west runway at Bergstrom.[71]

2. Develop joint use at Bergstrom Air Force Base and reduce the role of Robert Mueller to general aviation use.

3. Develop a new air carrier facility at Tims [Tim's Airpark] and keep general aviation at Robert Mueller.

4. Develop a new air carrier and general aviation facility at Tims and close Mueller.

Cost was a primary consideration: $30 million for maintaining both general aviation and air carrier operations at Mueller, compared to $40 million for moving air carrier operations to Bergstrom. In summary, joint use of Bergstrom was the more favorable choice. The report also considered noise problems if air carrier growth was allowed to continue at Robert Mueller. By 1995, the noise level within the CNR 115 noise contour, containing 403 acres of residential development, or roughly 2,200 residents, would be considered "unsuited for residential housing." In addition, located within the CNR 100 contour were nine schools and several hospitals that were also considered to be incompatible. In terms of air traveler's convenience, the report also projected the average 1995 airport driving times to Mueller (14 minutes) and Bergstrom (22 minutes) and cab fare to Mueller ($3.90) and Bergstrom ($5.90). The consultant concluded the report with two basic recommendations to the Austin City Council: one, develop a program for joint use of Bergstrom Air Force Base; and two, develop a master plan for interim air carrier and future general aviation facilities at Robert Mueller Municipal Airport.[72]

Specifically, Speas Associates identified Bergstrom Air Force Base as Austin's primary choice for a permanent air carrier facility, while questioning Mueller's future. And since the Bergstrom issue depended upon political decision making at the highest echelon, there was no certainty the use of that facility would ever materialize. Furthermore, regardless of what level of service the City Council chose for Mueller, three critical factors clouded its future: a restricted landing area, overlapping air space with Bergstrom, and increasing neighborhood complaints. One factor, however, remained patently clear: a new or renovated airport carried a hefty price tag. Although no one could predict the future with any level of certainty, the complex of issues relating to the airport matter was destined to enliven debate within all sectors of Austin society, further retarding the process of political decision making.

Fifty-eight private aircraft await service at Browning Aerial Service on Mueller's west side. Austin's second air traffic control tower appears adjacent to the Browning hangar. Photo by Crowe Photography.

Source: Browning Aerial Service, Inc.

Source: Robert L. Ragsdale Estate.

Ragsdale Flying Service operated from a steel hangar on Mueller's east side. Offering sales, service, charter flights, and flight training, the Ragsdale organization became one of the major fixed base operations in Texas. Austin's first airline passenger terminal, a small square building, appears at left center. Official City of Austin Photograph no. 483(M), November 28, 1960.

Women played an active role in Austin aviation. This group, with a converted Cessna UC-78 "Bamboo Bomber," are, left to right, Mary Catherine Quist Edwards, Madge Janes, Pearle Ragsdale, Frankie Wilborn Lindsey, Mildred Miller, unidentified, Mary Ellen Pope Jackson, unidentified, Edna Hammerman, and Janet Jackson Shelton.

With the growing popularity of private flying after World War II, Ragsdale Flying Service explored department store sales. E. M. Scarbrough's priced this Piper "Cub" at $2,165.

Source: Robert L. Ragsdale Estate.

C. G. (Red) Cross, with his pre–World War II Curtiss "Robin," was one of the first Austinites to use aircraft in their businesses. An automobile parts dealer, Cross operated stores in Austin, San Antonio, and Del Rio. He also served as Mueller's airport manager during World War II. Photo by Neal Douglas.

Max Westerman, the Department of Public Safety's first pilot, with the department's first airplane, a Ryan "Navion" acquired in 1950. By 2003, the department owned sixteen aircraft, operated by twenty-seven pilots, based at nine different locations in the state.

Source: Texas National Guard. Photo via Tom Hail

Three Texas National Guard Hiller OH-23 light observation helicopters in formation over Camp Mabry parade ground, from which fixed-wing aircraft also operated, 1964. The north-south runway is visible at left.

Source: Browning Aerial Service, Inc.

To better serve the growing corporate aviation industry, Browning Aerial Service established a transient passenger terminal adjacent to the Browning hangar in 1963. The terminal contained facilities for conferences and corporate meetings. Aircraft being serviced are a Lockheed "Constellation" and a Martin 404. Photo by Bill Malone Photography.

Source: Austin History Center, Austin Public Library, PICA 15898.

Vice President Lyndon Baines Johnson addresses the audience at the May 27–28, 1961, dedication of Austin's new Robert Mueller airport terminal building. Austin architects Fehr and Granger won the 1958 *Progressive Architecture* "Best in the Nation" award for the terminal design.

Aerial view of Robert Mueller Municipal Airport in the 1990s, when the facility reached maximum expansion. Because of the surrounding development, extending the 7,000-foot main runway to the 9,000 feet required by modern jetliners appeared impractical.

Walter E. Long (1986–1973), prolific author-historian and secretary-manager of the Austin Chamber of Commerce from 1914 to 1950, probably more than any other individual helped advance the cause of Austin aviation.

Source: Austin History Center, Austin Public Library, PICA 30732.

Inspirational sign displayed during construction of Austin-Bergstrom International Airport. The Denver airport opened months behind schedule and millions over budget because of a malfunctioning "state-of-the-art" baggage system.

The Barbara Jordan Terminal at Austin-Bergstrom International Airport opened on May 23, 1999. In 2002, the ten airlines and five cargo carriers serving Austin reported annual totals of 6,720,668 passengers and 285,896,271 pounds of cargo. Photo courtesy of John Edward Linden Photography.

CHAPTER 8

ERA OF
INDECISION

ALTHOUGH the site of Austin's future municipal airport remained in doubt, two facts were abundantly clear: first, Robert Mueller Municipal Airport would continue to provide the city's commercial air service for the present and, second, the facility fell far short of meeting either current and future traffic needs. That situation would be a continuing challenge for the Austin City Council, and until that civic body could make a final decision on Austin's future air service, maintaining and renovating Mueller would be a constant drain on the city's financial resources, as well as one of its most politically divisive issues.

On February 22, 1976, some fifteen years following the opening of the $1.3 million Mueller terminal, city officials dedicated a $2 million,

21,000-square-foot passenger convenience facility. The new addition included an enclosed passenger loading concourse, six passenger waiting lounges, enclosed loading bridges, and an enlarged air-conditioned baggage claim area. Besides terminal expansion, the renovation program included installing a new $100,000 instrument landing system (ILS) on runway 13R.[1] The second ILS afforded electronic guidance systems for aircraft approaching either of the airport's two main runways. At the conclusion of the dedication ceremony, Congressman J. J. (Jake) Pickle addressed Mueller's primary asset: "I feel this airport is one of the most convenient of its kind and size in the United States." That very convenience would prove to be a major obstruction in future airport decision making.

In searching for a solution to Austin's airport problem, joint use of Bergstrom Air Force Base appeared to be the Austin City Council's most logical choice. On July 8, 1976, Councilwoman Betty Himmelblau introduced a motion proposing that, one, the council instruct the city manager to pursue joint use of Bergstrom Air Force Base and submit appropriate documentation and inquiries to federal officials and, two, authorize Speas Associates to complete the Master Plan Study for Robert Mueller Airport.[2]

Some three month later, the consultant submitted to the city council the "Request for Joint Use of Bergstrom Air Force Base by the City of Austin." The city proposed using approximately 260 acres of undeveloped Air Force property west of the primary runway and extending to U.S. Highway 183. The city would, in turn, acquire an additional 300 acres, which, when added to the Bergstrom property, would provide space for a commercial air terminal, cargo, parking, and other support facilities. However, that plan would require relocating U.S. Highway 183 a distance of some two-and-one-half miles west of the present location. The proposed transition of air carrier operations from Mueller to Bergstrom Air Force Base could be accomplished in eight to ten years, would serve the city beyond the year 2000, at an estimated cost of $27,175,000. Furthermore, Mueller would remain as the city's interim air carrier terminal until the transfer of air carrier operations to Bergstrom was accomplished, whereupon Mueller would be reduced in size and used exclusively for general aviation.[3] The council accepted the report verbatim. On October 12, 1976, Mayor Jeffrey M. Friedman wrote Col. A. J. Parker, Base Commander, Bergstrom Air Force Base, supporting the joint use plan and pointing out that, in his opinion, it would in no way interfere with the Air Force's mission.[4] And the council awaited the Air Force's answer.

In the meantime, changes were occurring in the airline industry that would further impact Mueller. During the 1960s, intrastate airlines, a category not recognized by the Civil Aeronautics Board, began forming in California, and spread rapidly throughout the nation. Those local air carriers, operating within a state without federal restrictions, began competing aggressively with the established federally certificated trunk line carriers. Air Southwest, formed in Dallas, Texas, on March 15, 1967, received an intrastate certificate from the Texas Aeronautics Commission on February 20, 1968.[5] Immediately challenged in the courts by the established carriers, the United States Supreme Court ultimately ruled against the complainants, and on June 17, 1971, the company, renamed Southwest Airlines, inaugurated high-frequency, low-cost Boeing 737-200 service to Houston and San Antonio.

On December 1, 1976, the Texas Aeronautics Commission approved Southwest Airline's application to serve five additional Texas cities, including Austin. The Austin service, scheduled to begin in mid-July, was delayed some two months by political skirmishing over a lease agreement and additional construction at Mueller to accommodate the new airline. The short-haul airline, preferring the convenience of close-in airports like Houston's Hobby and Dallas' Love Field, did not provide service to either Houston Intercontinental or the Dallas–Fort Worth Regional airports. With Austin's pending application to move all air carrier service to Bergstrom Air Force Base, the city manager foresaw the possibility of having to maintain air carrier service at Mueller solely for the convenience of Southwest Airlines. To avoid such a possibility, the city agreed to give Southwest the lease necessary to begin service to Mueller "only if the airline would sign a letter [of] agreement giving the city blanket authority to determine which airport Southwest would serve."[6] The airline, considering that provision an "illegal demand," terminated negotiations. Finally, on March 23, the two parties reached an agreement; Southwest would serve Austin through Mueller.

Meanwhile at Mueller, construction continued on a $150,000 Southwest Airlines expansion project, which included an additional three thousand square feet of terminal space for ticket counters, baggage conveyors, an operations office, additional paving, and security fencing. Finally, on September 15, 1977, a full-page ad in the *Austin American-Statesman* announced the arrival of not only a new airline, but a new concept in promoting low-cost, high-frequency air travel: "On Southwest Airlines you can fly for less than it costs for you to drive. Just $15 start our fares for fun, and from $25 get your business done."[7] The new airline helped contribute to the Mueller congestion; the 510,030 enplanements in 1977 represented an 18 percent increase over the previous year. Air freight gain was even more impressive, showing a 29 percent gain, while airmail grew 14 percent.[8]

The growth in Austin air traffic could be credited in part to the Chamber of Commerce's ongoing promotion of increased air carrier service to the city. To the Chamber, increased air service was synonymous with progress, and progress was the lifeblood of urban culture. On November 23, 1977, the Chamber, on behalf of Braniff International Airways and Delta Airlines, offered a motion before the Civil Aeronautics Board in Docket No. 31236, supporting increased Austin–San Antonio–Atlanta air service. Also, on April 17, 1978, the Chamber, supported by the City of Austin, presented supplementary exhibits and testimony in Docket No. 32143, in the same case, and ten days later offered rebuttal exhibits. The CAB subsequently awarded that service to Delta Airlines.[9] And all the while the Austin airport quandary continued. In December 1977, Speas Associates presented its third report to the Austin City Council, elaborating on the master plan for Robert Mueller Municipal Airport, essentially, more of the same with financial projections: "Airport revenues are projected to increasingly exceed the cash cost of operating the airport, by an amount increasing from roughly $200,000 in 1976 to nearly $1,500,000 by 1985."[10] That projection did not include future costs of landing field and runway renovations.

Bergstrom Air Force Base, however, remained Austin's most optimistic, yet elusive hope for a future air carrier airport. With no response from the mayor's October 12, 1976, request for joint use, members of the city council, nevertheless, reaffirmed its interest in expediting the joint use plan.[11] And again the council awaited an answer from Washington. Time, of course, was critical, as the next Speas report reaffirmed. "Impact of Recent Changes in the Aviation Industry," presented to the city council in January 1978, addressed the unexpected growth of Austin airline enplanements, which far exceeded previous forecasts. The consultant attributed that growth to lower airfares, higher frequency of flights to Austin's air trade markets, and increased cost of surface transportation. Those factors further exacerbated other pending problems: the Mueller terminal building would have to be doubled in size by 1995, and all the while growing neighborhood apprehension increased the chance of litigation. In conclusion, the consultant urged the city council that, if joint use of Bergstrom failed to develop, the council should immediately launch a site selection plan to identify a new airport facility.[12]

Speas' prophetic warning materialized on January 19, 1978; the Austin City Council received a communication from the Department of Defense rejecting the city's request for joint use of Bergstrom Air Force Base.[13] Refusing to be denied and not ready to consider a new airport site, Mayor Carole McClellan embarked immediately for Washington to further appeal Austin's request for joint use of Bergstrom.[14] That proved to be wasted effort. Joe F. Meis, assistant deputy secretary of the Air Force at the Pentagon, refused the council's request, citing Austin's heavy commercial air traffic, which he believed would not be compatible with the Air Force's Bergstrom mission. However, the deputy secretary agreed to consider the city's alternative plan to build a new air carrier runway west of the present Air Force runway, as previously cited in a Speas report.

Contrary to Mayor McClellan's enthusiasm for constructing a new $40 million air carrier runway adjacent to Bergstrom, or the $68 million option of expanding Tim's Airpark, other council members thought it advisable to explore other alternatives. Councilman Lee Cooke suggested seeking a new airport site outside the city, as had Dallas and Fort Worth, while Ron Mullen questioned spending more money on additional consulting work. Dick Hodgkins, chairman of the Citizens' Advisory Committee, prevailed: he felt an additional study was needed in order for his committee to make a valid recommendation to the city council.[15]

The Citizens' Advisory Committee, however, had about run its course. On February 2, 1978, the council abolished the Advisory Committee and established the Airport Task Force Committee, chaired by Dr. S. H. Dryden, a licensed pilot.[16] The task force committee assumed a four-fold agenda: (1) assess the current and projected statistical data as it affected air carrier operations at Mueller, (2) consider the feasibility of further pursuing the joint use of Bergstrom, (3) explore other airport site options, and (4) determine expansion potentials if Mueller were to remain at its present location. The answer to item two was immediately forthcoming. On March 20, Mayor McClellan met with Joe F. Meis, Air Force deputy assistant secretary, during an unannounced visit he made to Bergstrom Air Force Base. Meis clarified two salient points for the mayor: Bergstrom Air Force Base was not under consideration for closing or relocation and joint use of the facility with the City of Austin was not possible, either then or in the foreseeable future.[17]

With the matter of joint use apparently settled, the task force committee addressed the remaining issues. On April 6, 1978, they approved a motion that Mueller would function at the present location through 1995, but with extensive terminal remodeling to accommodate additional airlines. In addition, the committee recommended that the city council begin immediate site selection work to determine a location for future air carrier facilities.[18] The council responded on August 3 with an ordinance amending the 1978–1979 Annual Operating Budget to appropriate $10,571 from the Airport Fund Balance to match a Federal Aviation Administration grant of $95,138 for an airport site study.[19]

With the search for a new site underway, unrest in the Mueller neighborhoods continued to mount. On March 29, 1978, Emile Jamail, owner of an office complex at 4920 North Interregional Highway, filed suit against the city, charging that low-flying aircraft were damaging his business. Jamail asked for $150,000 in damages, claiming he was having difficulty in keeping tenants in his two-story office building.[20] West of the airport, another irate citizen took even more drastic steps in response to the low-flying aircraft. Seventy-year-old John Henderson, who lived at 5009 Duval Street, called the airport operations manager, threatening to shoot down the planes unless he got some relief from the noise. In response to his threat, the Federal Bureau of Investigation arrested Henderson and a federal judge ordered him to undergo psychiatric testing. Henderson's neighbor, Dinah Acord, a University of Texas student, also shared Henderson's concern. She said the noise was so bad she planned to move at the end of the semester. "You don't need an alarm clock [to wake you up] in the morning," she explained, "The first flight at 7 A.M. knocks me out of bed." [21] And there was scant hope of improvement. On October 24, 1978, Congress passed the Airline Deregulation Act, freeing airlines to choose the cities they serve.[22] With Austin's growth as a travel market, air traffic around Mueller was destined to increase, along with the noise, pollution, and citizens' complaints.

Meanwhile, representatives of the Speas organization quietly surveyed the Central Texas countryside, seeking the ideal 3,200-acre site for a new municipal airport. They purposely withheld the results of the study, pending a scheduled announcement at the April 12, 1979, meeting of the Austin City Council. And then suddenly, without warning, the airport issue escalated to a new level of volatility. The *Austin American-Statesman*, under the federal Freedom of Information Act, acquired from the Fort Worth

Federal Aviation Administration office a map citing the three primary sites for the proposed airport. Those sites were rural farming areas located near Manor, Pflugerville, and Decker Lake, all within eighteen miles of Austin. When the citizens of those communities read the report, they were outraged; so was Speas chief consultant, Ray Kusche. "He said detailing of the sites will 'create unrest and unhappiness among the people who live in those areas,'" the *American-Statesman* reported, "It could cause people to start forming committees to counteract this thing."[23]

Kusche was correct; when the California consultant scheduled public hearings at Manor on May 8 and at Pflugerville on May 9, he was forewarned "to bring the police."[24] Kusche, however, did not bring the police, but, when he entered the Manor High School gymnasium and faced some eight hundred irate citizens carrying anti-airport placards, he no doubt sensed his vulnerability. And his reception the following night at Pflugerville differed little from the Manor encounter. After Kusche outlined plans for the proposed airport, the local citizens articulated their complaints: loss of valuable farmlands, a threat to their established rural lifestyle, aircraft noise, traffic congestion, and reduction of the local public school tax base. Some responded emotionally; Diane Sheiler exclaimed, "It is our HOME! Homes!!—People, that's what this is all about! Our Homes!!!" Some argued logically. Responding to Kusche's explanation that the prime consideration in airport location is its adjacency to the air travel demand center, Patrick Gannon pointed out that since "the majority of people that use the Austin airport reside in the northwest quadrant of the city . . . [then] why isn't the airport there?" Others, in opposing the issue, were more emphatic. Jimmy Sanderson complained, "Now they want to stick the new airport two miles north of me. Well, if there is anybody here from the City of Austin, I can tell you . . . where to stick that new airport."[25]

Regardless of their individual bearing, the people representing Manor and Pflugerville made themselves abundantly clear; they did not want an airport in their communities. Meanwhile, the citizens of Austin awaited an answer, which was not immediately forthcoming. On June 10, Speas vice president Ronald Ahlfeldt announced a further delay in making the final report on the airport site selection. He was awaiting additional studies on anticipated air traffic increases at Bergstrom Air Force Base. With the addition of a new training squadron operating forty-two RF-4C "Phantom" jet aircraft, flights out of Bergstrom were expected to increase from the current

576 a month to more than 1,200. According to Ahlfeldt, the impact of increased Bergstrom air traffic could determine which site is chosen for the new airport. And still the city waited.

Finally, on September 20, 1979, Speas executive Ray Kusche made his final report to the Austin City Council; there were no surprises. The two-inch-thick volume, entitled "Site Selection Study for Air Carrier Airport," represented a comprehensive analysis of nine possible airport sites (of an original fifty-one candidate sites), all located within some twenty miles of the city. Each site was evaluated on the basis of comparative cost, property considerations, access, airspace analysis, environmental impact, and engineering considerations. Existing airports at San Marcos and Georgetown were evaluated, but disqualified as alternate sites. The three sites chosen for the city council to consider for a future air carrier airport consisted of areas of open farmland north of Decker Lake, northeast of Pflugerville, and east of Manor. In further analysis, Kusche explained that increased training activities at Bergstrom would create airspace management problems that should eliminate the Decker Lake site from consideration. Also, the Pflugerville East site, located further from the centers of demand, would require the construction of major new access highways, and was not a viable candidate for consideration. In brief summary, "the Manor East–Alternate B location must be preferred."[26] There were obvious advantages; the proposed terminal site, located adjacent to U.S. Highway 290, was only eighteen miles from Austin. But there were inherent problems: fifty-four families living in New Katy, a small community fronting U.S. Highway 290 on the south, would have to be relocated.

Instead of reaching a conclusion, the final report marked the beginning of a lengthy and tedious process that could take years to reach fruition, which Mayor Carole McClellan fully understood: "We have some pretty deep and heavy discussions to take place here." She made that statement in the presence of some fifty Manor residents who attended the presentation wearing cotton corsages, symbolizing the prospective airport's threat to the rich farmlands surrounding the Manor site. Although about six thousand acres adjacent to the airport site would have restricted use, farming would be allowed up to the airport property boundaries. That, however, did not appease Jim Archer, leader of the Manor Concerned Citizens Group, who declared, "We are saving our ammunition. Ninety percent of the people out there are ready to fight." The following day the *Austin American-Statesman,* not wanting to engage in a word battle with its neighbors to the east, editorialized: "Airport at Manor not a great idea." The newspaper, its editor reasoned, had a better idea.

> Well, there's another site with compatible air traffic patterns—the current airport, Robert Mueller, the airport handily near downtown and handy otherwise: The city owns the first thing in the way of expansion, the golf course. And, by moving a subdivision or two, there is no apparent reason the Mueller tarmac couldn't be extended clear to Ed Bluestein Boulevard . . . Any flight-path conflicts with BAFB [Bergstrom Air Force Base] could be worked out, surely.[27]

And so the City of Austin reached a new level of quandary in its quest for a permanent air carrier airport. The city's only newspaper appeared to be ignoring the obvious. All data clearly indicated Mueller's days as an air carrier airport were numbered. In mid-1978, using 1976–1978 statistics, Speas Associates had issued a revised fifteen-year traffic projection, predicting annual Mueller passenger boarding increases from 1.4 million passengers to 2.1 million by 1995. That meant, at peak hours, an airliner would be taking off or landing every two minutes. Austin voters subsequently approved $7.6 million for an interim Mueller expansion program, designed to accommodate increased traffic demands for the next decade.[28] That led to the construction of a new 25,000-square-foot, rotunda-shaped extension on the north side of the terminal building, with an additional concourse to house five new passenger gates and a new aircraft freight handling area.[29] Aviation Director Roy Bayless welcomed the prospect of an enlarged terminal but took exception to the newspaper's suggestion of "moving a subdivision or two" and taking over the adjacent golf course to expand the airport. The runways could, indeed, be extended, but that would not solve the primary problem at Mueller. "We need an airport of 3,200 acres," Bayless insisted, "and you cannot put an airport of that size on 700 acres."[30]

Some six weeks following Ray Kusche's airport site selection report, members of the Austin City Council were still not convinced that Manor was the best location for a new airport. Councilman Ron Mullen's comment probably best reflected the views of the council, as well as the electorate: "I'm not convinced of anything yet. I'm surprised by the number of people who have told me it should remain where it is." Understandably, the council was torn between two issues: the ability of the city to qualify for 80 percent federal funding for a new, $122 million airport and the future of Bergstrom Air Force Base. Ray Kusche expresses the latter dilemma: "I really wring my hands over that. To build a new airport and then have the Air

Force pull out of Bergstrom." The pending proposal to build parallel but separate air carrier runways immediately west of Bergstrom was one option to ensure use of at least part of that Air Force facility. It also was an option Airport Director Roy Bayless could support. He had already advised Kusche to come to the next council meeting prepared to discuss establishing a runway west of U.S. Highway 183 parallel to the main Bergstrom runway and to bring cost estimates for a new study on that option.[31]

Ray Kusche's appearance at the November 12, 1979, city council meeting ignited a new political firestorm. Supported by Mayor McClellan and City Manager Dan Davidson, Kusche withdrew his Manor "East" recommendation, saying cost and safety factors made that plan unacceptable, and instead recommended pursuing the Bergstrom "West" plan. Emotions were mixed. Some thirty residents of the Delwood II subdivision attending the meeting urged the council not to abandon plans for the new airport; they wanted Mueller closed. Their spokeswoman, Vivian L. Bettis, explained: "We are most concerned and we feel we are living in a potentially dangerous area." The *Austin American-Statesman,* on the other hand, viewed the issue solely as a fiscal matter; "So after four years and $250,000, the city is back to square one." The newspaper continued to support an enlarged Mueller and urged the city "to take another look at what it already has, and work from there."[32] But there remained the matter of some 390 families in the Del Valle area that would have to be relocated, and the thousands of school tax dollars lost, if the Bergstrom "West" plan materialized. And those voices were destined to grow louder.

On August 6, 1981, the Austin City Council submitted a formal request to the Air Force to develop an air carrier facility on the west side of Bergstrom Air Force Base, previously described as the Bergstrom "West" plan.[33] That plan provided for the construction of a 9,000-foot runway approximately one mile west of the main Bergstrom runway. Highway 183 would separate the two airports, with a taxiway built over the highway, facilitating joint emergency operations. Also included was a plan to shift small, private aircraft to an unidentified new facility for general aviation; Mueller would be closed and the property sold to pay for the new Bergstrom "West" facility. On September 21, the Federal Aviation Administration announced its endorsement of the proposal, saying the plan would "'enhance a safe, expeditious movement of air traffic' and reduce the number of homes adversely affected by noise from military and commercial flights."[34]

Again, there appeared the familiar sight of placard-carrying citizens pro-testing locating a new Austin airport near their homes. Meeting at the main entrance to Bergstrom Air Force Base on October 30, Enrique Lopez, spokesman for the one-hundred-member Montopolis Neighborhood As-sociation, complained that the planned expansion of the air base would "swallow up" their neighborhood, while the north-south flight path over Allison Elementary School "could seriously impair the education of our children." By December 16, when the Austin City Council scheduled a public hearing in Municipal Auditorium, Lopez' supporters had grown to more than three hundred. Homeowners, businessmen, educators, and one influential legislator came to oppose the city's Bergstrom "West" plan; more than seventy-one people signed cards to address the council. "'I have come to bury Bergstrom West, not praise it,' declared State Representative Gonzalo Barrientos, who said more aircraft traffic would severely hurt schools and neighborhoods." Amid the voices of protest, only one, Roy Bayless, supported the issue, but all to no avail.[35]

On January 5, 1982, Mayor Carole McClellan received a ten-page letter from Lt. Gen. Charles Blanton, deputy Air Force chief of staff, citing twenty-nine "minimum requirements that must be addressed prior to any further consideration," before talks could proceed on the city's proposal. The three most critical requirements called for the city to be held liable for all aviation accidents (including those involving Air Force planes); a one-year termination notice on the city's use of the facility; and the city to cover a section of U.S. Highway 183 to prevent an accidental landing on the highway. For all practical purposes, these requirements brought an end to the Bergstrom "West" proposal.[36] On February 11, by a vote of a six to one, the council terminated the Bergstrom "West" plan. Further negotiations with the Air Force appeared futile.

Councilman Ron Mullen, however, saw an alternative. He suggested the council end the two-year indecision on the Manor site. "If we put if off, we will bury our heads in the sand and hope it goes away." Still the council lacked consensus; for Mayor McClellan, the loss of Bergstrom "West" merely heightened Mueller's appeal. "I remain persuaded that Austin will require a new airport within the next 15 to 20 years," she stated in a coun-cil memo. "However, it now appears to me that neither the citizens, the avi-ation community, nor the airlines are prepared at this time to support the relocation."[37] In one respect, the mayor was correct; Southwest Airlines board chairman Herb Kelleher had previously established the carriers' position in that matter: "There is a possibility that we would not agree voluntarily to shift our operation to a new airport."[38] And still the council remained in a react mode.

During the mid-1980s, while the Austin City Council debated the Manor "East" and the Bergstrom "West" issues, a near tragedy occurred at Robert Mueller airport that, but for a miracle, could have multiplied the airport problem manifold. At approximately 2:30 on Sunday afternoon, August 10, 1980, a DC-9 airliner, approaching Mueller from the west, was cleared to land on runway 13-R. Just before touchdown, the captain saw approaching from the east the one weather phenomenon pilots fear the most—a tornado! Applying full power, the captain climbed the DC-9 steeply to the right and departed the area to the south. Moments later the tornado, packing 500-mile-an-hour winds, churned through the east side of Mueller, striking two of Ragsdale Aviation's operating sites. Seventy-four airplanes were damaged, forty totally demolished. Ironically, many of the aircraft caught in the tornado's wrath were just flown in from Galveston, Corpus Christi, and Victoria to escape Hurricane Allen. Total damage exceeded $10 million. Howard Barker, Ragsdale Aviation treasurer, viewed the positive side of the tragedy. "The tornado struck when traffic was light and few people were around," he explained. "Lives would have been lost had it been a week day."[39] The terminal area on the west side of the field was spared, as were other areas of the airport.

In the meantime, in a matter totally unrelated to the tornado, negotiations were underway that would have far-reaching impact on the City of Austin and would stimulate economic growth far beyond the vision of most citizens. It began with an idea. Members of the business community, concerned with an economy dependent largely on state and federal income, were seeking measures to broaden the city's economic base. The Austin Chamber of Commerce, led by a staff of consultants from the University of Texas Bureau of Economic Geology, launched a cooperative effort to diversify the economy, focusing on the burgeoning electronics industry. The Chamber recorded its first success in 1960; that year International Business Machines opened an Austin division to manufacture IBM Selectric typewriters. Texas Instruments followed in 1966, Motorola in 1974, and Advanced Micro Design in 1979. According to one major study, the watershed event in Austin's high-tech development occurred in 1983, when the city won the nationwide competition for Microelectronics and Computer Technology Corporation. The key ingredient in those negotiations was a

$20 million incentive package assembled cooperatively by Gov. Mark White, the University of Texas College of Engineering, and the Austin business community.[40] That event set in motion the forces that created the new Central Texas high-tech growth economy. It was the early shock waves of that economic boom that frustrated the Austin City Council as they grappled with the growing inadequacies of Robert Mueller Municipal Airport. Their efforts were crucial to Austin's future growth; *Fortune* magazine rated air service fifth in the top criteria for attracting new industries.[41]

The February 11, 1982, six-to-one vote to terminate the Bergstrom "West" proposal did, in essence, end the McClellan council's direct involvement in the airport issue. On May 15, 1983, a new council headed by Mayor Ron Mullen inherited that responsibility. With new members Sally Shipman, Mark Rose, and Mark Spaeth joining carry-over members John Trevino, Charles Urdy, and Roger Duncan on the council, Mayor Mullen appeared, at least in the beginning, to follow a familiar script. In January 1984, he appointed attorney Pike Powers to chair a new ten-member Austin Citizens' Airport Task Force.[42] With a new task force, another consultant could not be far behind. At the October 12 meeting, the Task Force authorized Bovay Engineers, Inc. to prepare a summary of data for airport planning that included Alternatives D, G-1, and G-2 for use in its final deliberations. And so, the more things changed, the more they stayed the same.

Essentially, the Bovay report summarized and updated the 1979 Speas report with specific cost projections. Alternative D expanded Robert Mueller Municipal Airport for air carrier service and relocated general aviation to an unidentified reliever airport. That plan required the acquisition of approximately thirty-five acres of land for two parallel nine-thousand-foot runways at an estimated cost of $39,866,000. Those thirty-five acres contained an unspecified number of dwellings, the source of deep concern for many citizens living near the airport. Alternatives G-1 and G-2 addressed the Manor "East" site. Plan G-1 provided for the acquisition of a 12,000-acre tract, allowing for ownership of all property within the overall noise contour, while plan G-2, a 5,300-acre outlay, encompassed only the inner noise contour. According to the report, the estimated cost of the new airfield was $74,482,000, with estimated land acquisition costs of $177,408,000 and $78,355,000 for Alternatives G-1 and G-2, respectively.[43] While Bovay researched the three options, the Task Force solicited citizen input.

By October 18, after some eight months of meetings, the Task Force appeared no nearer to a final decision. Mueller remained the stumbling block. While some members seemed to favor the Manor site, John Cutright and Hugh Higgins questioned the need for a new airport. Meeting in closed session, and in the presence of a land appraiser, became another point of contention. On October 17, Cutright tried to halt the closed sessions, but his motion failed for lack of a second.[44] Powers, however, maintained the meetings would be closed as long as the discussions involved real estate. Tensions mounted, and the following day both Cutright and Higgins walked out of the meeting, arguing that the topic, an updated report on the 1979 Speas airport site study, should be discussed publicly.

The following week, John P. Machado, Bovay project manager, made his formal report to the Task Force. There were no surprises; Manor "East" was the preferred site, while expanding Mueller and building a reliever airport for general aviation was considered a "fallback position." The Task Force accepted Machado's report on a nine-to-one vote. John Cutright cast the dissenting vote, claiming a new airport was not needed and recommending the matter of closing Mueller airport should be left for voters to decide. Cutright stated further he would write a minority report.[45] On November 15, Chairman Pike Powers presented the Citizens' Airport Task Force Final Report to the Austin City Council. Cutright's signature is the only one missing from the report. Again, there were no surprises. The Task Force recommended that all air services, both general aviation and commercial air carrier, be relocated and the city acquire fifty-three hundred acres of land for a new airport, plus an additional ten thousand acres surrounding the proposed site for controlled development. In addition, the city should create an airport authority to immediately begin the task of implementing the recommendations. The report recommended further that Mueller be closed and the existing site be sold in conformity with FAA regulations.[46]

John Cutright also delivered his minority report to the council. He recommended that Mueller retain its current status, serving both air carrier and general aviation. In the future, should expansion become necessary, Cutright advised that restrictions be placed on the type of aircraft that could use Mueller and general aviation be diverted to a reliever facility. In addition to the immediate application of noise abatement procedures in the vicinity of Mueller, he recommended that the city council give serious consideration to San Antonio mayor Henry Cisneros' proposal for an Austin–San Antonio regional airport.[47] Finally, Cutright maintained that the need for a new airport had not been proven, and he urged the city council to conduct further financial studies to confirm his position. That did not occur.

At last, the Austin City Council had a firm recommendation from a citizens' committee to take positive action in the airport matter. On November 29, the council voted to accept the Task Forces' recommendation to relocate the airport and set January 19, 1985, as the date for a public referendum on the issue. Mayor Ron Mullen agreed to place the issue on the ballot. With the benefit of hindsight, he added, "If we had taken that advice 10 years ago, we would be well on our way to affording a new airport. I'm convinced that if we don't move now, the alternative some day will be an airport 30 to 40 miles away."[48]

At that point the mayor, believing the move to Manor was a certainty, made a courageous, if politically risky, decision. However, there was precedent for his plan. Long before construction began on the Dallas–Fort Worth International Airport, a group of Dallas and Fort Worth business leaders, attempting to avoid land speculation, either purchased or optioned land for that development before the matter became politicized. Their vision saved the two cities millions of dollar. Mullen hoped to do the same for Austin. He had learned that Charles Carpenter, one of the largest landowners at the Manor "East" site, had acquired over two thousand acres to develop a residential community for low-to-medium income families. In early 1985, Mullen arranged a meeting with Carpenter, where he explained:

> I believe we will be able to pass a referendum to move the airport to Manor. . . . If it gets moved there, you will make money because you already own land there. You can help us if you will go out and tie up in options the property we are going to have to have. And I will tell you that we will pay you, not a profit, but what you paid for it, plus what your carrying costs are. You will make your profit on the property you already own.[49]

Mullen found Carpenter surprisingly receptive to the proposal. And there was good reason. When Carpenter originally acquired the Manor property, he believed if the Austin airport was ever moved from its present location, it would be to Bergstrom Air Force Base. Therefore, with funding assured, Carpenter began making land purchases. However, the more recent specter of an airport near Manor adversely altered his plans; airports and housing developments are not compatible. When Carpenter decided to shift from residential to commercial development, his lending institution withdrew his financing. For Carpenter, Mullen's proposal came at a most opportune time; commercial land developments adjacent to a major airport could be equally remunerative. Using personal funds, plus bank loans, Carpenter continued acquiring property near the Manor "East" airport site.[50]

Meanwhile, with the approaching airport referendum, political positions quickly polarized, with familiar names assuming leadership roles. Pike Powers represented "Citizens for a Safe and Affordable Airport," while his former Task Force adversary, John Cutright, spoke for "People to Save Mueller Airport." In addition to slogans, political campaigns require funding. By January 16, 1985, the pro-Mueller group had raised $29,233, while the opposition reported $39,410 in contributions. Newspaper ads, radio commercials, and "Move It" yard signs helped define campaign positions. On Wednesday night, January 16, four days before the election, the Austin Jaycees sponsored a voter forum where Cutright and Powers debated the airport issue. Cutright charged the opposition was waging a "campaign of lies and distortions" and using cost estimates that were too low in an attempt to persuade voters to abandon Robert Mueller Airport. Powers argued that, while Mueller is a temporary solution to the city's air carrier needs, "This is the last opportunity we'll have to do it right. If we wait until 2005 or 2010, there won't be a convenient place to move it." Two days later Austin voters went to the polls to consider twenty propositions affecting the city's future. Proposition 1, to relocate the airport, failed by 748 votes.[51]

Interpretation of the outcome of the nonbinding referendum differed according to one's political position. To those opposing the move to Manor, it indicated that Austin citizens believed Mueller was adequate, liked its convenience, and opposed the cost of building another airport. Others, who supported the move to Manor, believed voters had been misinformed on the issues relating to change. Nevertheless, the matter was largely academic; current airport policies were destined to continue. On March 20, 1986, the council awarded a consulting firm, The Greiner Austin Team, a $1,270,000 contract to make environmental impact and design studies for the expansion of the Mueller terminal. Tim Ward, who was appointed aviation director in October 1985, supported the study.[52]

While the Greiner Team compiled data, Donald Engen, administrator of the Federal Aviation Administration, further prodded the Austin City Council to action, urging them to "decide quickly the future of Robert Mueller Municipal Airport or face possible federal intervention." "Federal intervention" meant flight restrictions on Austin air service. Engen sent similar directives to Denver, St. Louis, Los Angeles, and Boston. The *Austin American-Statesman* created further pressure for the council by questioning the growing expenditures of outside consultant services. "So far this year alone, the city has committed more than $2 million to pay private consultants to study problems ranging from the airport (again) to affordable housing." Asking "Are these expenditures necessary?" the editor went on to question motivation. If the idea is to make a final determination on whether the airport needs to be expanded or moved, "that's one thing. But if the idea is to keep hiring consultants until the council in power at the time gets the answer it wants, that's another."[53] The newspaper probably failed to get the response it was seeking; the city council would indeed seek the advice of other consultants in a more-than-a-decade-long attempt to resolve the problem of Robert Mueller Municipal Airport.

During the Austin City Council's marathon airport discussions, most interest centered on future air carrier operations, with scant concern for general aviation. That drew the attention of private pilots, who wanted to be assured a base for their operations. Executive Air Park, formerly Tim's Air Park, was the last remaining private airfield in the Austin metropolitan area and the site frequently mentioned as the logical reliever airport for Mueller. One of the owners, John E. Simmons, appeared before the city council in November 1985 to propose the city purchase the 131-acre airfield on West Dessau Road. Jim Bassett, representing the Texas Pilot's Association, supported the purchase; Aviation Director Tim Ward opposed the issue, as did City Manager Jorge Carrasco. Ward believed the field was too small and there would be an air space conflict with Bergstrom and Mueller; the $12.5 million price tag bothered Carrasco.[54] In addition, the Federal Aviation Administration had a vested interest in the matter and urged the city to buy Executive Air Park to relieve the private plane traffic at Mueller. The FAA's interest stemmed from the $4.5 million grant in 1984 to improve the Executive Air Park.[55] And so the matter stood. Also, during the mid-1980s, other important changes in general aviation were occurring at Mueller; the two long-standing fixed base operations, Browning Aerial Service and Ragsdale Aviation, terminated service. In April 1984, the Bill Milburn Company purchased Ragsdale Aviation, and three years later Signature Flight Support acquired Browning Aerial Service.

In August 1986, when the Greiner Team presented its initial report to the city council with data from multiple consultancies at the council's disposal, the council still faced a double quandary on the airport issue. On the one hand, they agreed unanimously the airport should be moved; however, the 1985 nonbinding referendum was too close to give the council an accurate gauge of the public's feeling on the issue. And there remained the immediate problem of keeping Mueller operative until establishing a new landing site. The council moved on both matters. On December 3, 1986, they agreed to hold another election the following autumn to determine Mueller's future, and the following April 16, authorized funding for interim renovations at the airfield. Of the total $7.6 million expenditure, a $5.7 million federal appropriation reduced Austin's responsibility to $1.9 million, which local airport revenues would provide. The renovations included paving on runways, taxiways, and parking aprons.[56]

And in the process of major decision making, the council, ignoring the *American-Statesman*'s earlier admonition, engaged still another consultant to *again identify* the most desirable replacement site for a new metropolitan airport. The Turner Collie & Braden firm essentially did a repeat performance of the 1979 Speas Report, and again chose the Manor "East" site.[57] With a mandate from the consultant, all that remained was a citizens' concurrence, and for that Councilwoman Sally Shipman had a plan: "What we need to do is to show on a ballot what it will cost to keep Mueller where it is and what it will cost to build it on the new site."[58] And a new campaign was underway. During the ensuing weeks, Austin became involved in an orgy of campaign activity. Some meetings were sedate: East Austin ministers, who were members of Austin Interfaith, met to express concern that expanding Mueller would force a massive relocation of homes and churches in that area. Other meetings were thought provoking: Tim Ward, aviation director, stated that if the voters decide to build a new airport, the "estimated $60 million cost of interim improvements [to Mueller] could be cut in half or more because of the certainty that the new airport would be built." Later that same day the Austin City Council voted to hold the airport referendum on November 3, 1987.

With the election day set, the campaign rhetoric grew more intense. Former council member Les Gage pointed out that if Austin voters elected to spend some $400 million for a renovated Mueller, they could end up with a facility that still disrupts people's lives. Others agreed. On October 4, one month before the election, a group of East Austin citizens held a barbecue on the parking lot of an East Seventh Street carpet store. Surrounded by "Move the Airport, not East Austin" campaign signs, State Representative Lena Guerrero told the crowd that if Mueller is expanded,

"Where we're standing is the end of the runway." Mayor Frank Cooksey challenged the group, "Don't talk about anything else [but the election] for a month," while State Representative Wilhelmina Delco countered, "Talking a good cause is not enough. We lose a lot of issues important to our people because we assume that if we think it is a good issue, everybody will."

The airport issue had grown into far more than an East Austin concern. On October 14, members of three north Austin neighborhood associations—Allandale, Crestview, and Brentwood—assembled at the Austin Community College Business and Technical Center to hear a panel debate the airport issues. Discussions focused primarily on costs: $728 million in revenue bonds to relocate the airport east of Manor versus $1 billion in bonds to expand the current site. In addition, on October 28, the five Travis County commissioners approved a resolution urging residents to vote to move the airport, while the *Austin American-Statesman,* assuming a complete editorial about-face, agreed that moving the airport was indeed a good cause: "The voters have to make an intelligent decision, and the only one on the ballot is to support construction of a new airport near Manor by voting 'For' Proposition 1."

On November 3, the Austin voters also did a complete about-face, approving Proposition 1. The vote was 56 percent for moving the airport, and 44 percent against. For Proposition 2, funding for long-term expansion of Mueller, the margin was even greater, but in the opposite direction: only 12 percent for and 88 percent against. And so the Austin City Council had promoted the proposition to build a new airport east of Manor and the electorate responded with a clear mandate. Austin citizens next looked to the council for action.

CHAPTER 9

CITY ON A TIGHTWIRE

I N the wake of the November 3 election, the Austin City Council appeared to fulfill the voters' highest expectations. Subsequent discussions at city hall focused on expediting the airport projects: selling the revenue bonds to begin land purchases for the Manor "East" site and launching interim improvements at Mueller. The council furthered its commitment on December 10, 1987, by passing a resolution to fulfill the "intent, goals, and objectives regarding development of a new airport near Manor, Texas." In response, City Aviation Director Tim Ward stated construction could begin as early as January 1989. To facilitate that operation, the city council engaged the Turner Collie & Braden engineering firm to complete the federally mandated environmental impact study on the Manor site, and approved Hunter Industries' $3.9 million contract to expand aircraft parking aprons at Mueller and rebuild two taxiways.[1] The council also instructed the Planning and Growth Management Department to determine the best method of annexing a strip of property to connect the city with the Manor "East" site.

And then the tempo slowed. At the May 6 council meeting, Mayor Pro Tem John Trevino, attempting to boost minority participation in constructing the new airport, delayed the appointment of an airport project manager. He argued the delay would give four minority-owned firms an opportunity to revise their proposals. The debate, however, continued at the June 2 meeting, until the council selected Turner, Collie & Braden for the $1,488,850 assignment. But that decision was only temporary. In the meantime, former council member Lee Cooke, who had defeated Frank Cooksey as mayor in the May 28 election, stated he wanted a voice in choosing the project manager. His choice was Fluor Daniel, Inc., originally the council's second choice. Between Cooke and council newcomer Robert Barnstone, the Turner Collie coalition fell apart. A five-month voting deadlock ensued, and finally, during a late-night session on November 3, the council chose the firm Sverdrup/Gilbane, Inc. as project manager.[2] But that did not end the matter; there would be further delays. Some six weeks later, Acting City Manager John Ware advised the city council that the Sverdrup/Gilbane proposal eliminated the fine the company would have to pay if minority or women-owned business fell below 85 percent of the project.[3] Negotiations continued until January 12, 1989, when the council approved the revised version of the contract.

Considering the many individuals interested in relocating the airport, selecting the project manager seemed to mark the beginning of a new era in those negotiations. People wanted action. "The opening shot of what appears to be a recharged effort to wring some airport action out of the council came at this week's council meeting," wrote Arnold Garcia Jr. He reported that Sam Griswold, an organizer of Citizens for Airport Relocation (CARE), urged the council to "get moving and to think positive thoughts about overcoming obstacles to building an airport in Manor." Griswold emphasized that in the thirteen months since the voters approved moving the airport, "two words sum up the progress toward complying with the mandate—not much." Garcia further noted the formation of a new group, the Airport Landowners League, composed of Manor area farmers who also were concerned with council inactivity. Former county commissioner

David Samuelson, a member of that organization, stated in a press release: "Small property owners within the footprint of Austin's new airport have been held hostage by the City of Austin since the voters approved the new airport." Homer Biggerstaff, one of the five organizers of the Landowners League, explained that while he was interested in selling his property, he was "mostly interested in having something happen. 'Either build (the airport) or stop it, just leave me alone.'"[4]

On February 2, 1989, the Austin City Council, bowing to growing public pressure, approved Mayor Pro Tem Sally Shipman's resolution to begin Manor land purchases, possibly as early as August. The Shipman resolution, which passed on a 5-2 vote, drew immediate fire from fellow council members Robert Barnstone and Mayor Lee Cooke. Barnstone's earlier resolution prevented any land purchases until some $50 million had been committed for that phase of the project.[5] However, as the council's Manor momentum continued, political wounds were soon healed. On March 21, environmentalists and federal aviation officials settled a lawsuit over an environmental study of the Manor airport site, and the city council selected consultant design teams for the project. On a 7-0 vote, the council chose the Austin architectural firm Page-Southerland-Page and the New York airport planning firm Thompson Consultants to complete the initial design of the terminal building. P & D Technologies and Murfee Engineering, both local firms, were selected to complete the overall master plan design.[6]

While the city council continued grappling with the Manor development, construction crews were already working on the final phase of a $15 million expansion at Mueller. Design changes included four new airline boarding gates, a baggage claim conveyor, expanded ticket counters, and a new air freight building located at 4005 Airport Boulevard. The terminal expansion incorporated the original air cargo facility located adjacent to the Mueller terminal.[7] In the meantime, the political spotlight switched to Manor. On May 18, Austin mayor Lee Cooke and other city officials met with some two hundred fifty area residents in Manor High School to reassure them that land purchases could begin as early as August.[8] While the mayor offered no firm date, he at least provided the first concrete assurance that the city intended to fulfill its promise to open a new airport there by February 15, 1995. While Cooke's reception was neither warm nor hostile, the Manor meeting fell far short of its mark; the Austin mayor could not provide specific answers the landowners sought.

Austin residents who lived adjacent to Mueller airport shared similar frustrations with the Manor area landowners. They too wanted answers, as well as having the airport moved—to Manor, or anywhere. They wanted to be free of the noise, danger, and congestion. But unlike their Manor neighbors, East Austin citizens had support in the Texas Legislature, specifically Representative Wilhelmina Delco. On May 10, 1989, one week before Mayor Lee Cooke appeared at the Manor High School meeting, Representative Delco introduced House Bill No. 2848, a noise abatement bill, which focused specifically on the Mueller issue. The text of the bill specifies as follows:

> This section applies only to an airport owned by an incorporated city, town, or village [and] . . . not later than December 31, 1991, [the city, town, or village will] provide adequate soundproofing and noise reductions devices for all public buildings within the 65 or higher average day-night sound level contour of the airport . . . or not later than March 31, 1990, contract to purchase at least 10 percent of the real property required for the site of a replacement airport . . . and, not later than December 31, 1996, provide a replacement airport . . . Any interested person may bring suit in a court of competent jurisdiction to enforce this section, and the court may grant appropriate relief.[9]

While Representative Delco's bill failed to pass, an identical companion senate bill, S.B. 1707, introduced by Senator Gonzalo Barrientos of Austin, passed the Senate on May 9, 1989, was approved on June 16, and became effective on August 28, ninety days after adjournment.[10]

While the city council may not have been intimidated by the noise abatement legislation, they were well aware of its existence and continued to move forward with the Manor airport project. On June 8, the council approved an agreement with five of the major carriers serving Austin, establishing terminal rental and landing fees at Mueller. That agreement also addressed the first phase of the Manor project, including preliminary terminal design work in which the airlines would participate. It also paved the way for the September 7 sale of $30 million in revenue bonds to finance the initial Manor land purchases. While that session proceeded rather mildly, with only Robert Barnstone's dissenting vote, such was not the case when the council addressed the land purchases. In describing the bad manners exhibited at the December 7 council meeting, journalist Arnold Garcia Jr. wrote, "There are better displays of manners at hog troughs than there were during Thursday's Austin City Council discussion of how land for the Manor airport will be bought. Recrimination, insinuation, cheap shots, innuendo and even race baiting dwarfed the issue at hand."[11] The problem was procedure. While the council majority supported discussing the details of each purchase in closed session and then voting on the contract in public, Robert Barnstone and George Humphrey, for different reasons, disagreed. The council resolved the matter by agreeing that each purchase would not be finalized until the council voted in open session.

And then it happened. All the vocal bloodletting went for naught. The banner headline in the January 28, 1990 *Austin American-Statesman* told the entire story: "U.S. to Study Closing Bergstrom." Secretary of the Air Force Donald Rice had previously advised United States Representative J. J. Pickle of Austin that Bergstrom Air Force Base was included on a list of several military installations "to be studied for possible closure." [12] That announcement threw the local political establishment into shock. Mayor Lee Cooke called for an immediate moratorium on Manor land purchases; other council members disagreed, realizing the fate of Bergstrom probably would not be known for more than a year. And there remained in the background the specter of Senate Bill 1707; if Manor land acquisitions did not begin by March 31, soundproofing public buildings near Mueller appeared mandatory.

Such was the quandary the city council faced. On the one hand, Bergstrom, once the panacea for Austin's airport dilemma, was likely to become available, while on the other, Manor landowners were still being held hostage by the city council. And even if Bergstrom became available with its 3,971 acres and a 12,250-foot runway, Austin voters had already approved moving the airport to Manor and authorized $72 million in bonds to purchase that land. But overshadowing all other factors in that baffling political equation was the likelihood the city could lose one of its largest employers, the United States Air Force. Bergstrom employed some eight thousand military and civilian residents and in 1989 pumped an estimated $533 million into the Austin economy.[13] But regardless of the outcome, there would be both winners and losers. There was no way the airport issue could be resolved to everyone's satisfaction.

As the debate erupted in the wake of the January 28 announcement, Mayor Lee Cooke assumed the unenviable task of serving as both judge and advocate in the face of increasing dissatisfaction. On January 30, he refereed a rowdy and sometimes hostile town meeting at Austin's Pearce Middle School. The audience of some two hundred included Northeast Austin residents who complained about the city's delay in moving Mueller. Equally angry were southeastern Travis County residents fearful that Bergstrom would become Austin's new municipal airport, plus impatient Manor citizens still demanding answers about Austin's plans to build an airport there. "Members of the crowd sometimes shouted at each other and sometimes at the mayor—but all for different reasons," one journalist wrote. The mood was more subdued the following night in the Manor High School cafeteria. Faced with a moratorium on land purchases, Manor residents appeared resigned to the fact that, with the possibility of Bergstrom becoming available, there could be no immediate answers to their questions. Cooke had already stated his priority at the Pearce Middle School meeting: "My first priority is Bergstrom and my second priority is dealing with the Manor airport."[14]

Hostility, however, regenerated the following day in the city council meeting. By the time the bickering and name-calling ended, the council passed resolutions calling for the Air Force to keep Bergstrom open, approved a study of the air base as a possible municipal airport site, and placed a sixty-day hold on Manor land purchases. That prompted Manor landowners to consider legal action against the City of Austin. They sought the advice of high profile Austin attorney Roy Minton, who advised them to "get yourself a lawyer and get trucking and tell the city of Austin . . . to fish or cut bait."[15] Cooke, meanwhile, moved ahead in his effort to save Bergstrom as an Air Force facility. After appointing Austin attorney Pike Powers co-chairman of the Save Bergstrom Task Force, Cooke, in a February 8, 1990 memo, outlined for him ten "new missions that we should consider for Bergstrom Air Force Base." Those included reassigning overseas Air Force reductions to Bergstrom, retaining the 10th and 12th Air Force headquarters and the NCO training academy at Bergstrom, relocating the Panama Southern Command headquarters to Bergstrom, and creating "a national transition training center at Bergstrom to transition military and civilians into private sector jobs."[16] The Greater Austin Chamber of Commerce also supported the campaign to save Bergstrom. On June 22, the chamber issued a press release stating that within the past three days, twenty-two community leaders from Austin made thirty-eight contacts in Washington, D.C., to support retaining Bergstrom as an active Air Force base.[17]

While news from Washington brought scant hope of keeping Bergstrom active, the prospect of its availability as a municipal airport generated new interest. On April 20, City Manager Camille Barnett released a new study of the base, indicating the city could save $108 million by using Bergstrom, instead of building a new facility at Manor. That information prompted the city council to suspend all but a fraction of the work on the proposed Manor airport. Time, however, was a factor. That same day homeowners living near Mueller filed suit against the city, hoping to force the closure of that facility. There was a measure of irony in the timing; the same day the homeowners filed suit, city and airline officials held a ribbon-cutting ceremony for the soon-to-be-completed Mueller terminal addition. The new section included ticket counters for Southwest, Northwest, and America West airlines, plus four new gates for Southwest Airlines.[18] " 'It's not a fix,' city aviation director Charles Gates said of the terminal expansion. 'It's just a little Band-Aid put on to carry us over to a new airport.' " [19]

The social, political, and economic ramifications of the ribbon-cutting greatly transcended the significance of that event. The latest addition to Mueller occurred, in part, in response to explosive growth in the airline industry, especially as it applied to the Austin market. Totally aside from neighborhood complaints, Mueller had far outlived its usefulness. Two factors, both closely interrelated, helped deem it so. First, the Airline Deregulation Act of 1978 opened all markets to all carriers.[20] The increased number of carriers serving Austin soon reflected that change. In 1971, for example, only two trunk line carriers, Braniff and Continental, served Austin, plus two regional carriers, Texas International and Rio Airways. In 1977 Southwest Airlines, another regional carrier, entered the Austin market. Second, by 1981, the burgeoning Austin high-tech economy and the air travel it stimulated had attracted three more major carriers, Eastern Airlines, Delta Airlines, and US Air, plus two regional carriers, Texas Star and Emerald. By 1985, American Airlines, Trans-World Airlines, and Pan American World Airways, plus four regional carriers were serving the Capital City. (Braniff International Airways terminated service on May 12, 1982.) Growth continued and, by 1990, nine major trunk line carriers, including United Airlines, plus two regional carriers were serving the Austin market through a greatly outdated Mueller. Furthermore, expanding air travel was a statewide phenomenon; by January 1, 1991, some thirty Texas cities had scheduled airline service.[21]

Air traffic data, combined with urban statistics, provide an even clearer perspective of the changes that were occurring in the Capital City. During the decade of the 1970s, enplaned passengers at Mueller increased 231 percent, from 268,488 to 887,905, and during the 1980s they increased 128 percent, from 887,905 to 2,022,269. Increases in air freight were even more striking. During the 1970s revenue tons grew 104 percent, from 572.61 to

1,165.61, but in the 1980s, they advanced 735 percent from 1,165.61 to 9,733.12 tons. Austin was clearly becoming an industrialized market. And furthermore, airmail loadings also increased, but to a lesser degree, up 47 percent in the 1970s and 117 percent during the 1980s.[22]

Another factor stimulating airline traffic was concurrent population growth. During the 1970s, Austin population increased 37 percent, from 251,808 to 345,890, and during the 1980s, 25 percent, from 345,890 to 465,622.[23] Closely related to population increases was the city's geographic expansion. Austin encompassed 81 square miles in the 1970s but by 1980 had grown to 129 square miles, an increase of 59 percent. However, during the 1980s, the city registered its greatest expansion, a 74 percent increase, from 129 to 225 square miles.[24] Thus, Walter Long's high expectations were gradually being fulfilled; the Capital City was achieving a large measure of what he envisioned as urban progress, a matter that would stimulate debate during the ensuing decades. By the 1990s, socially, culturally, economically, as well as geographically, Austin had become a vastly different city, creating unprecedented demands on the city government. And still one of the most pressing was the airport issue.

All the while, both parties in the ongoing drama played a waiting game; Austin looked to Washington for a break in the Bergstrom matter while Manor looked to Austin. News that could benefit one party meant almost certain defeat for the other. With scant prospect for future land sales at the Manor site, the original investors were left with no choice. On July 2, 1990, the Carpenter Development Company filed for Chapter 11 bankruptcy protection,[25] and on July 19 the United States Department of Defense released a Bergstrom Air Force Base environmental impact statement that essentially terminated its use as a military base. According to the study, active combat units would be either deactivated or transferred and the military and civilian workforce phased out. After December 31, 1992, only the Air Force reserve units would be retained, along with a token civilian force and a caretaker unit of some fifty people.[26]

Although the city council had adopted a resolution to establish the new municipal airport at Bergstrom, Mayor Lee Cooke continued his balancing act, attempting to hold all interests in abeyance until the Bergstrom matter was definitely settled. Failure carried specific penalties. Should the city delay Manor land purchases indefinitely, provisions of Senate Bill 1707 could force the city to soundproof public buildings near Mueller. And the growing discontent of Manor area landowners was a certain matter to be dealt with in the future. Nevertheless, the case for a municipal facility at Bergstrom was further strengthened on February 14, 1991, when the Citizens' Task Force on the Economic Conversion of Bergstrom Air Force Base issued its final report. The task force concluded: "If fully developed, the Bergstrom site has the capacity to handle future projected air passenger demand at Austin well into the twenty-first century."[27]

Subsequently, a new city council led by Mayor Bruce Todd attacked the airport issue with renewed vigor. Bolstered by President George H. W. Bush's approval of the base closure list, the council approved a $2.2 million study on the conversion of Bergstrom into a municipal airport. Prior to the July 11 vote, Mayor Todd stated: "There seems to be a mood on the council to move with deliberate speed . . . to try to resolve an issue that has faced this city for a long, long time."[28] The council's foresight was further confirmed on July 30, when the House of Representatives overwhelmingly approved closing thirty-four United States military bases, including Bergstrom Air Force Base.[29] That essentially insured Bergstrom's closing; only highly unlikely action by both houses of Congress could change the outcome.

With Bergstrom's availability as Austin's future airport site virtually assured, the city council began working toward that end. There still remained, however, the aborted Manor airport issue. Following more than a decade of strained relations, the new city council moved to avoid future litigation with irate Manor landowners. At the December 20th meeting, the council voted not to issue $698 million in bonds Austin voters authorized in 1987 for construction of the projected Manor airport.[30] The council, in turn, filed a request with the Federal Aviation Administration to transfer the original $112.5 million Manor airport grant to the projected Bergstrom Air Force base conversion.[31] On March 11, 1992, they moved another step forward in the Bergstrom matter by setting May 1, 1993, as the date for a public referendum on constructing a new municipal airport at the former Air Force base.[32] The council's earlier defensive legal maneuver, however, fell short of its goal. On June 16, 1992, six Manor landowners filed suit against the City of Austin, former mayor Lee Cooke, former council member Robert Barnstone, and two companies employed by the city, alleging they conspired to obstruct attempts to move the airport to Manor. The plaintiffs, who sought damages for lost profits, decline in property values, and mental pain and suffering, pleaded for an unspecified cash settlement.[33]

The year, however, ended on a positive note. On November 26, Congressman J. J. Pickle announced that the Air Force attorneys had ruled that most of the Bergstrom Air Force base property would revert to the City of Austin without cost.[34] That included acquisition of 113 acres of paved runways, aprons, and taxiways, more than 800,000 square feet of buildings planned for reuse, plus some sixty buildings available for use during airport construction.[35] News of the total acquisition cleared the way for the city council to move forward immediately with plans for the new airport. On December 13, the council appointed Parsons Brinckerhoff to coordinate the development of the project. The management contract, expected to cost as much as $20 million, would span an estimated six years.[36]

The May 1, 1993, airport referendum received the approval of 63 percent of the Austin voters, thereby authorizing the city council to borrow $400 million to build a new airport at the Bergstrom site and close Robert Mueller Municipal Airport.[37] Change indeed was in the offing. Long before the May election, the military exodus from Bergstrom had begun. Flight operations terminated in October 1992, the base hospital closed in February 1993, the clinic in May, and the pharmacy and acute care clinic in June. The main store, commissary, dorms, billeting, and the officers' club were the last to close.[38] By September 30, the streets and thoroughfares were empty, the aircraft parking ramps vacant, the runways strangely silent. Each vacant building standing in ghostly silence gave mute testimony to Bergstrom's half-century role in three armed conflicts and various international emergencies. But now, the mission complete, it was time to say farewell. At five o'clock in the afternoon, some three hundred people, many Bergstrom veterans, watched quietly as a color guard lowered the United States flag, which they handed to Col. Scott Madole, whose final responsibility was to march to the front gate and officially close the base. One era in Austin aviation history had just ended; another was about to begin.

The same day Bergstrom Air Force Base closed, Mayor Bruce Todd received confirmation from the Federal Aviation Administration that Austin would receive up to $91 million in federal funding for the airport to be constructed at the Bergstrom site. That included transferring funds from the original Manor airport project to the current $583 million Bergstrom project, scheduled to open in two phases. Cargo operations were to begin in 1996, and passenger service to follow in the fall of 1998. The new airport, however, needed a name, which the city council provided on November 2. In a 6-0 vote, they named the projected facility Austin-Bergstrom International Airport.[39] Mayor Todd, who suggested the name, made his choice to honor those who had served their country at the base as well as the Austin native for whom the base was named originally. All that remained was to begin construction, and that began symbolically on November 19, when eleven public officials, using silver-plated shovels, moved the first earth for what would be Austin's new municipal airport. "'We have put to rest all apprehensions, doubts and questions about our future,' said Congressman Jake Pickle. 'The doubters and naysayers can take a back seat because Austin is flying forward.'"[40]

On Monday morning, March 6, 1995, the first contingency of workmen entered the main gate of the former Air Force base to begin construction on the largest public works project in the city's history. A small supervisory staff with support personnel began positioning equipment and establishing workstations in several vacant buildings. They embarked immediately on rebuilding the airport's south access road. That same day a group of Austin civic leaders, headed by Mayor Bruce Todd, traveled to Washington to help expedite the project. They had meetings scheduled with the Department of Defense to urge the final cleanup of the former Air Force base, with the Federal Aviation Administration to discuss further funding for airport construction, and with former United States senator Alan Dixon, chairman of the Base Closure and Realignment Commission, to appeal the Pentagon's recent recommendation to disband the Air Force Reserve base at Bergstrom. The Washington trip yielded a measure of success. On August 14, the Federal Aviation Administration awarded the city $30 million to remove four Del Valle schools from the proposed flight path. That was in addition to an earlier $37.5 million noise mitigation allotment for the school district.[41]

Meanwhile, construction continued at the new airport. In late October the Federal Aviation Administration began erecting a new control tower and radar control facility. With cargo operations scheduled to begin the following year, air traffic control was a priority consideration. Airport construction also weighed heavily on the city council's time; important decisions had to be made. By January 1996, the council was locked in debate over the type of urinals—low-flush or no-flush—to be installed in the new terminal. "The toilet talk illustrated a classic Austin debate," the *American-Statesman* reported, "pitting strong environmental interests against budget and operations concerns."[42] Practicality, however, won out; low-flush urinals emitted less odor.

The council also addressed more critical airport issues. On January 9, they opened bids for the new terminal. Pelzel-Phelps, a joint venture of Pelzel & Associates, a local firm owned jointly by Mary Guerrero-Pelzel and Hensel Phelps, submitted the low bid, $100 million. The Pelzel-Phelps bid encountered immediate council opposition: first, it was $5 million over budget and, second, Pelzel & Associates had previously sued the city over a contract. Also, Morganti Texas, the third-lowest bidder, claimed the bids of Pelzel-Phelps and Hyman/Samcorp, the second-lowest bidder, were incomplete. To resolve the matter, the council voted at the February 8 meeting to reject all bids and rebid the project. That proved to be a wise decision. When the council opened the new bids at the June 26 meeting, Morganti National, Inc. [Morganti Texas] submitted the lowest bid, $87.2 million. That, however, did not end the matter. On July 17, State District Judge Joe Hart ordered that the city could not enter into a contract with Morganti until after a hearing requested by Aviation Contractors, Inc., the second-lowest bidder in the rebidding. That company claimed two of Morganti's subcontractors were not qualified for the project. Faced with contraction delays that could cost the city $140,000 per day, the council agreed to pay the plaintiff $190,000 to drop the suit.[43]

With the passenger terminal under contract, the city council focused next on the cargo complex. To develop the 165,000-square-foot cargo port, the council approved $11.7 million in bonds, to be repaid by revenues generated by Austin CargoPort Development, the independent agency operating that facility.[44] With three major cargo air carriers already contracted to serve Austin, time was of the essence. Less than one month later, on October 1, more than 150 people participated in the ground-breaking ceremonies on the extreme north end of the airport complex.[45] Construction began immediately. The council next faced the formidable task of disposing of acres of existing structures on the former Air Force base to make way for passenger terminal construction. The 45 duplexes located in the path of the new east runway were the most pressing problem. Eventually, the city found new owners for about 125 of the 257 duplexes on the base and for 65 single-family homes; most went to private developers, nonprofit groups, or the city housing program.[46] Other duplexes were sold in a public drawing for ten dollars each, while 40 other houses and related structures yielded $26,420 at public auction. Structures not sold and moved off the base were scheduled for demolition.

By late November, John Almond, airport project director, reported construction was progressing on schedule; rehabilitation of the 12,250-foot west runway was complete, and work on the east runway and terminal aircraft parking apron was ahead of schedule. At that time, about five hundred workers were on site; by summer that number would increase to two thousand. Progress, however, was not without problems. There remained the looming threat of the State Aircraft Pooling Board to force Mueller to remain open to accommodate its fleet of state-owned aircraft. The state's argument had merit; part of the problem of relocation was cost. At the new airport, the city would charge the state about $66,000 a year to lease land, where the state would have to build a new headquarters building and aircraft hangars to replace the facilities it already owned at Mueller. In addition, there was a city-imposed fuel fee, 2 percent higher than at Mueller.

There was also the matter of convenience; access to state aircraft was important to the Pooling Board's air operation. During 1995, the state's twelve executive-type aircraft transported more than eleven thousand state employees nearly 600,000 miles on state business. Originally, the city promised the state a prime location near the main entrance to the field; however, when that site was reassigned to the air cargo carriers, the city unilaterally selected another location at the far southeast corner of the airport for the state aircraft. That site, accessible only by a back entrance from U.S. Highway 183 and Burleson Road, was some three miles from the airport's main entrance on Texas Highway 71. Travel time to the new airport was another problem. Mueller was only a ten-minute drive from the state complex, while the new location, some fifteen miles from the Capitol area, was accessible only via a circuitous, traffic-congested route through largely residential sections of the city.

All factors considered, the issue would not be easily resolved; powerful personalities, representing equally powerful interests, were eager to defend opposing sides of the issue. The State of Texas was represented by Billy Clayton, former Speaker of the House and present chairman of the State Aircraft Pooling Board, and by Pete Laney, who was the current Speaker, a former chairman of the Pooling Board, and a private pilot. Defending the city's position were former congressman J. J. (Jake) Pickle, Austin mayor Bruce Todd, former Austin mayor Roy Butler, attorney Ron Kessler (former chairman of the Greater Austin Chamber of Commerce), and the *Austin American-Statesman,* which editorialized in behalf of moving the state fleet to the new airport. Again the city found itself in a particularly precarious position. Should the state force the city to keep Mueller open, then the city would have to deal with the citizens of East Austin, who had been promised that once the new airport was open, Mueller would be closed.

The State of Texas, possessing the right of condemnation, negotiated from a position of power. And to further ensure its advantage, should the matter have to be resolved in court, the state engaged a commercial appraiser to place a specific value on its land and assets at Mueller. At that point another interested party entered the stalled negotiations—general aviation. The private pilots, also wanting Mueller to remain open, supported the state's cause. Norman Scoggins, head of air traffic operations at Dallas–Fort Worth International Airport, and Kirby Perry, an Austin architect and longstanding supporter of private aviation, represented that group. Both were private pilots and affiliated with the Aircraft Owners and Pilots Association, a national private pilots' lobby that supported some two hundred fifty area pilots in their effort to keep Mueller open. General aviation was indeed a factor to be considered. In 1995, there were 47,331 licensed pilots in Texas, plus 25,923 fixed wing aircraft and 917 helicopters registered to the owners.[47]

Ultimately, the State Aircraft Pooling Board and the City of Austin came to terms; on April 24, 1997, the city council approved a contract with the State of Texas. The city agreed to sell the State of Texas 282 acres at Mueller for an estimated $29 million; to purchase the Pooling Board's 20-acre Mueller site for about $5 million; and to spend another $3 million on roads, drainage, and other improvements near the Pooling Board's new location at Bergstrom.[48] That also cleared the way for the transfer of the aviation facilities of both the Texas National Guard and the Department of Public Safety to the new airport. The only losers in the settlement were the private pilots. With the scheduled closure of Mueller in May 1999, they would have the options of renting hangar space at Bergstrom for what many considered prohibitive prices or of moving their aircraft to another airport in another Central Texas town. Understandably, most private pilots felt abandoned by the city.[49]

As construction on the new airport progressed, city planners discovered certain necessary design changes. On March 19, 1997, the city council voted to double the number of parking spaces in the airport garage. That change expanded the garage plan from 1,800 public spaces to 3,500, and increased the total airport cost from $638 million to $663 million.[50] On March 30, workmen erected the first steel structure of the new terminal building, to be named in honor of former congresswoman Barbara Jordan.[51] Amid the beehive of construction activity, air cargo operations from the new airport began on June 30, 1997. With the 12,250-foot runway, air cargo jets could fly nonstop from Austin, Texas, to Tokyo, Japan, without having to make an intermediate fuel stop. And still there emerged other design changes, adding additional costs to the city. On July 2, airport officials recommended to the city council a proposal to add five additional gates to the passenger terminal, still under construction. "We are outgrowing our facility as we build it," said John Almond, the new airport project director. That proposal, the fourth increase in the city's portion of the cost since the development of the 1993 Airport Master Plan, set the city's share at $546,800,000.[52]

With airport construction on schedule and approximately 50 percent complete, the city council voted on January 22, 1998, to plan the annexation of a portion of Del Valle. Unlike previous annexation proposals, Del Valle residents offered no opposition. Most felt they were already citizens of Austin as the city provided utility service to that area. Under the limited-purpose annexation, the landowners would not have to pay city taxes, could vote in city elections (but not on bond issues), and would begin receiving city sewer service, police and fire protection, and street lights. Most everyone seemed happy; residents of Richland Estates were the exception. Those living in the fifty-seven-house subdivision, located some five hundred yards north of the cargo port, began voicing their complaints concerning the late-night aircraft noise, the fumes, and a mysterious black substance that collected on their roofs and automobiles. And they felt it was only going to get worse. By February 1998, there were already some thirty daily takeoffs and landings at Bergstrom. Once the airport became fully operational, they argued, there would be more than five hundred daily flights. "We were told that we wouldn't be invaded—and it is an invasion," complained Philip Vela, president of the Richland Estates Neighborhood Association. They wanted action; instead, they received technical analyses. City officials contended the odor was not jet fumes, but automobile fumes from Texas Highway 71, while a Texas Natural Resource Conservation Commission study determined the black substance was a combination of pollen, common minerals, and tire-rubber dust, nothing related to air cargo jets. City officials did agree to update the noise study of the area, which some Richland Estates residents had requested. On May 19, the study complete, the city announced plans to purchase an undetermined number of homes near the new airport, which included some in Richland Estates.[53]

By May 31, with only three hundred twenty-eight days to the scheduled May 2, 1999, airport dedication, 63 percent of the project was complete and still within budget. Airport Director Charles Gates articulated the city council's uneasy anticipation: "One year out is like in basketball—this is crunch time and our goal is not to go into overtime."[54] Six months later construction crews, still on schedule, began attaching the first passenger loading gate, Gate 4, at the Barbara Jordan Terminal, reaching a four-year milestone in terminal construction. In the meantime, increasing air traffic at Mueller continued to verify Austin voters' foresight in moving commercial air operations to Bergstrom. By October 31, 1998, passenger traffic for the year reached 5,028,202, up 2.13 percent over 1997, while air cargo for the same period totaled 195,374,638 pounds, an 18.68 percent increase.[55] While the Mueller air traffic controllers continued to coordinate the more than one hundred fifty daily flights of the eight commercial carriers serving that site, their counterparts at Bergstrom began clearing flights on the just-completed 9,000-foot east runway. With official dedication of the new facility less than five months away, the project, in aviation terminology, appeared to be on final approach.

However, disruptive side issues developed. One of the most critical—and enduring—was street access to the new airport. Mueller's convenient central location merely intensified the matter. As early as June 1990, while the city council debated the Manor versus Bergstrom issue, council member Smoot Carl-Mitchell foresaw the problem. He predicted that a traffic study would reveal that going to Manor would be much more convenient than a trip to Bergstrom. Apparently the city council failed to benefit from Carl-Mitchell's vision. Some eight months before the scheduled airport dedication, the street access problem still had not been addressed. Richard Kriss, a frequent flyer who lived in West Austin, raised the critical question: "How am I going to get there?" . . . "'It's gridlock today, and it's going to be gridlock when the airport opens,' he said angrily. 'I don't care about all the improvements to that airport—I can't get to the stupid thing.'"[56] While still in Washington, Congressman J. J. Pickle, another frequent flyer, urged Austin policy makers "to start thinking of the new Austin airport as a chance to show how different forms of transportation can be linked."[57] Pickle's advice also went unheeded. There were, however, multiple role models for the Austin policy makers to follow. During the 1990s, three major metropolitan areas dedicated new airports—Pittsburgh, Denver, and Orange County, California. And even-more-specific examples were nearby:

Texas' three major municipal airports—Dallas–Fort Worth, Houston, and San Antonio—were all connected to the downtown areas by freeways. Yet, referring to Bergstrom, Richard Kriss still wondered, "How am I going to get there?"

State Representative Ron Wilson of Houston created another disruptive side issue. On March 2, he filed a bill in the Texas Legislature that would keep Mueller open if any of the commercial airlines elect to continue operating there. Although no city is mentioned by name, the bill was so worded that it applied only to Mueller. The House promptly approved the measure and sent the bill back to the Senate, where it died. Yet, amid the local outcry over the issue, Mayor Kirk Watson ignored it, dispatching a "Dear Friends" invitation to the dedication of the two runways at Austin-Bergstrom International Airport on Saturday, April 17. The west runway was dedicated to the late President Lyndon Baines Johnson, and the new east runway was named in honor of former congressman J. J. (Jake) Pickle. Honored guests were United States Senator Kay Bailey Hutchinson, Congressman Lloyd Doggett, and United States Secretary of the Air Force F. Whitten Peters. Secretary Peters also participated in the ceremonial transfer of the airport property from the Air Force to the City of Austin.[58]

A week preceding the runway dedication, contractors conducted a successful trial run on the mechanized baggage conveyors in the Jordan Terminal.[59] City officials attending the demonstration questioned the wisdom of a May 2 dedication. The east concourse, for example, appeared ready for passenger accommodation, but further west, fresh drywall was being sanded and workmen were still tiling the restrooms. It was obvious the project had entered crunch time; overtime appeared inevitable. But any delay carried obvious penalties: $2 million monthly losses in airport rental revenues and $2 million monthly payments in capitalized interest on airport revenue bonds that the city had to begin making in May. The decision lay, however, not with the city, but with the airlines, the primary tenants of the $115 million terminal. Their concern was neither unpainted walls nor unfinished restrooms, but loading gates still under construction. The airlines prevailed; the city moved the airport opening forward to Sunday, May 23.

While the three-week delay created fiscal problems for the city council, it also whetted the appetites of Austin citizens to see what they were getting for their 690 million tax dollars. In a fiesta-like atmosphere, the City of Austin held an open house on Saturday and Sunday, April 24 and 25, at the 600,000-square-foot Barbara Jordan Terminal. To avoid overcrowding, H.E.B. stores distributed 100,000 free tickets. The response was overwhelming; by Thursday, April 22, about 50,000 tickets had been claimed. Police estimated that as many as 16,700 people toured the terminal every three-hour interval during the open house. The high point of the two-day event occurred as Bennie Criswell and Rose Mary McGown, two sisters of former United States Representative Barbara Jordan, joined Mayor Kirk Watson in the Saturday morning ceremonial ribbon-cutting. Before the ceremony, Watson, addressing the crowd of some four thousand visitors waiting to enter the terminal, said, "I think you'll be impressed." Visitors' comments were uniformly positive.[60] While the visitors admired chief designer Lawrence Speck's architectural creation, they were also entertained by some of Austin's prominent recording artists. Also, the East and West food courts featured typical Texas food with an Austin flavor: Schlotzsky's sandwiches, Matt's El Rancho Mexican food, Salt Lick barbecue, and Amy's ice cream.[61]

The Austin-Bergstrom open house forecast the beginning of the end of Mueller. On May 5, John Almond, now director of Facilities and Operations at both Austin-Bergstrom and Mueller, wrote Mueller fixed base operators that all air operations were scheduled to cease at midnight, May 22, 1999. After that time, no aircraft would be allowed to land at Mueller, and control tower operations would cease at the same time. "Within thirty days after closure," Almond continued, "all airplanes must be removed from [Mueller]. Runway 17-35 will be used for airplane departures only. Runways 13R-31L will be barricaded closed. Departures will only occur during daylight hours between 0800–0900 hours and 1400–1500 hours, Monday thru Friday . . . Airside Operations will coordinate the departures with Austin-Bergstrom International Airport . . . Airfield demolition efforts may be in progress, which prohibits uncontrolled departures."[62] That letter also signaled a change that was to occur in Austin general aviation. Convenience for Austin-area private pilots would become a thing of the past.

Three days later when Air Force One landed at Austin-Bergstrom at 5:04 P.M. some three thousand people had waited three hours to see the president of the United States, William Jefferson Clinton. Mayor Kirk Watson, accompanied by Congressman Lloyd Doggett, extended official welcome to the first major passenger aircraft landing at the new airport. In his six-minute response, which covered a number of unrelated topics, the president cited the conversion of Bergstrom Air Force Base as a model for other communities to follow.[63] The president's visit seemed to set the stage for an even more dramatic production, the official dedication of Austin-Bergstrom International Airport on Sunday, May 23. That drama, however, began the night before at Mueller, with the traditional farewell for the last scheduled passenger aircraft to leave the airport. At 9:54 P.M., as an honorary ground crew of fifteen escorted Continental Airlines Flight 1691 as it backed away from Gate 4, two fire trucks, one on either side of the plane, sent streams of water arching over the Boeing 737. That event marked the end of an era that began some sixty-nine years before.

The departure of Flight 1691 cleared the way for a mass exodus from Mueller, led by a caravan of rental cars. Then came the departure of six airliners that terminated their flights at Mueller on the evening of May 22 but would originate their morning takeoffs from Austin-Bergstrom. Also, there was the departure of the seventh airliner, Southwest Airlines "Lone Star 1," a publicity short hop from the old facility to the new one for some 125 notable Austinites, including Mayor Kirk Watson, council members Daryl Slusher and Gus Garcia, and former congressman J. J. Pickle and his wife, Beryl. It was a civic joy ride, soaring above Austin at five thousand feet for no other purpose than to toast four years of hard work that yielded Austin-Bergstrom International Airport. "Lone Star 1" landed there at 10:55 P.M., appropriately on the Jake Pickle runway, and subsequently deposited its occupants at the new Barbara Jordan Terminal. And there was one final exodus from Mueller. Shortly after one o'clock the following morning, a bizarre parade of people herding motorized baggage carts, mobile passenger loading stairs, air-conditioning generators, tugs, flatbed trucks, and just about every piece of equipment ever seen on an airport ramp, all flanked by a fleet of police cars and two fire trucks, began moving slowly along the seven-mile route to Austin-Bergstrom to prepare for the first airline departure at 6:09 that morning.

When the airport officially opened at 4:00 A.M., all was in readiness. American Airlines Flight 1604 departed on schedule after the passengers received their "Official Honorary Passenger" certificates from Mayor Kirk Watson. The first incoming aircraft, American Airlines Flight 1911, landed at 7:49 A.M. Arriving passengers were met at the gate and served coffee by city and airline officials. While Mayor Watson cut a ceremonial ribbon to celebrate the occasion, two fire trucks sprayed the aircraft with the traditional arches of water. Airline operations were underway at Austin-Bergstrom International Airport. A crowd estimated at between twenty and thirty thousand visited the airport on opening day. Although airport officials reported some glitches—a passenger loading bridge that malfunctioned and a broken conveyor belt—nothing caused significant delays. Meanwhile back at Mueller, departing passengers continued arriving during the day, unaware that that facility had closed and the new airport had opened. Access to Austin-Bergstrom still remained a problem for frequent flyer Robert Kriss, who arrived there on opening day on a flight from Dallas. "One thing about Mueller—you can get there, but you can't park. Here, you can park, but you can't get there." [64]

In the meantime, Austin's best all-time entertainment continued at the Capitol complex, where some legislators looked upon Houston representative Ron Wilson as the master of bad timing. Four days before the May 23 Austin-Bergstrom airport dedication, in the waning days of the session, Wilson introduced another Save Mueller bill. "The Houston Democrat, an expert on House rules," the *American-Statesman* reported, "was able to attach it to an amendment to the routine DPS [Department of Public Safety] bill." [65] Under Wilson's amendment, the Department of Public Safety would acquire Mueller through condemnation and operate it for law enforcement and general aviation. Amid the outcry of opposition, Wilson maintained the validity of his proposed legislation. "'If I'm wrong, I'll donate my plane to charity,' said Wilson, a pilot who doesn't own a plane.'" [66] Senator Gonzalo Barrientos of Austin, who opposed the measure, threatened to shut down the Senate with a filibuster if it approved Wilson's bill. Barrientos' maneuver succeeded; on Saturday May 29, the Senate killed the proposal that would have kept Robert Mueller Municipal Airport open.

While Senator Barrientos remained the hero to Austin citizens who were living near Mueller, the private plane owners saw in State Representative Ron Wilson, regardless of his legislative objectives, their last hope to keep their airplanes in Austin. Considering the cost, inconvenience, and limited space at Austin-Bergstrom, that facility offered a partial solution to only a portion of Austin's some five thousand private pilots and more than four hundred aircraft owners. To further complicate the issue, on June 23 would come the closure of Austin Executive Air Park, formerly Tim's Air Park, where some one hundred private planes were based. [67] The only option left for the private aircraft owners was to remove their aircraft to one of the twelve regional airports located within fifty miles of Austin. [68] Kirby Perry was one of the last pilots to leave Mueller. It was a sad farewell on Sunday afternoon, May 20, when he took off in his single-engine Piper "Lancer," bound for his new base at the Horseshoe Bay airport. That facility, located an hour's drive from Perry's Austin office, precluded his using the aircraft in his business.

And so there were losers, but there were also winners. Austin-Bergstrom International Airport emerged a proven winner, exceeding everyone's expectations in traffic volume. During October 1999, the new airport served 603,905 revenue passengers, an 11.70 percent increase over October 1998, while cargo operations, both domestic and international, for that same period reached 21,882,416 pounds, a 13.48 percent increase.[69] The new airport was indeed serving a fast-growing city. By 2000, Austin's 656,562 citizens occupied about 265 square miles, extending from Round Rock on the north to Buda on the south.[70]

Austin-Bergstrom International Airport, however, represented far more than statistics; the spirit of Walter E. Long and Max Bickler and their belief in urban progress seemed to pervade every aspect of the operation. Their vision, their hope, and their belief in the future of commercial aviation had indeed reached fruition, and helped build a city far beyond the imagination of either. That architectural edifice, however, was not about just Walter Long and Max Bickler; it symbolized the expectations of many civic leaders who foresaw Austin's social, cultural, and economic potential and helped build a city that turned the vision into reality. Nor did Austin-Bergstrom have its beginning on the morning of March 6, 1995, when the first crew of workmen began rebuilding the airport's south access road. Its origins reach much further back in time, to that October morning in 1911 when Cal Rodgers landed the first airplane in Austin, to Camp Mabry and Penn Field, to the early barnstormers in their Curtiss "Jennies" who first awakened Austin citizens to the potentials of commercial aviation. Austin grew on ideas, ideas for the future, and finally it happened. Austin-Bergstrom International Airport stands today as a tribute to all who have gone before, each of whom gave some part of themselves to make it possible.

CONCLUSION

O NE underlying theme of twentieth-century American history is the expanding role of aviation in business, industry, and national defense, as well as private flying. The American geographic and philosophical circumstances deemed it so. "The sheer immensity of our country, its width and breadth, provided a natural environment for the airplane. The dynamism of the American outlook did the rest," wrote aviation historian Patricia Strickland.[1] By the very nature of aviation, the American city emerged as the focal point of that development, and within the broad scope of that experience, each individual city responded within a strongly similar pattern. Therefore, Austin, Texas, when examined within that context, emerges as a microcosm of a national phenomenon. Austin, like

Muncie, Winston-Salem, Tallahassee, and Tulsa, reacted to the total complex of forces, both local and national, and established an aviation infrastructure to serve that community's individual needs. Yet, when projected nationally, a marked commonality emerges, and within that projection local events assume added relevance.

The excitement ignited by Cal Rodgers' Austin appearance, for example, was essentially a national phenomenon; the initial appearance of manned flight, wherever it happened, was an unprecedented and lasting experience and had a far-reaching impact on the future of aviation. Also, the University of Texas, which sponsored the School of Military Aeronautics, was one of six state universities in the nation that also trained aviation cadets for World War I military service. Likewise, the University's School for Radio Operators had affiliates in 120 other colleges and universities across the nation. In addition, there was precedent for Walter Long's leadership in establishing Penn Field, Austin's first landing field. During World War I mobilization, civic leaders in four other Texas cities aided the military in opening six other military airfields in their respective areas. And as the nation later geared up for World War II, the Civilian Pilot Training Program, and later the War Training Service, sponsored locally by the University of Texas and Austin High School, had affiliates in 1,121 other educational institutions in forty-eight states, plus Alaska, Hawaii, the District of Columbia, and Puerto Rico. The program's success was equally astounding: more than 400,000 students won their wings while operating 7,585 training aircraft.[2] Locally, Ragsdale Flying Service and Browning Aerial Service contributed to that effort. The establishment of the Del Valle Army Airbase (later Bergstrom Air Force Base) during World War II was also part of an expanding nationwide network of Air Force training bases that included seven similar facilities in Texas.

Federal legislation, while stimulating the growth of commercial aviation, at the same time helped disseminate further the use of air transportation in more areas of the nation. The passage of the Air Mail Act of 1925, and the subsequent extension of airmail service, necessitated the establishment of adequate landing facilities, which led to the proliferation of municipal airports. When Austin's Robert Mueller Municipal Airport opened on October 30, 1930, there were in Texas alone 133 airports in service; nationally, by 1970, there were more than 10,000. In the post–World War II era, with the abundance of landing facilities and the huge number of military-trained pilots, private flying grew dramatically. By the mid-1960s, some 160 corporate and privately owned aircraft were based at Austin Mueller airport; by 1970, the nation's general aviation fleet totaled 130,806 aircraft, comprising 95 percent of all 133,814 licensed aircraft in the United States.[3]

In the post–World War II era, worldwide expansion of all forms of air transportation forced readjustments in the local aviation infrastructure. Many municipal airports built in the 1930s had become encased by development, restricting expansion necessary to accommodate the high-performance aircraft of the period. That happened in New Orleans, Kansas City, Chicago, Denver, Dallas, and Washington. The same was particularly true in Texas; however, Austin's response to change differed markedly from that of the state's other major cities. While the civic leaders of San Antonio, Houston, Dallas, and Fort Worth anticipated change and purchased suburban land for new airports well in advance of the need, Austin hesitated. Some fifteen years elapsed between the first airport study that cited closing Mueller as one option and the initial announcement that Bergstrom Air Force Base would become available as Austin's next municipal airport. (Austin was not alone in acquiring a former Air Force base as a municipal airport; the same occurred in Cincinnati, Pittsburgh, Chicago, and Spokane.)[4] In retrospect, Austin, besides lacking the foresight to acquire suburban land for an eventual new airport, differed from the other four major Texas cities in airport development in two other significant aspects: one, those cities maintained their original close-in airports for general aviation and, two, they provided freeway access to their new municipal airports. The lack of freeway access to Austin-Bergstrom International Airport remains an obvious blemish on Austin's air service.

How Austin-Bergstrom International Airport came into being, its inherent problems, and its ultimate success was all about progress, urban and economic progress. Furthermore, progress in its multiple forms is part and parcel of the American psyche. It was that fundamental belief in progress that drew the first immigrants to the Atlantic Coast and ultimately drove them westward, filling up the land. During their overland trek they cleared the forests, established farms and ranches, developed the natural resources, created industries, and built cities, visible trophies of progress. American cities became meccas where people of vision and imagination gathered to exchange items of value with the belief that those values would grow and produce other items of greater value. In Austin, Texas, those items of exchange were essentially ideas.

In "Cities of Ideas," journalists Bill Bishop and Mark Lisheron identify Austin as one of twenty metropolitan centers in the nation "that by 2000 had higher than average rates of both innovative and technological production" plus growth rates double the national average.[5] Austin, with a 54 percent growth rate in the 1990s, followed the national pattern and emerged at the turn of the century a city vastly different from the one that celebrated the Mueller airport dedication on October 14, 1930. Within that time span, population increased from 51,286 to 656,562, essentially the byproduct of progress, a phenomenon identified by author Larry Landau "as an obvious fact and forgone conclusion" in American life.[6]

Progress may be a foregone conclusion, but it leaves in its wake social, cultural, economic, and philosophical problems to solve. In Austin some of those problems have been articulated as a growth versus no-growth philosophy, the "Save Our Springs" movement versus bigger and better condos on scenic hillsides, or secluded hiking paths versus sprawling shopping centers. Urban progress may also be evaluated in terms of what has been lost as well as in terms of what has been gained. On the minus side was the loss of small town innocence and provincialism: Thursday night band concerts and audience sing-alongs at Zilker Park, twenty-two-cent movie matinees at the Capitol Theater, the diving tower at Deep Eddy, the PK Grille, the Nighthawk restaurants, Fritz's Barn, the lunch counter at Woolworth's, downtown shopping on Saturday nights, and city streets free of traffic congestion. On the positive side, as a byproduct of progress, the Capital City has achieved a measure of urban sophistication that includes expanded educational, recreational, and cultural opportunities that include neighborhood parks, playgrounds, and libraries; a ballet society; an opera company; a symphony orchestra; live theater; expanded medical care, including some fifteen hospitals and medical centers; and unlimited shopping facilities. In balancing the present with the past, it can be argued that progress has indeed left a positive imprint on the Capital City.

And so we come to the end of this nine-decade survey of aviation activity in Austin, Texas. It is a huge leap from that October day in 1911 when Cal Rodgers first landed his Wright biplane at Austin's Ridge Top Annex to the opening of Austin-Bergstrom International Airport on May 23, 1999. That story, in itself, provides additional insight into how and why the city grew, but projecting those local events into a national context yields an additional dimension to the broader knowledge of the topic. And while Richard Kriss, whomever he may be, may still find automobile travel to Austin-Bergstrom International Airport difficult, there are many others who seem to have found a way. And still it grows.

NOTES

Preface

1. Joseph J. Corn, *The Winged Gospel: America's Romance with Aviation, 1900–1950*, p. 135.

Introduction

1. In 1910, the population of Austin was 29,860 and Forty-fifth Street marked the city's northern boundary.

2. For a comprehensive study of the Wright brothers' achievements, see Walter J. Boyne, *The Wright Flyer: An Engineering Perspective,* and Marvin W. McFarland, ed., *The Papers of Orville and Wilbur Wright.*

3. Charles Howard Gibbs-Smith, *Aviation: An Historical Survey from Its Origins to the End of World War II.*

4. Boyne, *The Wright Flyer,* p. 1.

5. Eileen F. Lebow, *Cal Rodgers and the Vin Fiz: The First Transcontinental Flight,* p. 41.

6. Ibid., p. 40.

7. Ibid. For more information on Glenn Curtiss, see C. R. Roseberry, *Glenn Curtiss: Pioneer of Flight.*

8. Gibbs-Smith, *Aviation,* p. 157.

9. Commodore Matthew Calbraith Perry headed the 1853–1854 naval expedition that forced Japan to enter into trade and diplomatic relations with the West after more than two centuries of isolation. Commodore John Rodgers dictated the peace terms to the Algerian pirates, while a granduncle, Commodore Oliver Hazard Perry, won the Battle of Lake Erie and sent the famous message, "We have met the enemy and they are ours." Calbraith Perry Rodgers also planned a naval career but failed his physical at the United States Naval Academy because of partial deafness.

10. Lebow, *Cal Rodgers,* p. 60.

11. David Young and Neal Callahan, *Fill the Heavens with Commerce: Chicago Aviation, 1855–1926,* p. 45.

12. Anticipating accidents along the route, Hearst stipulated that while the aircraft could be repaired, and even rebuilt, the winner must use the same plane throughout the flight. Hearst believed such a flight "would encourage prosperity for millions, advance the knowledge of aerial science and navigation, and, best of all, put America 'at the head of all aviation activities, just as America was first to perfect the art of flying.'" Ibid., p. 71.

13. Calbraith Rodgers was not without competition in the transcontinental flight. Robert Fowler was already flying eastward from San Francisco, while James West departed from

Governor's Island, New York, three days before Rodgers left Sheepshead Bay. Subsequently, both Fowler and West abandoned the flight.

14. Tom Mahoney, "The First Airman across America," *The American Legion Magazine,* March 1965, p. 21.

15. With the power plant located behind the pilot, the propeller pushes the aircraft forward. Later types of planes, having the power plant located in front of the pilot and being pulled forward by the propeller, were designated "tractors."

16. Ibid., p. 23.

17. Lebow, *Cal Rodgers,* p. 99.

18. Mahoney, "The First Airman," p. 50.

1. Cal, Glenn, Bennie, and the Origins of Austin Aviation

1. The name of the real estate development appears in two forms, Ridge Top and Ridgetop. The latter remains in current usage.

2. Historians Lebow (*Cal Rodgers,* p. 169) and Walter E. Long (*Wings over Austin,* p. 5) cite Rodgers' fee as $150; the *Austin Daily Statesman* places the amount at $200.

3. *Austin Daily Statesman,* October 21, 1911.

4. Corn, *The Winged Gospel,* p. 4.

5. Roseberry, *Glenn Curtiss,* p. 286.

6. *Austin Daily Statesman,* November 5, 1911. Camp Mabry was established in 1890 as a summer encampment of the Texas Volunteer Guard, a forerunner of the National Guard.

7. Ibid., November 22, 1911.

8. Ibid., November 23, 1911.

9. No published accounts of airplane landings in Austin were found for this period.

10. *Austin Daily Statesman,* January 6, 1913.

11. Carroll V. Glines, *The Compact History of the United States Air Force,* p. 66.

12. *Austin Daily Statesman,* see appropriate dates.

13. Benjamin D. Foulois, with Carroll V. Glines, *From the Wright Brothers to the Astronauts,* p. 21.

14. Glines, *Compact History,* p. 56.

15. Roseberry, *Glenn Curtiss,* p. 397. The original operations model, the JN-2, was extremely unstable in the air, which resulted in several fatal accidents. The 1915 version, the JN-3, was used during Pershing's Punitive Expedition into Mexico. Its poor performance made it unsuited for field operations. The next developmental model, the JN-4, appeared in 1916; more than six thousand were produced for the Signal Corps. Powered by a 90-horsepower, water-cooled Curtiss OX-5 engine, the JN-4 could attain a maximum speed of seventy-five miles per hour and cost $5,465. In addition to the production at the Hammondsport, New York, plant, Glenn Curtiss produced the Canadian version of the JN-4, frequently referred to as the "Canuck."

16. That site is presently bounded by North Lamar Boulevard, Forty-fifth Street, and Guadalupe Street.

17. *Austin Daily Statesman,* November 24, 1915. Captain Foulois remembered, "The only mixup came when Lt. Joe Carberry was leading the formation between Waco and Austin. A strong wind blew him off course, and we followed him. After discovering his error, each of us landed at various places, asked directions, and then flew on our own to Austin." Foulois, *From the Wright Brothers,* p. 121.

18. *Austin Daily Statesman,* November 23, 1915.

19. Ibid.

20. Col. Frank Tompkins, *Chasing Villa: The Story behind the Story of Pershing's Expedition into Mexico,* Appendix B, p. 243. Captain Foulois reported that "during the first month's operation of the Squadron, March 19th to April 20th, five of the eight airplanes taken into Mexico were wrecked and one, which was damaged in a forced landing . . . was abandoned, so that on the 20th only two airplanes . . . remained. . . . They were flown back to Columbus, N.M., and ultimately condemned and destroyed."

21. Foulois, *From the Wright Brothers,* p. 136. See also Maj. Gen. Benjamin D. Foulois, ". . . And Teach Yourself to Fly," *Reader's Digest,* October 1960, pp. 50–54.

2. Austin, the University of Texas, and World War I

1. Ernest R. May, *The World War and American Isolation, 1914–1917,* p. 3.

2. Lewis L. Gould, *Progressives and Prohibitionists: Texas Democrats in the Wilson Era,* p. 161.

3. Foulois, *From the Wright Brothers,* pp. 147–148.

4. Ibid., pp. 145–146. Preparing the 1916 budget, the Aviation Section of the Signal Corps requested "a little over 1 million dollars." On March 4, 1915, Congress appropriated only $300,000. "At that time the entire Aviation Section consisted of only 29 officers, 155 enlisted men and less than 20 planes" (Glines, *Compact History,* p. 67).

5. May, *The World War,* p. 42.

6. In the election of 1916, when Woodrow Wilson defeated the Republican nominee, Charles Evans Hughes, his supporters claimed, "He kept us out of war."

7. On March 3, 1915, Congress established the National Advisory Committee for Aeronautics (NACA) to conduct research in aviation.

8. Telegram from Robert E. Vinson to F. W. Graff, University of Texas Presidents Office Records, T. S. Painter Records, The Center for American History, University of Texas at Austin, Box VF 13/E.b. Cited hereafter as Painter Records, UT-CAH. The six universities invited to the Toronto conference were Massachusetts Institute of Technology, Cornell University, Ohio State University, the University of Illinois, University of California, and University of Texas. In *Wings over Austin,* Long, former manager of the Austin Chamber of Commerce, wrote: "The Chamber paid the expenses of Dr. Vinson to and from Washington, and for his stays there on some eleven trips. The Manager of the Chamber was kept in Washington throughout the fall and part of the winter of 1917." (Although Walter

Long and the Austin Chamber of Commerce played a major role in promoting aviation for Austin, Chamber records for that period were not available for this research.) As compensation for his three-day meeting in Toronto, Dr. J. M. Bryant received $150.53, which covered railroad transportation, meals, telegraph, telephone, and tailor. Painter Records, UT-CAH.

9. Dr. Theophilus S. Painter later served as president of the University of Texas, from 1946 to 1954. Information that follows on the professors' experience at RFC headquarters in Toronto is from "History of the School of Military Aeronautics," unpublished manuscript prepared by Dr. J. M. Bryant, University of Texas, July 10, 1919, in Painter Records, UT-CAH; cited hereafter as Bryant Manuscript. Quotations are from pp. 8, 10, 11, 14, and 16. RFC Lieutenant Pack's name is also spelled Peck.

10. Telegram from J. M. Bryant to Robert E. Vinson, May 8, 1917, Painter Records, UT-CAH.

11. In general, the following information on the organization and operations of the School of Military Aeronautics is derived from the Bryant Manuscript. Unless otherwise noted, quotations are from that manuscript (pp. 21, 23, 81, 102, and 107).

12. After the war Percy Pennybacker joined the Texas Highway Department, later the Texas Department of Transportation, as a bridge engineer, where he remained until retirement. Theodore L. Bellmont, who served as athletic director for the University of Texas at Austin, expanded the scope of intercollegiate athletics at that institution and was one of the first four named to the Longhorn Hall of Honor in 1957. Bellmont Hall on the University campus is named in his honor.

13. In Dr. Vinson's report to the University Board of Regents, he cites May 21, 1917, as the date the School of Military Aeronautics opened. The University was to receive $50 per student for an eight-week course. Brackenridge Hall ("B" Hall) rental was $4,800 annually; the initial lease ran from June 30, 1917, to July 1, 1918. Painter Records, UT-CAH.

14. "Little Campus" included ten brick buildings containing some 100,000 square feet of floor space, plus a parade ground.

15. Interview with Mrs. John A. McCurdy, her daughter Marian, and her son-in-law, Richard Robertson, Austin, Texas, February 9, 1998.

16. *Austin Statesman,* December 10, 1917.

17. Ibid., January 20, 1918.

18. *The Daily Texan,* March 20, 1918. The University of Texas also operated a concurrent military automobile mechanics program, the Air Service School of Automobile Mechanics, at facilities provided at Camp Mabry.

19. Weekly Progress Reports, Air Service School for Radio Operators, Texas War Records, UT-CAH, Box 2J342. Hereafter Weekly Progress Reports are generally cited in the text by date.

20. Weekly Progress Report, August 5, 1918. Thirteen of the most advanced students were sending and receiving fourteen words per minute, while the two slowest reported only eight words per minute.

21. *The Daily Texan,* March 29, 1918.

22. A copy of the lease drawn between H. D. Gruene, John Marbach, and Harry Landa, all of New Braunfels, Texas, and the Austin Chamber of Commerce is in the Walter E. Long Collection at the Austin History Center, Austin, Texas. Dated March 3, 1917, the lease terminated on January 1, 1919. The initial rent was $3,180, and the lease was renewable for $10 per acre paid in advance. The actual acreage provided for in this document was 316.25.

23. Letter from Walter E. Long to Lt. Col. C. G. Edgar, April 15, 1918; Walter E. Long to Lt. Newell Thomas, Fort Sam Houston, Texas, April 17, 1918. Long Collection, Austin History Center, Austin Public Library, cited hereafter as Long Collection.

24. Penn was killed in an airplane crash in Italy on May 20, 1918.

25. *Austin Statesman,* April 19, 1918.

26. Long, *Wings over Austin,* p. 19.

27. *Austin Statesman,* February 25, 1918. Other Kelly Field cadets were not as fortunate. In 1917 and 1918, plane crashes at Kelly Field and in the surrounding area became so frequent the Air Service organized "wrecking crews" to recover the damaged aircraft. A crew consisted of a senior officer or a sergeant, a mechanic, plus two or three assistants. The crews traveled in heavy trucks that pulled a flat bed trailer sufficiently large to carry a JN-4 aircraft with wings disassembled. After receiving a crash report, a "wrecking crew" went to the crash site to recover the damaged aircraft. John M. Loeblin, *Memories of Kelly Field, 1917–1918,* UT-CAH.

28. Austin Chamber of Commerce Annual Report, 1918. Copy in author's files.

29. *Austin Statesman,* July 31, 1918.

30. Contract, dated August 1, 1918, creating the Penn Field Radio School; contract agreement between J. F. Johnson and R. E. Vinson, University of Texas Presidents Office Records, 1907–1968, UT-CAH, Box VF 13/E.a.

31. *Austin Statesman,* July 31, 1918.

32. Ibid., September 22, 1918. Major George W. Littlefield's gifts to the University of Texas include a fund to promote the study of Southern history, purchase the Wrenn Library, build the Littlefield Dormitory, and construct the south entrance to the campus, which commemorates Southern statesmen. See also J. Evetts Haley, *George W. Littlefield, Texan* (1943), and R. E. Vinson, "The University Crosses the Bar," *Southwestern Historical Quarterly,* vol. 42 (1939–1940).

33. *Wings over Austin,* p. 19.

34. *Austin Statesman,* October 10, 1918.

35. Weekly Progress Report, November 17, 1918.

36. Bryant Manuscript, pp. 55–57. Besides the School of Military Aeronautics, the other war emergency schools operated by the University of Texas and their enrollments were the Air Service School of Automobile Mechanics, 5,106, and the Air Service School for Radio Operators, 1,731. Enrollment for the three schools totaled 13,795. These totals do not include the Students Military Training Corps.

37. Ibid., p. 172. See also Painter Records, UT-CAH, Box VF 13/E.a.

38. R. E. Vinson to Col. A. L. Fuller, May 5, 1919, Painter Records, UT-CAH, Box VF 13/E.a. At that point the School of Military Aeronautics account had not been resolved.

39. The purchase of land by the United States government requires an act of Congress; however, during World War I, Congress delegated that authority to the secretary of war.

40. Letter from the Chairman, Board of Control, United States Army Schools, University of Texas, to President R. E. Vinson, University of Texas Presidents Office Records, UT-CAH, Box VF 13/E.a.

41. *Austin Statesmen,* July 17, 1919. Sam Sparks, a resident of Travis County, was president of the Texas Trust Company of Austin, Texas. After Sparks acquired the property, the Woodward Truck Body Company manufactured wooden truck bodies in the Penn Field buildings until the plant was destroyed by a tornado on May 22, 1923. The buildings were reconstructed and later occupied by the Woodward furniture factory.

42. Letter from Commanding Officer to Dr. R. E. Vinson, August 8, 1919, UT-CAH, Box VF 13/E.a.

43. *Austin Statesman,* September 4, 1919. Since the United States government issued the final check after the terminal date for collecting the Texas War Records, no record of that transaction is found in this collection.

3. Barnstormers, Businessmen, and High Hopes for the Future

1. Glines, *Compact History,* pp. 83–84. See also David Anderson, *The History of the United States Air Force,* and Alfred Goldberg, *A History of the United States Air Force.*

2. Nick A. Komons, *Bonfires to Beacons: Federal Civil Aviation Policy under the Air Commerce Acts of 1926 and 1938.*

3. The Curtiss JN-4 "Jenny" was well adapted for landing on unprepared surfaces, specifically cow pastures. With modified high-lift wings, it could be landed as slowly as thirty-five miles an hour. In the event the water-cooled V-8 ninety-horsepower OX-5 engine failed, the Jenny's slow landing speed favored survival. For more information on the Curtiss JN-4, see Paul O'Neil, *Barnstorming and Speed Kings.*

4. The initial transcontinental flight departed Mineola, New York, at 6:30 A.M. on September 8, 1920, carrying four hundred pounds of mail. The scheduled three-day trip was forty-two hours less than the time specified in the train schedule. The 2,651-mile flight included stops at Cleveland, Chicago, Omaha, Cheyenne, Salt Lake City, Reno, and San Francisco. *Austin Statesman,* September 9, 1920.

5. *The [Austin] Statesman,* May 1 and 3, 1919.

6. The Austin Chamber of Commerce Annual Report for 1923.

7. Letter from Max Bickler to Lt. Robert D. Kapp, March 13, 1923, Max Bickler Collection, Austin History Center, Austin, Texas. Cited hereafter as Bickler Collection, AHC.

8. Max Bickler to Capt. Burdette S. Wright, March 17, 1923; Bickler to Charles J. Glidden, April 23, 1923; and Glidden to Bickler, April 23, 1923. Bickler Collection, AHC.

9. Max Bickler to Maj. H. H. Hickman, May 21, 1923; Paul Henderson to Max Bickler, May 29, 1923. Bickler Collection, AHC.

10. Long, *Wings over Austin,* pp. 20–21. The two biplanes operated by Watson and McClelland were identified as Lincoln Standard LS-5s. Long cites the acreage in the Webb Ruff property (University Airport) as 178 acres. However, according to the Travis County land records, Webb Ruff purchased a 138-acre tract from C. A. Nelson on September 28, 1926, which became his base of operations, known as University Airport. That facility had no affiliation with the University of Texas. Office of the County Clerk, Travis County Texas, Recorded vol. 225, page 590, September 28, 1926. R. B. Dickard and Associates owned the 62-acre site occupied by the Austin Air Service. Because of the itinerant nature of barnstorming and the early fixed base operators, no other records of these local operations exist.

11. *The Statesman,* February 2 and 3, April 20, 27, and 28, and May 2, 1926.

12. Ibid., June 6, 11, and 26, August 9, and September 19 and 25, 1926.

13. Ibid., June 13 and July 11, 1926. Benny (Benjamin O.) Howard later developed a series of racing planes, many of which he flew himself. He also manufactured commercial aircraft and later became a test pilot for Douglas Aircraft Corporation.

14. *The Sunday American-Statesman,* September 4, 1927.

15. *American-Statesman* (Combined Edition), September 5, 1927. Competition winners were as follows: 20 miles speed race, 90-hp and under, Howard Woodall of Dallas flying a Travelair; altitude race, 2,000 feet and down, Howard Woodall; Landing to Mark, Reginald Robbins of Fort Worth flying a Standard biplane; Acrobatic Flying, Upside Down Flying, and the Free-for-All Speed Race, Howard Woodall. Aircraft types represented were Travelair, Swallow, Eaglerock, and Standard. Since Grace McClelland had collected the prize money from Austin merchants, pilots from the Austin Air Service were disqualified from competition. Pilots from University Airport represented Austin. According to the newspaper report, Stratton had completed only five of the twelve hours of instruction then required for student flyers.

16. Komons, *Bonfires to Beacons,* p. 21.

17. *Airmail Act of 1925, United Statutes at Large* 43 (1925): 805–806. This was also known as the Kelly Air Mail Act, sponsored by Congressman Clyde Kelly of Pennsylvania. The contracts were let under competitive bidding; the transfer to private operations was completed in September 1927. (Initially, *airmail* was spelled as two words.)

18. *Air Commerce Act of 1926, United States Statutes at Large* 44 (1926): 568–576. This act provided for navigation facilities, airworthiness of aircraft, periodic examinations for pilot proficiency, dissemination of weather information, establishment of air traffic rules, and designation of federal airways.

19. "On May 21 [1925] Howard E. Coffin announced the formation of National Air Transport [NAT]. Capitalized at $10,000,000, with $2,000,000 already paid in by the company's organizers, NAT represented 'the most ambitious attempt to promote air transportation

in the country.' Its board of directors—a veritable Who's Who of the nation's financial and industrial establishment—included Philip K. Wrigley, Lester Armour, William A. Rockefeller, C. F. Kettering, and John Hays Hammond." William M. Leary, *Aerial Pioneers: The U.S. Air Mail Service, 1918–1927,* p. 224. By 1928, Wright Aeronautical stock had passed General Motors in price. Wright stock reached an all-time high of $214, a gain of $15 per share over the previous close. *The Statesman,* May 15, 1928.

20. *The Statesman,* May 13, 1926.

21. Text of a public address on the promotion of airmail for Austin, Texas, Bickler Collection, AHC.

22. *Austin Statesman,* April 29, 1926.

23. Unidentified newspaper clipping, dated May 31, 1926, Airmail Service File, AHC.

24. *Austin Statesman,* September 15, 1926.

25. Charles A. Lindbergh, *We,* p. 136.

26. R. E. G. Davis, *Airlines of the United States since 1914,* p 56.

27. Advertisement for Air Mail Service, Post Office Department, Washington, D.C., June 15, 1927. Braniff Collection, History of Aviation Collection, University of Texas at Dallas.

28. *Austin Statesman,* August 1, 1927.

29. *Austin American,* December 29, 1927.

30. *Austin Statesman,* February 6, 1928. Southbound, the Texas Air Transport airmail plane departed Dallas at 7:45 A.M.; Fort Worth, 8:15; Waco, 9:20; Austin 10:25; San Antonio, 11:15; and arrived at Laredo at 12:55 P.M. Northbound, the plane departed Laredo at 2:55 P.M.; San Antonio, 4:15; Austin, 5:10; Waco, 6:25; Fort Worth, 7:15; and arrived at Dallas at 7:47. Air Mail File, AHC.

31. Unidentified newspaper clipping, dated February 7, 1928, Airmail Service File, AHC.

32. Competition from an efficient system of public ground transportation was another deterrent to the development of airline passenger traffic. However, the future development of commercial air transportation would virtually eliminate most forms of scheduled ground transportation.

33. Albert E. Blomquist, *Outline of Air Transport Practice,* p. 17.

34. *The Austin Statesman,* March 25, 1929; August 25, 1926; April 1, 1931.

35. *Sunday American-Statesman,* October 3, 1926.

36. Text of public address, "Air Mail Service," Bickler Collection, AHC.

37. Letter from Hunter Barrett, Fort Worth, Texas, November 8, 1999. A. P. Barrett received a bachelor of science degree from East Texas State Normal College, and a law degree from the University of Texas in 1905. He was elected to the Texas Legislature while still attending the University. He was the youngest member ever elected to the legislature and the youngest member of the Senate.

38. Interview with Frank Taylor, Round Rock, Texas, November 20, 1999.

39. Telephone interview with A. P. Barrett, November 3, 1999.

40. C. R. Smith was elected president of American Airlines in October 1934, at the age of thirty-five. Also see Robert J. Serling, *Eagle: The History of American Airlines.*

41. *The Austin Statesman,* August 19, 1927. Two planning engineers for the City of Austin, identified as "Koch and Fowler," had already submitted plans for an airport located in downtown Austin. The new city plan, distributed publicly on February 12, 1928, recommended locating "an airport on the south bank of the Colorado river between Congress avenue and the I&G.N [International-Great Northern] railroad . . . just north of Barton Springs road . . . It would be convenient of access to the downtown district of Austin [and] for air mail delivery to the post office" (*The Sunday Morning News, City Plan Supplement,* Austin, Texas, February 12, 1928). A group of fourteen Austin civic leaders funded this apparent one-time publication. No other reference to *The Sunday Morning News* has been found.

42. *American-Statesman,* March 4 and May 19, 1928.

43. Janet R. Bednarek, *America's Airports: Airfield Development, 1918–1947,* pp. 178–179.

44. "List Of Sites Offered For Airport," Bickler Collection, AHC.

45. Claire L. Chennault, who as a general became air advisor to Gen. Chiang Kai-shek and formed the Flying Tigers to combat Japanese air superiority.

46. Lt. C. C. Chennault to Hon. P. W. McFadden, July 20, 1928, Bickler Papers, AHC.

47. Ibid. Neither the Matthews nor Giles properties appear on the original list of available sites. Lt. Chennault rejected the University Airport site because of its remote location, as well as its "rolling" and "irregular contours." He dismissed the Austin Air Service field because of its "small and . . . irregular shape." The Austin Air Service field would eventually be incorporated with the municipal airport acreage. Lt. Chennault considered the remaining sites as "unsatisfactory from practically every consideration mentioned heretofore." Chennault Report, Bickler Papers, AHC.

48. Robert Mueller Municipal Airport Land Acquisition Folder File 4905, City of Austin Engineering File Room. When the City of Austin completed the municipal airport expansion on September 28, 1962, ninety-nine different parcels of land had been acquired, totaling some one thousand acres.

49. Max Bickler to Leigh Wade, Consolidated Aircraft Corp., Buffalo, New York, September 5, 1930. Bickler Collection, AHC. The "flicker light" emitted a code identifying the airport; the "ceiling light" determined the height of the cloud base. Since the City of Austin Public Works Department administered the airport construction, no separate accounting of those expenditures are available.

50. *Austin American,* October 15, 1930.

51. Platform guests included Mrs. Dan Moody and son Dan Jr., representing the governor; J. K. Berreta, San Antonio, vice president of the National Aeronautics Association; Mrs. W. M. Randolph, widow of the late United States Air Service pilot for whom Randolph Field (later Randolph Air Force Base) was named; and Army Air Corps pilot Lt. Lester J. Maitland, who, accompanied by Lt. Albert Heggenberger, made the first nonstop flight from Oakland, California, to Hawaii.

52. *Description of Airports and Landing Fields in the United States,* Airways Bulletin No. 2 (Washington, D.C., Department of Commerce, Aeronautics Branch, September 1, 1931), pp. 140–141.

53. Ibid.

4. A Bright Side of the Great Depression

1. *Texas Business Review,* July 28, 1932, p. 203.

2. Information and quotations in this and the following paragraph are from *Aero Digest,* January 1930, p. 92; February 1930, p. 202; and September 1930, p. 68.

3. *Austin American,* February 25, 1931.

4. *Fort Worth Star-Telegram,* November 1, 1931.

5. Powered by a Pratt & Whitney 450-horsepower, SC-1 radial engine, the Lockheed "Vega" had a maximum speed of 185 miles per hour. David Donald (gen. ed.), *The Complete Encyclopedia of World Aircraft,* p. 569. Hereafter cited as *Encyclopedia of Aircraft.*

6. The Saturday, May 16, 1931, edition of the *Austin American* contains only a brief announcement of the inaugural Bowen flight that was to occur the following day. There was no follow-up coverage of the first flight, as on previous occasions, and no mention of a traditional airport welcoming ceremony accorded the carriers.

7. Photocopy of a Bowen Air Lines brochure dated May 17, 1931, Aviation Collection, University of Texas at Dallas; interview with Jim Criswell, San Antonio, Texas, August 9, 1999. Jim Criswell was the person responsible for spreading the "wagon sheet."

8. *Aero Digest,* November 1930, p. 130.

9. Ibid., June 1930, p. 164.

10. Long, *Wings over Austin,* p. 23.

11. *Austin Statesman,* October 14, 1930.

12. *Aero Digest,* September 1931, p. 92. Aviation progress stimulated local interest in the industry. In 1931, Walter Wade Everts of San Antonio formed Everts Aero Motors, Inc., to manufacture a new type of aviation engine of his own design. W. F. Smith, former superintendent of Tips Engine Works of Austin, planned to construct the engine, while A. Vallance, an associate professor of engineering at the University of Texas, served as technical advisor. There is no record of this engine ever being manufactured. (*Aero Digest,* January 1931, p. 112).

13. Ibid., September 1931.

14. *Austin American,* September 14, 1931.

15. *Fort Worth Star-Telegram,* November 1, 1931.

16. *Aero Digest,* March 1932, p. 44; July 1932, p. 43; April 1933, p. 24.

17. Letter from C. R. Smith, Vice-President, American Airways, Inc., Southern Division, Love Field, Dallas, Texas, to Adam Johnson, City Manager, City of Austin, July 27, 1931.

Austin Chamber of Commerce Files, Austin History Center, cited hereafter as Chamber of Commerce Files. The 1933 Austin Chamber of Commerce Annual Report placed the amount of the transaction at $8,000 (p. 48). The actual cost of the hangar was $6,900, according to *Aero Digest* (January 1933, p. 81).

18. *Aero Digest,* January 1932, p. 81.

19. 1932 Austin Chamber of Commerce Annual Report, p. 59.

20. Letter from William J. Mackenzie, Airport Specialist, to Chief, Airport Section, Aeronautics Branch, Department of Commerce, Washington, D.C., April 23, 1932, Aviation Collection, AHC. The Air Commerce Act empowered the Aeronautics Branch of the Department of Commerce to rate airports. However, the rating system was voluntary; ratings ranged from A to E. "'A' airports had extensive lighting systems including beacons, boundary lights, obstruction lights, a landing area flood-lighting system, and all-night operation of all lighting equipment." (Komons, *Bonfires to Beacons,* pp. 45–46.) No record of the rating accorded Robert Mueller Municipal Airport could be found; however, since Mueller was considered an "all weather" facility, it probably received an "A" rating.

21. 1934 Austin Chamber of Commerce Report, p. 55.

22. Criswell interview, August 9, 1999.

23. Interview with Sam Wilborn, Austin, Texas, June 26, 1997. Sam Wilborn soloed after three hours and fifteen minutes of instruction; the average was ten hours. His first passenger was his mother. "Dead stick landing" is an aviation term meaning landing an airplane without power. The Curtiss-Wright "Junior" was a small two-place aircraft designed for primary flight instruction. Wilborn later graduated from medical school and became a successful Austin pediatrician. He owned several different airplanes, logged some five thousand hours, and continued flying until the age of 82.

24. *Aero Digest,* August 1933, pp. 28 and 36.

25. *American Statesman,* July 1, 1933. It remains unclear when the city's contract with Gifford Flying Service ended. Immediately following Naylor's death, Webb Ruff's cousin Rudolph (Doc) Haile managed the municipal airport under a temporary agreement.

26. Proclamation, Governor Miriam A. Ferguson's Records (RG301); Letter from C. R. Smith to Gov. Miriam A. Ferguson, December 15, 1933, Archives and Information Services Division, Texas State Archives.

27. Komons, *Bonfires to Beacons,* p. 225.

28. *Air Mail Act of 1925,* pp. 805–806.

29. Postmaster Walter Folger Brown believed that "there was no sense in taking this government's money and dishing it out . . . to every little fellow that was flying around the map and was not going to do anything . . . to develop aviation in the broad sense. Mail subsidies should go to the well-financed lines capable of providing a first-rate passenger service over long continuous routes. . . . Opening the old mail routes to competitive bidding was unthinkable. It was the surest way to perpetuate . . . the existing chaos." Komons, *Bonfires to Beacons,* p. 198.

30. U.S. Congress, House, *Amended Air Mail Act,* H. Rpt. 1209, 71st Congress, 2nd Session, 920, 2–4.

31. Foulois, *From the Wright Brothers,* p. 236. See also Robert M. Kane and Allan D. Voss, *Air Transportation,* p. 28.

32. Kane and Voss, *Air Transportation,* p. 29.

33. Komons, *Bonfires to Beacons,* p. 263. See also U.S. Congress, Senate, *Revisions of Air-Mail Laws, Hearings before the Committee on Post Offices and Post Roads,* 73d Cong., 2d Sess., 1934, p. 70. The latter provision was directed to aviation holding companies like United Aircraft, which owned the Boeing Company, which designed and constructed the airframe; Pratt-Whitney, which built the engine; Hamilton Standard, which manufactured the propeller; and United Airlines, which operated the mail and passenger service.

34. *Aero Digest,* June 1934, p. 56.

35. *Air Mail Act of 1934, U.S. Statutes at Large* 48 (1934) 933–939.

36. *Austin Statesman,* September 19, 1934.

37. City of Austin, Texas, Appropriations—Engineering Department, for the years 1932, 1933, 1934, and 1935, AHC.

38. 1936 Austin Chamber of Commerce Report, pp. 61–62.

39. *Fort Worth Star-Telegram,* March 21, 1935.

40. William F. Salathe to Max Bickler, March 21, 1935, Bickler Collection, AHC.

41. *Sunday Austin Statesman,* April 7, 1935.

42. *American Statesman,* May 22 and 27, 1935.

43. 1936 Austin Chamber of Commerce Annual Report, p. 62.

44. Roger Bilstein and Jay Miller, *Aviation in Texas,* p. 46.

45. *Fort Worth Star-Telegram,* February 16, 1936.

46. 1936 Austin Chamber of Commerce Annual Report, pp. 62–63.

47. 1937 Austin Chamber of Commerce Annual Report, pp. 87 and 89.

48. Donald C. Walbridge to President, Austin Chamber of Commerce, March 19, 1936, Chamber of Commerce Files. On February 15, 1936, the Works Progress Administration released $21,090,965 for 410 airport and airway projects, to employ approximately 50,000 men. Twenty-five of the projects had been completed. Those included two airport projects under construction in Texas: Galveston, level landing field, $2,465; and Fort Worth, construct runways, $12,143. Works Progress Administration, Press Release, March 29, 1936, Chamber of Commerce Files.

49. Chamber of Commerce Files: Walbridge to Max Bickler, March 19, 1936; Bickler to Morgan, March 23, 1936; Stuart Bailey to Walter Long, August 31; Thad Holt, Assistant Administrator, Works Progress Administration, to Congressman James P. Buchanan, December 28, 1936.

50. City of Austin Appropriations, Airport Division, 1937, AHC.

51. Bednarek, *America's Airports,* p. 179.

52. *Encyclopedia of Aircraft,* pp. 357 and 571.

53. Kane and Voss, *Air Transportation,* p.31.

54. 1938 Chamber of Commerce Annual Report, p. 71.

55. *American Statesman,* October 19 and October 27, 1937.

56. Ibid., August 25 and October 2, 1938.

5. War Training Returns to the University

1. Foulois, *From the Wright Brothers,* p. 142.

2. Patricia Strickland, *The Putt-Putt Air Force: The Story of the Civilian Pilot Training Program and the War Training Service, 1939–1944,* p. 3.

3. *Aero Digest,* May 1939, p. 36.

4. Strickland, *The Putt-Putt Air Force,* p. 4.

5. *Civilian Pilot Training Act, U.S. Statutes at Large* 53 (1939), pp. 855 ff.

6. Letter from Walter E. Long to Hugh Herndon, December 7, 1939, Non-College Civilian Pilot Training Program File, Long Collection, Box AR Q.2, AHC. On October 31, 1931, Hugh Herndon and Clyde E. Pangborn made the first nonstop flight from Tokyo to Wenatachee, Washington. They covered the 4,500 miles in forty-one hours and thirteen minutes.

7. Memo from C. M. Duncan to Walter E. Long, June 11, 1940, Long Collection.

8. Interview with Norbert Wittner, Austin, Texas, November 6, 1997. Courses taught at the Non-College Civilian Pilot Training Program included History of Aviation, Civil Air Regulations, Navigation, Meteorology, Parachutes, Aircraft and Theory of Flight, Engines, Instruments, and Radio Uses and Forms.

9. Interview with Lloyd Fry Jr., Liberty Hill, Texas, February 22, 1998. Other scholarship winners were Woodrow W. Bowden, Horace L. Holley Jr., Robert C. Wilson, William W. Barnes, Ellis A. Oualline, Glen W. Spencer, Eugene Bogle, Arthur L. Sentz, and Mary A. Miller.

10. Letter from Lt. C. Dibrell Fator to Board of Governors, Aviation Committee, Chamber of Commerce, Austin, Texas, January 24, 1940. Long Collection.

11. Foregoing data from Long Collection.

12. Minutes of a meeting of the Aviation Committee, January 27, 1940, and Letter from William B. Carssow to Senator Morris Sheppard, September 22, 1940, Long Collection.

13. Lloyd Alfred Fry Jr.'s "Student Pilot Log Book," on loan in author's possession.

14. Fry interview.

15. Ibid. Fry, however, did learn to land airplanes on concrete runways. Accepted for Army Air Corps cadet training in 1942, he graduated as a first lieutenant and served as a B-24 pilot during World War II. Following twenty-six years of service, Fry retired from the United States Air Force in 1968 as a lieutenant colonel with a command pilot's rating. His CPT training obviously served him well.

16. *The Daily Texan,* January 31, 1940. Dean Woolrich envisioned a time when the demand for aeronautical engineers would exceed that of petroleum engineers, one of the engineering department's stronger fields.

17. Letter from Dr. Homer Price Rainey to the University of Texas Board of Regents, September 6, 1940. University of Texas Presidents Office Records, Box 4Q49, Texas War Records, UT-CAH.

18. Contract between the University of Texas and the Civil Aeronautics Agency, dated September 14, 1940. Texas War Records, Box 4Q49, UT-CAH. In September 1940, St. Edward's University also received authorization to establish a CPT program for twenty students. That program operated from a field located one mile southeast of the campus.

19. Venton L. Doughtie, "CAA Pilot Training, The University of Texas, September 1940– August 1944," unpublished manuscript, Texas War Records, Box 4Q464, UT-CAH.

20. Woolrich to Rainey, November 4, 1940, Texas War Records, Box 4Q464, UT-CAH. Financially, the regular staff members fared only slightly better. W. J. Carter received $250 per month; H. D. Kent, $350 per month; and Venton L. Doughtie, $400 per month.

21. The flight school operators received from $270 to $290 for each student completing the flight course. Robert H. Hinkley, Chairman, Civil Aeronautics Authority, to University Presidents, August 5, 1939. Texas War Records, Box 4Q49, UT-CAH.

22. Interview with Richard Bloomer, Austin, Texas, November 12, 1997.

23. Ray Keenan narrative, April 9, 2000, in author's possession.

24. Ibid.

25. Nine of the forty-seven trainees who failed to complete the course withdrew to enlist in the Army Air Corps. Doughtie, "CAA Pilot Training," p. 3.

26. *Encyclopedia of Aircraft,* p. 359.

27. City of Austin Engineering File Room, Folder File 4909.

28. Reuben Rountree Report. Public Works Department, City of Austin. The initial appropriation was later increased to $446,000.

29. *Aero Digest,* February 1939, p. 24.

30. Interview with Robert L. Ragsdale, Austin, Texas, November 29, 1996. Robert L. Ragsdale, who contributed greatly to this research project, was not related to the author.

31. *American-Statesman,* February 18, 1942.

32. Undated Ragsdale interview.

33. C. G. Cross received a $250 monthly salary. Minutes of the City Council, City of Austin, Texas, March 12, 1942, p. 556. Cited hereafter as City Council Minutes.

34. *American Statesman,* April 10, 1942.

35. The original site, Del Valle, was named for a Spanish land grant. In 1940, the village had three stores and a population of approximately 100.

36. *Austin Statesman,* February 17, 1942.

37. City Council Minutes, February 16, 1942, pp. 538–539. In order to expedite the measure,

the council employed the legal procedure that allowed the three required readings of a resolution to be concluded simultaneously.

38. *Austin Statesman,* March 14, 1942.

39. Undated Ragsdale interview.

40. *Austin American-Statesman,* February 4 and 18, 1942.

41. This building, located near the present intersection of Berkman Drive and East Fifty-first Street, was not part of Hammill's CPTP operation but figured in his plan to establish an Air Corps primary flying school in Austin. When the Coleman, Texas, operation developed, he abandoned the Austin plan and offered to sell the building to Robert L. Ragsdale for $2,500. Since Ragsdale had no use for a structure that large, he rejected the offer. The Austin City Council minutes contain no record of what the city paid Hammill for the structure. Undated interview with Ragsdale.

42. *Austin Statesman,* February 20, 1942.

43. City of San Antonio Aviation Department.

44. *Aero Digest,* October 1942, p. 366. In October 1942, the Post Office Department increased Braniff Airways' airmail rate to 29.58 cents per airplane mile; former rates for the company's three contract airmail routes varied from seventeen cents to twenty-eight cents (pp. 365–366). The War Department announced in April 1942, it would "take over 25% of the 340 airliners still serving the civilian needs. . . . This means that with the latest subtraction, the airlines have delivered approximately 115 aircraft to the Army." *Aero Digest,* May 1942, p. 342.

45. *Austin Statesman,* June 2, 1942.

46. Ibid., May 9, 1942.

47. *Sunday Austin-Statesman,* May 24, 1942.

48. *Austin Statesman,* July 17, 1942.

49. Ibid., August 19, 1942.

50. Ibid., September 1, 1942.

51. Letters from Assistant City Attorney to J. M. Patterson Jr., Acting City Attorney, August 3, 1943, and from J. M. Patterson Jr. to Mayor Tom Miller, August 10, 1943, Legal Files, Bergstrom Air Force Base, Office of the City Manager, City of Austin, Texas.

52. *Austin American-Statesman,* May 12, 1999; S. Sgt. Robert A. Beggs, "Brief History of Bergstrom Air Force Base, Austin, Texas." Unpublished manuscript, copy in Austin History Center, cited hereafter as Beggs, "Brief History." The Del Valley Army Air Base, originally planned as a photo-reconnaissance facility, was reassigned as a troop carrier base. With the nation engaged in a global war, accelerated troop deployment became a key ingredient in strategic planning.

For more information on military bases, see *Air Force Bases: A Directory of U.S. Air Force Installations Both in the Continental U.S. and Overseas, with Useful Information on Each Base and Its Nearby Community* and Robert Mueller, *Air Force Bases,* vol. 1: *Active Air Force Bases within the United States of America on 17 September 1982.*

Other major Air Force installations established in Texas during World War II include Carswell Air Force Base, Fort Worth; Dyess Air Force Base, Abilene; Laughlin Air Force Base, Del Rio; Goodfellow Air Force Base, San Angelo; James Connally Air Force Base, Waco; Perrin Air Force Base, Denison; and Sheppard Air Force Base, Wichita Falls.

53. Performing "touch-and-goes" is a method of teaching a student pilot to land an airplane. Once the aircraft touches the runway, power is reapplied, and the pilot takes off, circles the field, and executes another "touch-and-go." Once on the ground, the aircraft is never allowed to come to a full stop.

54. Doughtie, "CAA Pilot Training," p. 13. See also Strickland, *The Putt-Putt Air Force*.

55. The N3N trainers, designed and build by the United States Navy Bureau of Aeronautics and powered by a Wright 235-horsepower engine, had a maximum speed of 126 miles per hour. Used extensively throughout World War II, the N3Ns were designated surplus soon after the war ended. *Encyclopedia of Aircraft*, p. 682.

56. Master Records, CAA-WTS Records, Box 4Q465, UT-CAH.

57. Rountree Report, p. 5, AHC.

58. Ragsdale interview, February 4, 1997.

59. Ned Preston, agency historian, Federal Aviation Administration, searched the Administration's records and could find no record of a control tower in Austin prior to 1945. Correspondence dated May 12, 2000.

60. Undated interview with Cathryn Batson, Austin, Texas; *Austin American-Statesman*, May 22, 1999.

61. City of Austin, Department of Aviation, Summary of Operating Revenues, Expenses and Transfers from 1929–1999, Office of the Controller.

62. City Council Minutes, January 21, 1943, p. 123.

63. Ibid., August 20, 1942, p. 38, and June 10, 1943, p. 225.

64. National Park Service, National Register of Historic Places, Registration Form, Ragsdale-Browning Aerial Service Hangar, Section 8, pp. 13 and 15.

65. Austin pilots and the aircraft they operated included realtor George Sandlin (Stinson); Louis Henna Sr. (Aeronca); Robert Coltharp (Fairchild photographic plane); Charlie Green and Dr. Joe Thorn Gilbert (Stinson); G. C. (Red) Cross (Curtiss "Robin"); and the Junior Chamber of Commerce Flying Club, operated by Joe Manor and Jess Allman (Aeronca).

66. Ragsdale interview, February 4, 1997. Other civilian flying included Civil Air Patrol squadrons that operated out of Mueller, St. Edward's Airport, and Doc Haile's Airport.

67. Ragsdale interview, November 11, 1996.

68. Beggs, "Brief History," p. 5.

69. Doughtie, "CAA Pilot Training," p. 24.

70. Beggs, "Brief History," p. 7.

71. Simmons to Painter, July 2, 1945, University of Texas Presidents Office Records, Box 4Q51, UT-CAH.

6. An Era of Peace and the Growth of Private Flying

1. John Morton Blum, *V Was for Victory: Politics and American Culture during World War II*, p. 333.

2. David M. Kennedy, *Freedom from Fear: The American People in Depression and War, 1929–1945*, vol. 9 of *Oxford History of the United States*, pp. 856 and 857.

3. Interview with Robert L. Ragsdale, Austin, Texas, July 1, 2000; interview with Bruce K. Hallock, Austin, Texas, June 15, 1998.

4. *Aero Digest*, September 15, 1945, p. 53. Bruce K. Hallock, also a graduate engineer, designed, built, and flew a roadable airplane. He quickly discovered the fallacy of the concept. The combined weight of the engine and transmission compromised the flying qualities of the airplane. And there was another problem: "It took me half a day to fold the wings on it." Hallock interview.

5. *Aero Digest*, May 1, 1945, pp. 56–57. See also other *Aero Digest* articles on military surplus aircraft: "AAF Contract Termination Procedure for Surplus Property disposal," December 1, 1944, p. 51; and "Relicensing of War Surplus Planes," October 15, 1945, p. 42.

6. Ragsdale interview, February 4, 1997. Most of the surplus aircraft purchased in the Austin area were warehoused at former Air Corps training fields at Cuero and Coleman, Texas. Combat-type aircraft was also available at bargain prices. Ragsdale also acquired and flew—but did not license—a North American B-25 and P-51 and a Lockheed P-38, which cost $175.

7. *Servicemen's Readjustment Act of 1944, U.S. Statutes at Large* 58 (1944), pp. 284–291.

8. *Certificate of Charges, Negotiated Contract No. 149r-ve-64, Aero-Tel Airport, Flight Training Course, Catalogue 1, October, 1946*, pp. 29–30. To enroll in the Commercial Pilot Course, each student was required to provide (1) Certificate of Eligibility, VA Form 1953; (2) an appropriate medical certificate; and (3) a valid CAA student or private pilot certificate.

9. *Austin Telephone Directory*, Classified Section, November 1944, p. 3.

10. Report to Internal Revenue Service, Austin Flying Service File, Aero-Tel Records, Office of James B. Cain, Athens, Texas. Cited hereafter as Aero-Tel Records.

11. Pfeil's family owned and operated The Model Airplane Shop, while Cain had a substantial inheritance that included stock in several major corporations.

12. Interview with James B. Cain, Athens, Texas, November 19, 1997. It remains unclear what flight equipment Pfeil was using prior to Cain's joining the company.

13. Ibid. Ragsdale Flying Service launched a similar promotion, exhibiting a Piper J-3 "Cub" in Scarbrough's Department Store in downtown Austin.

14. William D. Pfeil and James B. Cain purchased 53.95 acres of land from Lillian L. Roberts and husband A. P. Roberts on May 21, 1946. Recorded in Vol. 792, Page 614, Travis County Deed Records. Aero-Tel Records.

15. Cain interview.

16. Note in Aero-Tel Records.

17. Cain interview.

18. *Aero-Tel Catalogue 1,* October 1946, p. 5. Aero-Tel Records.

19. Financial Statement, Aero-Tel Records. Fixed assets, including buildings and grounds, totaled $73,636.88; thirteen aircraft valued at $31,369.25; unearned portion of G.I. Flight School Contracts, $50,569.47.

20. Aero-Tel Records.

21. G.I. Flight Report, March 1 through March 23, 1947. Hourly rates for the G.I. Commercial Pilot Course were as follows: dual instruction, 65 horsepower, $10 per hour; dual instruction, 145 horsepower or over, $18 per hour; solo practice, 65 horsepower, $8 per hour; solo practice, 145 horsepower or over, $15 per hour; and ground instruction, $0.70 per hour. Each student averaged five hours of ground school instruction and five hours flight instruction each week. Students were required to complete the course in a minimum of seven weeks and a maximum of nine weeks. Each student was allowed a minimum of seventy hours and a maximum of eighty hours for the combined solo, dual, and classroom instructions. *Aero-Tel Catalogue 1,* p. 12.

22. Financial Records, Aero-Tel Records.

23. Ibid.

24. Cain interview.

25. Coleman to Cain, February 25, 1948, Aero-Tel Records.

26. Aero-Tel Inventory, April 15, 1948. Aero-Tel Records.

27. Letter from C. G. Odell, Director, Flight Training Program, to C. D. Simmons, Vice President, The University of Texas, May 5, 1948. Aero-Tel Records.

28. The University of Texas kept the property several years before phasing out the flight training program. Cain next leased the facility to E. B. Sneed, who operated the field as his private airport. He held the property until 1960, when he sold it to a developer for about five thousand dollars an acre. With the profit from the sale, Cain resolved his entire indebtedness. Glastron Boat Company later occupied that site on Burnet Road.

   After establishing residence in Athens, Texas, Cain became eminently successful in business. As a prominent civic leader, he donated the multimillion-dollar Cain Center to the City of Athens. The Cain Foundation, of which James D. Cain serves as vice-president, provides funding primarily for scientific, medical, and educational institutions.

29. Interview with Charles Quist, Austin, Texas, August 11, 1999.

30. Interview with Mary Catherine Quist Edwards, June 9, 1998.

31. Hallock interview.

32. Mary Catherine Quist Edwards interview. There was some evidence that this particular student committed suicide.

33. Charles Quist interview. PEMEX is the national oil company of Mexico.

34. Hallock interview.

35. Charles Quist interview.

36. Vol. 906, pp. 67–68, Deed Records, Travis County, Texas.

37. Vol. 1261, pp. 374–376. Ibid.

38. *Aero Digest,* January 1947, p. 55 (Piper, "Lightplanes—Today and Beyond") and pp. 56–78.

39. Komons, *Bonfires to Beacons,* pp. 378–379.

40. John R. M. Wilson, *Turbulence Aloft: The Civil Aeronautics Administration amid Wars and Rumors of War, 1938–1953,* p. 60.

41. Austin Chamber of Commerce Annual Report, January 26, 1944, vol. 29, no. 190, p. 96. Dr. Frederick, who taught Air Transportation at the University of Texas, later joined the faculty of the University of Maryland and was associated with the Glen L. Martin Research Institute.

42. "Bill Long's 'Essair' Line," *Aero Digest,* September 15, 1945, p. 42. Maj. William F. Long was also the founder and president of the Dallas Aviation School, as well as Long & Harmon Airlines, which also served the Austin market in 1934. "Feeder line" was a short-haul concept designed to bring airline service to smaller urban areas not then being served.

43. Franklin M. Beck, "Executive Planes Lead the Way," *Aero Digest,* February 1947, p. 38.

44. Other Austin women pilots included Edna Hammerman and Mary Catherine Quist.

45. Interview with Ralph E. Janes III, Austin, Texas, November 29, 2000.

46. Ibid.

47. The twin-engine six/eight-passenger Beechcraft D-18 cruised at 185 miles per hour with a cruising range of some fifteen hundred miles. First flown on January 15, 1937, the D-18 series remained in production for eighteen years. Military versions included the C-45, AT-7, and AT-11.

48. Interview with Kenneth G. Cox, Austin, Texas, December 1, 2000.

49. Interview with Dabney Cauley, Austin, Texas, November 29, 2000. Herman Heep, a Phi Beta Kappa graduate of Texas A&M University (then College), later served as a member of the Board of Directors (Regents) and left "$250,000 to the College Development Fund, less $161,473 in contributions made during his lifetime." *Austin American-Statesman,* February 11, 1960.

50. Cox interview. Herman Heep was a charter member of the Headliners Club. Sen. Lyndon B. Johnson later purchased the "Lodestar" during his vice-presidential campaign.

51. Interview with Leonard Smith, Austin, Texas, November 29 and December 3, 2000. The 16–18-seat "Lodestar" cruised at 200 miles per hour, the Hawker-Siddeley DH 125 cruised in the 600 miles-per-hour range, while the Grumann "Gulfstream" seated 10/14 passengers and cruised at 355 miles per hour (*Encyclopedia of Aircraft*). Texas governor Price Daniel used a Beechcraft D-18, while Governor Preston Smith operated a Lockheed "Lodestar." Other members of the Austin business community using personal aircraft in their businesses in the late 1940s included C. G. (Red) Cross, automobile parts dealer with stores in Austin, San Antonio, and Del Rio, who flew a Curtiss "Robin." The Taylor Refining Company, which operated a refinery in Corpus Christi, first acquired a Republic "Seebee" and later a Cessna 195, and Porter Plumbing Company, a stateside heating and air conditioning contractor, operated a Cessna 170.

52. Interview with Mrs. Emma Browning, December 16, 2000. No documentation could be found confirming the purchase of these aircraft.

53. *Annual Report of the Game, Fish and Oyster Commission, State of Texas,* for the Fiscal Years of 1946–1947, 1947–1948, 1949–1950, and 1950–1951.

54. The Texas Aeronautics Commission (TAC) was created by House Bill 309, 49th Legislature. The commission was established to assist in the development of aeronautics in the state and to cooperate with the federal government and other states in establishing a uniform aviation system. In 1989, the commission became the Texas Department of Aviation, and in 1991, the Department of Aviation merged with the Department of Highways and Public Transportation.

55. "Some Notes on Early DPS Aviation," a narrative by Jim Boutwell, copy provided author by Max Westerman, Austin, Texas. Item cited hereafter as Boutwell narrative. Boutwell later operated Tim's Air Park in Austin and served as sheriff of Williamson County. It was Boutwell who "flew cover" during the University of Texas tower massacre on August 1, 1966, sustaining several bullet holes in his Taylorcraft.

56. Boutwell narrative.

57. Ragsdale interview, February 4, 1997.

58. *State of Texas, Department of Public Safety, Annual Financial Report, September 1, 1949, through August 31, 1950,* p. 4. North American Aviation subsequently sold manufacturing rights to the "Navion" to Ryan Aircraft Corporation of San Diego, California.

59. "History of the Aircraft Section," Department of Public Safety, Austin, Texas, p. 1. The low-wing, twin-engine Cessna 310 seated six people, including the pilot, and cruised at 160 miles per hour, with a high speed of 238. The four-place, single-engine "Navion" cruised at 150 miles per hour. Both aircraft were equipped with radio, full instrumentation, and tricycle landing gear.

60. Statistical data on all aircraft is taken from *Encyclopedia of Aircraft.* After receiving a certificate to extend it routes to South America, Braniff Airways, Inc., began using the trade name Braniff International Airways. The corporate name, however, remained the same.

61. In 1948, two air carriers scheduled 8,769 departures, carrying 35,739 enplaning passengers; in 1952 6,834 departures carried 46,517 passengers. *Enplaning Airline Traffic by Community,* Civil Aeronautics Administration, Office of Airports, Washington, D.C. Cited hereafter as *Enplaning Airline Traffic.*

The Austin Chamber of Commerce remained active in supporting improved airline service to the Capital City. In 1949, the Aviation Committee, in cooperation with the Civil Aeronautics Authority, hosted two public hearings in Austin, supporting applications for transcontinental airline service, with Austin and San Antonio as intermediate stops. Also, when competing airlines challenged Braniff's Austin-Houston service, a Chamber of Commerce representative appeared before the Civil Aeronautics Board in support of continuing Braniff's certificate. Austin Chamber of Commerce Annual Report, vol. 26, January 1951, p. 206.

62. 1936 Austin Chamber of Commerce Annual Report, pp. 62–63.

63. *Encyclopedia of Aircraft.*

64. *Austin American,* November 2, 1950.

65. *Austin Statesman,* December 1, 1951.

66. City Council Minutes, May 16, 1955.

67. *Austin Statesman,* May 17, 1955.

68. Rountree Report. Between May 30, 1956, and August 27, 1989, the City of Austin acquired 275.05 acres of land for airport expansion. Folder File 4905, Engineering File Room, City of Austin, 505 Barton Springs Road, Austin, Texas.

69. *Enplaning Airline Traffic.*

70. *Austin Statesman,* September 22, 1955.

71. *Austin American-Statesman,* May 13, 1956. This did not constitute an enthusiastic endorsement by Austin citizens. Less than 12 percent of the eligible voters went to the polls. Proposition No. 4, the airport item, carried by a margin of 3.2 to 1.

72. *Austin American,* September 9, 1957.

73. *Austin Municipal Magazine,* December 1958–January 1959, p. 10. Original sketches of the Austin airport terminal building appear in the January 1959 issue of *Progressive Architecture.*

74. The Austin City Council created the Department of Aviation on September 5, 1958. Col. Murphy formerly served as base commander of Bergstrom Air Force Base.

75. The Lockheed 188 "Electra II" was first flown on December 6, 1957. A total of 170 of them had been manufactured when production ended suddenly after two of the aircraft disintegrated in flight. One such accident occurred on a Braniff flight between Houston and Dallas. The fifty-passenger, 350 miles-per-hour Vickers "Viscount," first flown on July 16, 1948, inaugurated the world's first commercial passenger service by a turbine-powered aircraft, flying twice weekly between London and Paris. The fifty-passenger, 300-mph Convair 580, "Super Convair," had been converted to prop-jet power. All aircraft were pressurized. The commercial life of these aircraft was short-lived; airlines became more interested in turbo-jet (pure jet) rather in turbo-prop powered aircraft. *Encyclopedia of Aircraft.*

7. Mueller, Marfa, and the Gathering Storm

1. Vance E. Murphy, "The Soaring Sixties," *Austin in Action,* June 1964, pp. 28–29. Travel by private aircraft was becoming increasingly popular. The following year, 1961, Dallas County reported 881 civil aircraft; Harris County (Houston, Texas), 774; Cook County (Chicago, Illinois), 1,293; and Los Angeles County, 3,026. Aviation Department, Houston Chamber of Commerce.

2. *Austin American,* April 6, 1956.

3. Ibid., May 31, 1957. At that time Ragsdale was already leasing some thirty T-hangars that

the company had constructed individually. General aviation is a generic term used to identify all phases of private aircraft operation: personal, recreational, executive, corporate, industrial, and so forth. T-hangars are individual structures, shaped in the form of a T that
houses a single aircraft.

4. Record of Commercial and Military Aircraft Sales, Cessna Aircraft Company, Wichita,
Kansas. Faced with slow post–World War II aircraft sales and a backlog of sheet metal,
Cessna began manufacturing light patio furniture.

5. *Texas Business Review,* 24, no. 12 (January 1951), pp. 5 and 20.

6. *Aircraft Bluebook Price List,* Fall 2000.

7. Bobby Browning, who literally grew up in an airplane hangar, earned his private pilot's license before he could legally have a Texas driver's license. Living some five miles from Austin High School, he would offer to take classmates flying in his airplane if they would drive
him home from school in their car.

8. *Aircraft Yearbook;* Cessna Commercial Aircraft Sales. The all-metal Cessna 172 "Skyhawk"
was comparable in price and performance with the fabric-covered Piper "Tri-Pacer."

9. Cessna Commercial Aircraft Sales.

10. Robert L. Ragsdale interview, undated.

11. Some Austin doctors who were pilots were Edward Zidd, Harold Robinson, Albert
Lalonde, Donald Pohl, Curtis Hitt, S. H. Dryden, Frank Covert, Robert Morrison,
Dewey Cooper, E. B. Smartt, Seldon Baggett, Sam Wilborn, Darrell Faubion, Milner
Thorne, Billy Frank Johnson, Hardy Thompson, Robert Farris, William Turpin, Eugene
Schoch Jr., and Robert Ellzey.

12. All company records were lost when a tornado struck the Ragsdale hangar on August 10,
1980. In 1959, Ragsdale divided the company into two units. Capitol Aviation became the
regional wholesale distributor of Cessna products, while Ragsdale Flying Service, reorganized as Ragsdale Aviation, continued as the local retail dealer. Ragsdale later owned
Cessna distributorships in Dallas and Houston, with dealerships/FBOs in Fort Worth,
Austin, and San Antonio. With a combined staff of approximately two hundred, Ragsdale's service area included all of Texas, excepting the El Paso and Lubbock-Midland areas.
Dave Shanks, "Viewpoints on Business," *Austin American-Statesman,* September 10, 1967.

13. Ragsdale interview, March 12, 1997.

14. Ibid.

15. Interview with Morris S. Johnston, Austin, Texas, September 23, 1998. Other founding
members included Albert Ross, Larry Gray, Ted Cox, and Mary Ann Collins. As the club's
first president, Morris Johnston held membership card number one. While attending San
Antonio Community College, following service in the Air Force Training Command,
Johnson helped organize the Randolph Air Force Base Flying Club in 1953.

16. *The Longhorn Flying Club,* Austin, Texas 1957, club pamphlet, copy in author's files.

17. Letter from Morris S. Johnston to Robert Crutchfield, March 20, 1967. Copy in author's
files.

18. *Austin American,* September 10, 1967. The Longhorn Flying Club, Inc. operated affiliates in the following Texas cities: Austin, San Antonio, San Marcos, Abilene, Arlington, Dallas, Galveston, San Angelo, Fort Worth, Uvalde, Sugarland, Waco, Corpus Christi, Midland, League City, Victoria, and El Paso. Out-of-state club locations included Albuquerque, New Mexico, and Durant, Oklahoma. The University of Texas archives of the Center for American History hold no records of the Longhorn Flying Club. A former board member explained that, in all probability, no records exist; they probably were purposely destroyed. The Center for American History holds two clippings of a University Flying Club, which was not active during the Spring Semester, 2001. This account of the Longhorn Flying Club is based largely on interviews with Morris S. Johnston and a small personal collection of club papers he holds, plus interviews with B. H. Amstead and Robert L. Ragsdale. The Austin club was based at Ragsdale Flying Service.

19. On December 22, 1967, the ten-thousandth Model 150 the Cessna Aircraft Company produced was delivered to the Austin chapter of the Longhorn Flying Club, Inc. This aircraft bore the registration number N 22124. *Propwash,* newsletter of the Longhorn Flying Club, January 1968. Copy in author's files.

20. Ibid., July 1968.

21. Ibid.

22. In August 1968, the board of directors consisted of R. Patton Warren, president; Richard Lee Schlitz, vice president; B. H. Amstead, secretary; and Larry Meador, treasurer. All were University of Texas students except Amstead, who was assistant dean of Engineering and professor of Mechanical Engineering.

23. Timmerman did much of the construction himself. In installing the runway lights, he opened the trench for the underground electrical cables with a tractor-drawn turning plow. For aircraft tie-downs, he dug the holes with posthole diggers and poured the concrete, in which he set a metal ring attached to a chain. Interview with Theodore R. Timmerman Jr., Pflugerville, Texas, June 26, 2000.

24. Because of the difficulty in getting telephone service, Tim's Airpark listing does not appear in the Austin telephone directory until December 1961.

25. Telephone interview with Bobby Stanton, Georgetown, Texas, May 3, 2000.

26. There were individual lenders in Dallas, Fort Worth, and San Antonio that financed personal aircraft purchases, both for individuals and fixed base operations. The percentage rates were exorbitant; 18 percent was commonplace. And if the client missed a payment by one day, the aircraft was repossessed.

27. Telephone interview with Bob Wilson, Fredericksburg, Texas, June 15, 2001.

28. Undated interview with Walter S. Chamberlain, Austin, Texas.

29. Walter S. Chamberlain, "Financing of Small Aircraft by Installment Loan Departments of Commercial Banks" (master's thesis, Southern Methodist University, 1963), p. 2. See also Robert S. Knight, "Financing of Small and Medium Size Aircraft," *Bulletin of the Robert Morris Associates,* vol. 43, no. 11 (July 1961).

30. Other Austin banks also began making personal aircraft loans on the same basis as traditional automobile financing and at current bank rates. Bob Wilson began taking flight instruction at Browning Aerial Service and soloed in seven hours. He later sold the Piper "Tri-Pacer" at a $1,000 profit and purchased a high-performance four-place Mooney at Tim's Airpark, which he financed through University Savings and Loan. That venture had its downside. On a flight to Las Vegas, Nevada, the Mooney lost a propeller blade over Van Horn, Texas. Although the ensuing vibration severely damaged the flight controls, Wilson exhibited a veteran pilot's skill, crash-landing the Mooney on a rural ranch road. All passengers survived without injury. Wilson interview.

31. Stanton interview. With the profit from the sale of the flight school operation, Stanton and his father entered the land development business at Georgetown, Texas.

32. City of Austin, Department of Aviation, Summary of Operating Revenues, Expenses and Transfers from 1929–1999, AHC.

33. Ragsdale interview, February 4, 1997.

34. *Austin American-Statesman,* May 12, 1962. The Ragsdale Transient Terminal is presently identified as Building No. 3391 in the "Robert Mueller Municipal Airport Redevelopment and Reuse Plan, Prepared by ROMA Design Group and Associated Consultants, Administrative Draft, October 14, 1997," Building Services Division, City of Austin, Texas. Cited hereafter as ROMA Plan.

35. Interview with Mrs. Emma Browning, March 19, 1998. The Browning Transient Terminal is presently identified as Building NO. 3377 in the ROMA Plan. For more information on Austin business aviation, see Melissa Pitts Gaskill, "Private Wings on the Rise in Austin Business," *Austin,* November 1982, pp. 19–23; and Beverly Heider, "Executive Air Travel," *Austin,* August 1981, pp. 14–17.

36. *Austin American-Statesman,* October 28, 1967.

37. Interview with Kenneth G. Cox, Austin, Texas, January 15, 1998.

38. The three units were the 111th Aviation Group, the 322nd Aviation Company, and the 1249th Transportation Company. State of Texas Adjutant General's Department, General Orders No. 60, August 21, 1970, Files, Archives of the Adjutant General's Department at the Texas Military Forces Museum, Camp Mabry, Texas, cited hereafter as TMFM files.

39. In 1947, the Adjutant General's Department allocated two hundred dollars to maintain "runway for light aircraft" at Camp Mabry. Annual Report of the Adjutant General of Texas, August 31, 1947, TMFM files. The L-17 was the military version of the civilian North American "Navion."

40. Interview with Brig. Gen. Grady Matt Roberts, USA Ret., Austin, Texas, August 11, 1999.

41. TMFM files.

42. Report of Annual General Inspections—Section 1, December 12, 1960, TMFM files. In military terminology, helicopters are referred to as rotary-wing aircraft.

43. "Army Aircraft Maintenance Shop and Armory," Project Report, undated, TMFM files.

44. Bishop to National Guard Bureau, October 28, 1966, TMFM files.

45. *American-Statesman,* January 29, 1958.

46. See also special edition of the *Austin Statesman,* "12th Air Force Settled in New HQ Building," October 17, 1968.

47. *Austin Magazine,* November 1979, p. 30.

48. *Encyclopedia of Aircraft,* p. 168.

49. Between 1962 and 1972, air freight increased from 115,490 to 865,880 tons, while air express grew from 35,300 to 49,980 tons. *Enplaning Airline Traffic,* Calendar Year 1948, and *Airport Activity Statistics of Certified Route Air Carriers,* Prepared Jointly by Civil Aeronautics Board and Department of Transportation, Federal Aviation Administration.

50. *Austin Magazine,* November 1979, p. 30.

51. James N. Douglas undated interview with Harlan J. Smith, Minicassette 14, Side 2, Department of Astronomy Archives, Austin, Texas, cited hereafter as Astronomy Archives.

52. Bob Tull recollections, September 1, 2000, Astronomy Archives; interviews with Robert M. Browning III, Austin, Texas, July 2, 2001, and pilot Ingvar (Jake) Jacobsen, Austin, Texas, August 29, 2000. Browning records of this operation were not available for research.

53. Astronomy Archives: Robert M. Browning III to Charles Jenkins, April 2, 1969; Charles E. Jenkins to E. D. Walker, April 16, 1969; e-mail from Thomas G. Barnes to Karen Winget, September 18, 2000.

54. Harlan J. Smith interview, Astronomy Archives.

55. Barnes e-mail to Winget, Astronomy Archives. The *Daily Texan* is the University of Texas student newspaper.

56. Records of the University of Texas Accounting Office, courtesy G. Charles Franklin, Senior Vice President and Chief Financial Officer. All expenditures are from account number 18-0014-0150.

57. *Austin American-Statesman,* February 8, 1974.

58. *State Aircraft Pooling Act,* House Bill No. 1146, passed on March 28, 1979. The bill provided for "the custody, control, operation, and maintenance of all aircraft owned or leased by the state." House Bill No. 656, the Appropriations Act passed by the Sixty-Seventh Legislature in 1981, provided funding for the State Aircraft Pooling Board. The budget for Fiscal Year Ending August 31, 1982, totaled $3,781,255; that increased the following year to $4,054,332.

59. Harlan J. Smith interview, Astronomy Archives.

60. Bob Tull recollections, Astronomy Archives.

61. Courtesy Fritz Kahl, Marfa airport manager, whose facilities serviced the shuttle aircraft.

62. Background data provided by the State Aircraft Pooling Board; interview with Jerry Daniels, Executive Director, State Aircraft Pooling Board, Austin, Texas, July 10, 2001.

63. *Texas Airport Directory,* 1975–1976, Texas Aeronautical Commission, Austin, Texas.

64. *Statistical Handbook of Aviation,* Federal Aviation Administration.

65. Pike Powers, "Airport Task Force Seeks Citizen Input," *Austin Business Executive,* Au-

gust 1984, pp. 20–24. Cited hereafter as "Airport Task Force." The Citizens' Advisory Committee consisted of Dick Hodgkins (chairman), Tom Backus, June Barnes, Peter Coltman, Ralph Janes Jr., Jay N. Miller, William L. Nolen Jr., Frank D. Phillips, Charles P. Zlatkovich, and Col. Jerry Ranson, ex officio. Members of the Technical Committee were Roy Bayless, H. Merrill Goodwin, Dick Lillie, Maureen McReynolds, Jim Miller, Joe Turnus, and Max Ulrich.

66. Griffin Smith Jr., "The Most Dangerous Airports in Texas," *Texas Monthly,* April 1975, p. 64.

67. *Austin American-Statesman,* August 19, 1975.

68. Ibid., August 20, 1975.

69. Minutes, Austin City Council, June 5. 1975, Resolution 750605-4, pp. 558–559. It remains unclear why the city elected to sell 3.9 acres of land, located at the intersection of IH-35 and East Fifty-first Street, to the State of Texas to fund the consultant's initial $125,000 fee.

70. *Airport Site Selection Study, Summary Report,* City of Austin, December 1975. Prepared by R. Dixon Speas Associates, Los Angeles, California. Cited hereafter as Speas Report with appropriate date.

71. The east-west runway at Bergstrom Air Force Base would be for commercial air carriers. Before Bergstrom reached full development, there would have been space available for an east-west runway located between the flight line and Texas Highway 71.

72. Speas Report, December 1975.

8. Era of Indecision

1. *Austin American-Statesman,* February 27 and 29, 1976. In the original terminal design, the architect made no provision for passengers boarding the aircraft. Once they exited the terminal building, they walked unprotected across the parking ramp to the waiting aircraft, which they boarded by climbing portable steps.

2. Austin City Council Minutes, Resolution No. 760708-16, July 8, 1976.

3. "Request for Joint Use of Bergstrom Air Force Base by the City of Austin," October 1976, Speas Report. Reducing the size of Mueller would, in turn, reduce the length of runways 12R/30L, which would eliminate air carrier aircraft from that air space, and thereby eliminate the conflicting airspace between the two airports.

4. Letter from Mayor Jeffrey M. Friedman to Col. A. J. Parker, October 12, 1976, copy in author's file. There was precedent for this proposal. Several Air Force bases in the United States also served as commercial air carrier facilities. These included bases in Albuquerque, New Mexico; Charleston, South Carolina; Dover, Delaware; Eglin, Florida; Myrtle Beach, South Carolina; Palmdale, California; and Wichita Falls, Texas.

5. The Texas Aeronautical Commission was created in 1945 by House Bill 309, Forty-ninth Legislature. In 1989, the Commission became the Texas Department of Aviation, created by House Bill 94, Seventy-First Legislature, First Called Session. The Texas Department of Aviation, like the former Texas Aeronautical Commission, assists in the development of

aeronautics in the state and cooperates with the federal government and other states in establishing a uniform aviation system.

6. *The Daily Texan,* August 22, 1977. There was precedent for the city's concern in that matter. In 1972, the cities of Dallas and Fort Worth sued Southwest Airlines to force the carrier to move its operation from Love Field to the new Dallas–Fort Worth International Airport. A seven-year legal battle ensued. Southwest prevailed; operations continue at Love Field.

7. *Austin American-Statesman,* September 15, 1977.

8. *Statistical Handbook of Aviation,* 1977.

9. Austin Chamber of Commerce Records, AHC.

10. Speas Report, December 1977, p. 9-1.

11. Powers, "Airport Task Force," p. 21.

12. Speas Report, January 1978, pp. 1-1, 1-3, and 1-4.

13. Powers, "Airport Task Force," p. 21.

14. Mayor McClellan was accompanied to Washington by Dick Hodgkins, chairman, Citizens' Advisory Committee; Roy Bayless, Austin director of aviation; and Jim Miller, assistant city manager. In view of Bergstrom Air Force Base's current financial benefits to the city, some council members felt that further discussion of what apparently had become a sensitive issue was not in Austin's best interest.

15. Minutes, Austin City Council, January 30, 1978.

16. Powers, "Airport Task Force," p. 21. This body had the support of a Technical Advisory Committee, which included representatives of two local fixed base operators, Mrs. Emma Browning, president of Browning Aerial Service, and Kenneth Cox, vice president of Ragsdale Flying Service.

17. Letter from Mayor Carole Keeton McClellan to Members of City Council, March 20, 1978, photocopy in author's files.

18. Airport Study Committee Report, April 25, 1978, AHC.

19. Austin City Council Memo, August 3, 1978, p. 6, AHC.

20. *Austin American-Statesman,* March 30, 1978.

21. Ibid., December 1, 1978.

22. *Airline Deregulation Act of 1978, U.S. Statues at Large* 92 (1978): 1705–1754.

23. *Austin American-Statesman,* March 22, 1979.

24. Ibid., April 13, 1979.

25. Airport Site Selection Study, Supplemental Information, Speas Report, 1979, pp. 1, 4, and 9, AHC.

26. "Site Selection Study for Air Carrier Airport," Speas Report, July, 1979, AHC. "Alternate B" refers to parallel runways separated by 4,300 to 5,000 feet and a central passenger terminal. The north-south runway alignment minimized flight path conflicts with Bergstrom Air Force Base.

27. *Austin American-Statesman,* September 21 and 22, 1979.

28. Ibid., September 16, 1979.

29. *Austin Magazine,* August 1982.

30. *Austin American-Statesman,* September 16, 1979.

31. Ibid., November 4, 1979.

32. Ibid., November 16, 1979.

33. Austin City Council Minutes, August 6, 1981; Powers, "Airport Task Force," p. 21.

34. *Austin American-Statesman,* September 22, 1981.

35. Ibid., November 1 and December 17, 1981.

36. Ibid., January 6, 1982, and February 6, 1982. During the negotiations with the Air Force, Lockheed Missiles & Space Company was pressing the city to make a decision on the matter. The company subsequently acquired the property, where it erected a manufacturing facility.

37. Ibid., February 12 and April 17, 1982.

38. Ibid., September 16, 1979. Herb Kelleher undoubtedly based that statement on recent experience. Southwest Airlines had just won an extended legal battle with the cities of Dallas and Fort Worth, which allowed that airline to serve the Dallas–Fort Worth area through Dallas' Love Field, not Dallas–Fort Worth International Airport.

39. *Windsock,* No. 4, 1981, Marketing Division, Exxon Corporation, p. 7.

40. "Regional Case Study, Texas or 'how to create a knowledge economy,'" research study provided by Angelou Economic, Austin, Texas. See also *Austin, Texas: Building a High-tech Economy;* "The Perryman Economic Forecast: Short-term Outlook for The United States, Texas, and the Austin–San Marcos MSA," The Perryman Group, Fall 1998; and Jim Rapp, "The Austin Miracle," *TechWeb,* February 6, 1998.

41. *The Daily Texan,* March 4, 1990. Referring to Dallas–Fort Worth International Airport, historian Darwin Payne wrote: "The airport's success and the quick access it offers to the rest of the nation through direct flights has lured some 400 corporate headquarters to Dallas–Fort Worth since 1969," the date the airport opened. Darwin Payne, "The Feud That Built the World's Second Busiest Airport: Dallas vs. Fort Worth," *Legacies,* Spring 1999, p. 55.

42. Other members of the task force included Ben Head, vice-chairman, Lionel Aguirre, John Cutright, David Helfert, Hugh K. Higgins Jr., Glen R. Johnson, John M. Joseph, Rick McCulley, and Kathy Patman.

43. "Options Summary for the Austin Citizens' Airport Task Force, Alternatives D, G-1, and G-2," October 24, 1984, Bovay Engineers, Inc., Wasserman Library, LBJ School of Public Affairs Library. The previous city council had employed Bovay Engineers in June 1982 to update the city's Airport Master Plan study. "Options Summary," pp. 2–4.

44. *Austin American-Statesman,* October 18, 1984.

45. Ibid., October 25, 1984.

46. "Final Report, City of Austin, Citizens' Airport Task Force, November 15, 1984," Wasserman Library, LBJ School of Public Affairs, Austin, Texas.

47. "Austin Airport Task Force Minority Report" submitted by John Cutright, November 15, 1984, AHC.

48. *Austin American-Statesman,* November 30, 1984.

49. Interview with Ron Mullen, Austin, Texas, January 27, 2000. This was confirmed by an interview with Charles Carpenter in Austin, Texas, on May 28, 2000.

50. Interview with Charles B. and James R. Carpenter, Austin, Texas, May 18, 2001.

51. *Austin American-Statesman,* January 16 and 21, 1985.

52. Ibid., March 21, 1986.

53. Ibid., August 15, 1986.

54. Council Minutes, November 14, 1985.

55. *Austin American-Statesman,* November 5, 1987.

56. Ibid., April 17, 1987.

57. "Austin Airport Alternative Environmental Assessment," prepared by Turner Collie & Braden, Inc., Austin, Texas, July 1988, AHC.

58. This and following quotations on the airport referendum are from the *Austin American-Statesman,* May 13, August 27, October 4, October 18, and November 4, 1987.

9. City on a Tightwire

1. Minutes, Austin City Council, December 10, 1987. The fee for the Turner, Collie & Braden firm was $49,000.

2. Ibid., November 3, 1988; *Austin American-Statesman,* November 4, 1988. Incorporated in the final motion was a proviso that contract negotiations begin at $1.1 million.

3. *Austin American-Statesman,* December 14, 1988.

4. Ibid., January 7, 1989.

5. Council Minutes, February 2, 1989; *Austin American-Statesman,* February 3, 1989. The Shipman resolution was also viewed as overdue assurance to the ten carriers then serving Austin that the city did indeed intend to move forward on constructing the new airport at Manor. For a financial analysis of the proposed Manor airport, see "Briefing Paper, Preliminary 'Rough Cut' Financial Analysis New Airport Project," prepared for the Department of Aviation, City of Austin, October 1988, by Peat Marwick Main & Company, Airport Consulting Services, David Samuelson Private Collection, Manor, Texas. Cited hereafter as Samuelson Collection.

6. *Austin American-Statesman,* March 22, 1989. For the results of this endeavor, see "Master Plan for the New City of Austin Municipal Airport, Final Report," February 1990, Murfee Engineering Company, Inc., Page Southerland Page/Thompson Consultants International, and P&D Technologies. Samuelson Collection.

7. The air freight building was not included in the total cost of Mueller expansion. A private firm leased the land from the city, constructed the air freight terminal, and operated that facility privately.

8. Each property owner attending the meeting received a portfolio prepared by the City of Austin, entitled, "Property Purchase and Relocation Assistance; Information on How the City of Austin Will Acquire Property for the New Airport." Each portfolio contained ten items, which included an Information Brochure, Relocation Assistance Brochure, Property Owners List, Policy Document, and a List of Meeting Attendees. The Property Owners List contains 478 parcels of land, the largest being the 13 parcels of the Carpenter interests. The Relocations Assistance Brochure cited was *Your Rights and Benefits as a Displacee; Under the Federal Relocation Assistance Program,* U.S. Department of Transportation, 1986. Samuelson Collection.

9. *House Committee Report,* H.B. No. 2848, pp. 1–2, Regular Session, Seventy-First Legislature, January 10, 1989, to May 29, 1989, Texas Legislative Reference Library, Austin, Texas.

10. *General and Special Laws of The State of Texas,* Regular Session, Seventy-First Legislature, January 10, 1989 to May 29, 1989, S.B. No. 1707, pp. 4933–4934.

11. *Austin American-Statesman,* December 11, 1989.

12. Ibid., January 26, 1990.

13. Ibid., January 30, 1990. This figure was based on an Air Force report. A study assessing the economic and fiscal impact of the closing of Bergstrom Air Force Base, contained in a City of Austin Public Relations Office press release dated June 15, 1990, contained substantially different data. "The total economic impact of closing BAFB (including the estimated loss due to departure of local military retirees) is estimated to be $406.72 million, which represents 3.36% of the gross sales in the Austin MSA (1989 figures). That figure translates into a loss of 5,646 jobs, in addition to the 1,941 civilian employees, and 6,125 active and reserve military personnel at BAFB." Bergstrom Air Force Base File B2580, 1990, AHC.

14. Ibid., January 31, 1990.

15. Ibid., February 10, 1990. Minton represented Houston Lighting & Power in Austin's unsuccessful damage suite against that utility company.

16. Memo from Mayor Lee Cooke to Pike Powers, Co-Chair, Save Bergstrom Task Force, Samuelson Collection.

17. Greater Austin Chamber of Commerce Press Release, June 22, 1990. Bergstrom Air Force Base File B2580, AHC.

18. *Austin American-Statesman,* April 20, 1990. Concurrent with the lawsuit filing, Citizens For Airport Relocation (C.A.R.E.) distributed a leaflet stating: "Austin's Fun Fares at Mueller Are Over: What you can do to protect yourself from a city that squanders a mandate to move the airport. Join class action lawsuit. If you live in the 65 LDN contour shown on the back of this leaflet, join the class action lawsuit that is being organized. . . . We are working with national organizations and lawyers on the strictest ordinance that will be sustained in the courts." Samuelson Collection.

19. Ibid., April 23, 1990.

20. *Airline Deregulation Act of 1978. U.S. Statues at Large* 92 (1978): 1705–1754.

21. Aeronautical Activities in Texas, TDA Form 126, Revised January 1991.

22. *Statistical Handbook of Aviation, 1958–1989.*

23. Population Growth and Trends (1970–1994), City of Austin, AHC.

24. City of Austin, Department of Long Range Planning.

25. *Austin American-Statesman,* April 20, 1990. Charles Carpenter later released a list of partners in the Manor landholdings, which contained no names of local politicians.

26. Ibid., July 20, 1990.

27. Citizens' Task Force on the Economic Conversion of Bergstrom Air Force Base, Final Report, February 14, 1991, p. 28, AHC. Members of the Task Force were James M. Steed (chairman), Les Gage, Ray Reece, Nash Moreno Martinez, Joseph F. Trochta, and Gwendolyn Hill Webb.

28. Council Minutes, July 11, 1991; *Austin American-Statesman,* July 12, 1991.

29. Defense Base Closure and Realignment Commission Disapproval, Joint Resolution 308, United States House of Representatives, July 30, 1991.

30. Council Minutes, December 20, 1991; *Austin American-Statesman,* December 21, 1991.

31. Council Minutes, February 20; *Austin American-Statesman,* February 21, 1992.

32. Council Minutes, March 11, 1992, *Austin American-Statesman,* March 12, 1992. An election was required prior to June 1993 to inform the Air Force that an airport would be built at the site of the former Air Force base.

33. *Austin American-Statesman,* June 17, 1992. Lee Cooke and Robert Barnstone were later dropped from the suit. Plaintiffs in the case were Homer Biggerstaff, Jack Irwin, Frankie Slade Hughes, Marvin Casey, Robert Worley, and Alex Alexander. The companies sued were AR&R Inc., an Austin real estate acquisition and consulting firm, and Sverdrup/ Gilbane Corp. The suit was later dropped. As the result of the City of Austin's verbal commitment to build an airport near Manor, Texas, many landowners, advised to either move or dispose of their property, suffered severe hardship. They were never compensated.

34. *Austin American-Statesman,* November 27, 1991. The same day of the announcement, Myron H. Nordquist, Deputy General Council, Department of the Air Force, wrote Barry Hartman, Acting Assistant Attorney General, U.S. Department of Justice, "In our opinion, the Air Force must convey title to the land in question to Austin by quitclaim deed when the base is closed, retaining only a Reserve Force cantonment area. Improvements constructed with Government funds on the base may be removed or abandoned to the City in place, at the Air Force's option." Although there was no documented agreement between the City of Austin and the Army Air Corps when the base was opened, there was, however, legal precedent for the property to revert to the city. On August 12, 1991, Iris J. Jones, City Attorney, City of Austin, wrote Doug Baur, Acting Assistant General Council, Installations, SAFGCN, in Washington, D.C., arguing, "The lack of an agreement by the grantee of the land to convey to the person who furnishes the purchase money does

not necessarily defeat the claim of a resulting trust; however, there are certain defenses which are ordinarily availing." Samuelson Collection.

35. Some of the structures acquired by the city included an aircraft maintenance hangar (90,800 sq. ft.), an avionics building (30,541 sq. ft.), an engine shop (27,410 sq. ft.), ten dorms (273,698 sq. ft.), a hospital (93,682 sq. ft.), fourteen residential houses (33,909 sq. ft.), and six office buildings (30,124 sq. ft.). Also, almost one hundred additional buildings were available for the Air Force Reserves, approximately sixty buildings available for interim use during airport construction, plus "a significant number of buildings . . . also being considered as candidates for relocation." "Existing Facilities at Bergstrom Planned For Reuse," Bergstrom Air Force Base File B25880 1990, AHC.

36. Council Minutes, December 13, 1992; *Austin American-Statesman*, December 14, 1992. The council also planned to request the Federal Aviation Administration to reimburse the city for 75 percent of the contract cost. The Parsons Brinckerhoff firm was well known in Texas, having been part of a joint venture in developing the superconducting supercollider in Waxahachie, Texas. The Parsons Brinckerhoff team included seven subcontractors: Carter & Burgess, Austin, engineering; Corgan Associates Architects, Dallas, architectural design; Parshall & Associates, Austin, architects; Macias & Associates, Austin, land surveyors; Lee Flores, Austin, technical support; KLW, Austin, mechanical engineering; and Bonner & Tate, Austin, public relations.

37. *Austin American-Statesman*, May 2, 1993.

38. Closure Update, Bergstrom Air Force Base File, B2580 1990s, AHC.

39. Council Minutes, November 2, 1994; *Austin American-Statesman*, November 3, 1994. Other suggestions included Austin Peace Dividend Air Park, Austin International Airport at Bergstrom Field, and Stephen F. Austin International Airport at Bergstrom Field. Council action occurred on Stephen F. Austin's 201st birthday.

40. *Austin American-Statesman*, November 20, 1994.

41. Ibid., March 5 and August 15, 1995.

42. Ibid., January 9, 1996.

43. Ibid., January 10, January 26, February 8, February 9, June 27, July 10, July 18, July 26, and July 19, 1996. The readjusted Morganti contract totaled $98,081,788. In the rebidding, the Pelzel-Phelps firm was not considered; the bid was submitted thirty seconds after the bidding deadline.

44. Council Minutes, September 5, 1996; *Austin American-Statesman*, September 6, 1996.

45. *Austin American-Statesman*, October 2, 1996. The contracted cargo air carriers were Federal Express, Airborne Express, and Burlington Air Express. Austin CargoPort Development was owned jointly by Alan Graham and Ray Brindle. Other investors included former Austin city council member Lowell Lebermann and entrepreneur Walter DeRoeck.

46. Ibid., October 17, 1996.

47. Texas Department of Transportation, Aviation Division, Aviation Research Center, Austin, Texas, March 1, 1996.

48. Council Minutes, April 24, 1997; *Austin American-Statesman,* April 10, 1997, and April 25, 1997. The Pooling Board's location at the new airport was moved from the southern portion of the facility, entered off US Highway 183 and Burleson Road, to a more convenient location in the northeast section of the airport, entered from Texas Highway 71.

49. The private pilots also objected to both the location and the higher monthly hangar-rental costs at Austin Bergstrom, shown below.

	MUELLER		AUSTIN-BERGSTROM	
	T-Hangar	Common	T-Hangar	Common
Single Engine	$175	$200	None	$600
Small Twin	$245	$275	None	$725
Large Twin	$365	$375	None	$800

General aviation is located at Austin-Bergstrom International Airport near the site originally selected for the State Aircraft Pooling Board, accessible only off US Highway 183 and Burleson Road at the extreme south side of the airport. Common space refers to space in a large hangar shared with other aircraft. Source: Signature Flight Support, Austin-Bergstrom International Airport.

50. *Austin American-Statesman,* March 30, 1997. According the that plan, rental car agencies would pay for the majority of the expansion, by charging their customers two dollars per day, in addition to the normal rental cost. Any additional amount would be paid from normal airport revenues. In addition to the three-level parking garage, plans called for some 8,000 spaces in surface lots.

51. Councilman Eric Mitchell made the nomination, which passed unanimously. Council Minutes, June 23, 1997, Ordinance No. 970612-G.

52. *Austin American-Statesman,* July 3, 1997. The airport opened with twenty-five passenger gates.

53. Ibid., February 18, 1998, and April 20, 1999. The airport budget included $6 million for noise mitigation. Airport officials also announced that departing planes would have to climb to at least 3,000 feet, and to 4,000 feet between 10 P.M. and 6:10 A.M., before turning over the city.

54. Ibid., April 28, 1998.

55. Ibid., December 2, 1998. On December 29, Lynette Martin of Tulsa, Oklahoma, became the six-millionth passenger to pass through Austin Mueller Municipal Airport in 1998.

56. *Austin American-Statesman,* August 30, 1998.

57. Ibid., October 24, 1995.

58. "Dear Friend" letter from Mayor Kirk Watson, May 17, 1999. Municipal Airport File M8600, AHC.

59. The Austin-Bergstrom System was unlike the high-tech baggage system that delayed the Denver airport opening eighteen months.

60. *Austin American-Statesman,* April 25, 1999.

61. The open house cost an estimated $25,000, mostly to pay the performers. The Grand Opening Steering Group raised about $500,000 for opening festivities. H.E.B. stores printed the 100,000 visitor tickets.

62. Letter from John M. Almond, P.E., Director of Facilities, City of Austin—New Airport Department to Mr. Richard Tappero, General Manager, Signature Flight Support, 4909 Airport Boulevard, Austin, Texas. Copy in author's files.

63. *Austin American-Statesman*, May 8, 1999.

64. *Austin American-Statesman*, May 24, 1999.

65. Ibid., May 19, 1999.

66. Ibid., May 26, 1999.

67. In 1993, Centerline Properties, owned by Kirk Hays, Louis Durrett, Robert White, and Ron Bower, acquired Austin Executive Air Park from the Federal Depositors Insurance Corporation and operated it as a private airport until June 1999, when another group of investors, headed by Sandor Gottesman, purchased the property for commercial development.

68. Those regional airports were located at San Marcos, Georgetown, Burnet, Smithville, LaGrange, Lockhart, Giddings, Llano, Manor, Lakeway, Lago Vista, and Taylor.

69. File AF-M-8600 (8), Municipal Airport, 1990s, AHC.

70. City of Austin, Department of Long Range Planning.

Conclusion

1. Strickland, *The Putt-Putt Air Force*, p. 97.

2. Ibid., p. 111.

3. Ibid., p. 97.

4. Bednarek, *America's Airports*, p. 180.

5. *Austin American-Statesman*, December 22, 2002.

6. Larry Laudan, *Progress and Its Problems: Towards a Theory of Scientific Growth*, p. 2. See also J. B. Bury, *The Idea of Progress: An Inquiry into Its Origin and Growth*.

BIBLIOGRAPHY

Primary Sources

Correspondence

Barrett, Hunter. Fort Worth, Texas, November 8, 1999.
Preston, Ned. Agency Historian, Federal Aviation Administration, Washington, D.C., May 12, 2000.

Interviews (unless otherwise noted, interviews are by the author)

Barrett, A. P., November 3, 1999, by telephone.
Batson, Cathryn. Austin, Texas, undated.
Bloomer, Richard. Austin, Texas, November 12, 1997.
Browning, Mrs. Emma. Austin, Texas, March 19, 1998, and December 16, 2000.
Browning, Robert M., III. Austin, Texas, March 19, 1998, and July 2, 2001.
Butler, Roy. Austin, Texas, February 8, 2000.
Cain, James B. Athens, Texas, November 19, 1997.
Carpenter, Charles B. Austin, Texas, May 28, 2000.
Carpenter, Charles B., and James R. Carpenter. Austin, Texas, May 18, 2000.
Cauley, Dabney. Austin, Texas, November 29, 2000.
Chamberlain, Walter S. Austin, Texas, undated.
Cooke, Lee. Austin, Texas, June 28, 2000.
Cox, Kenneth G. Austin, Texas, January 15, 1998, and December 1, 2000.
Criswell, Jim. San Antonio, Texas, August 9, 1999.
Cutright, John. Austin, Texas, January 14, 2000.
Daniels, Jerry. Austin, Texas, July 10, 2001.
Delco, Wilhelmina. Austin, Texas, July 17, 2001.
Edwards, Mary Catherine Quist. Austin, Texas, June 9, 1998.
Fry, Lloyd, Jr. Liberty Hill, Texas, February 22, 1998.
Hallock, Bruce K. Austin, Texas, June 15, 1998.
Jacobsen, Ingvar. Austin, Texas, August 29, 2000.
Janes, Ralph E., III. Austin, Texas, November 29, 2000.
Jenkins, Charles E. Interview by E. D. Walker. April 16, 1969, Department of Astronomy Archives, University of Texas at Austin, Texas.
Johnston, Morris S. Austin, Texas, September 23, 1998.
Klappenbach, Rick. Sugarland, Texas, March 16, 1998.
McCurdy, Mrs. John A. Austin, Texas, February 9, 1998.
Mullen, Ron. Austin, Texas, January 27, 2000.
Pickle, J. J. Austin, Texas, January 25, 2000.
Puett, Nelson. Austin, Texas, December 4, 2000.

Quist, Charles. Austin, Texas, August 11, 1999.

Ragsdale, Robert L. Austin, Texas, November 11, 19, and 29, 1996; February 4, 1997; March 12, 1997; and July 1, 2000.

Roberts, Brig. Gen. Grady Matt. Austin, Texas, August 11, 1999.

Samuelson, David. Austin, Texas, January 13, 2000.

Simmons, John. Austin, Texas, July 18, 2000.

Shipley, George. Austin, Texas, September 5, 2001.

Smith, Harlan J. Undated interview by James N. Douglas, Department of Astronomy Archives, University of Texas at Austin, Texas.

Smith, Leonard. Austin, Texas, November 29 and December 3, 2000.

Stanton, Bobby. Georgetown, Texas, May 3, 2000.

Taylor, Frank. Round Rock, Texas, November 20, 1999.

Timmerman, Theodore R., Jr. Pflugerville, Texas, June 26, 2000.

Westerman, Max, Jr. Austin, Texas, June 1, 1998.

Wilson, Bob. Fredericksburg, Texas, June 15, 2001, by telephone.

White, Robert. Austin, Texas, July 13, 2000.

Wilborn, Dr. Sam W. Austin, Texas, June 26, 1997.

Wittner, Norbert. Austin, Texas, November 6, 1997.

Manuscript Collections and Public Records

Air Commerce Act of 1926. U.S. Statutes at Large 44 (1926): 568–576.

Airline Deregulation Act of 1978. U.S. Statues at Large 92 (1978): 1705–1754. *Air Mail Act of 1925. U.S. Statutes at Large* 43 (1925): 803–806.

Air Mail Act of 1934. U.S. Statutes at Large 48 (1934) 933–939.

Airport Site Selection Study, Summary Report. Prepared by R. Dixon Speas Associates for the City of Austin, December 1975. Other reports dated October 1976; January 1978 and October 1978; and July 1979.

Annual Report of the Game, Fish and Oyster Commission, State of Texas, for the Fiscal Years of 1946–1947, 1947–1948; and 1950–1951. Texas State Library, Legal Reference Division, Austin, Texas.

Archives of the Attorney General's Department, Texas Military Forces Museum, Camp Mabry, Texas.

Astronomy Department Archives, University of Texas at Austin.

"Austin Airport Alternative Environmental Assessment." Austin: Turner, Collie & Braden, 1988.

"Austin Airport Task Force, Minority Report," submitted by John Cutright, November 15, 1984.

Beggs, S. Sgt. Robert A. "Brief History of Bergstrom Air Force Base, Austin, Texas." Unpublished manuscript. Austin History Center.

Bergstrom Air Force Base, Legal Files. Office of the City Manager, City of Austin, Texas.

Bergstrom Air Force Base Collection, Austin History Center, Austin, Texas.

Bickler, Max, Collection. Austin History Center. Austin, Texas.

Boutwell, Jim. "Some Notes on Early DPS Aviation." Copy in Author's files.

Braniff Collection, History of Aviation Collection, University of Texas at Dallas.

"Briefing Paper, Preliminary 'Rough Cut' Financial Analysis New Airport Project," prepared for the Department of Aviation, City of Austin, by Peat Marwick Main & Company. Austin: 1988.

Bryant, Dr. J. M. "History of the School of Military Aeronautics." Unpublished manuscript, T. S. Painter Records, Center for American History, University of Texas at Austin, July 10, 1919.

Cain, James B. Aero-Tel Airport Records, Athens, Texas.

Carpenter, Charles B. Private Papers.

Chamberlain, Walter S. "Financing of Small Aircraft by Installment Loan Departments of Commercial Banks." Master's thesis, Southwestern Graduate School of Banking, Southern Methodist University, 1963.

"Citizens Task Force on the Economic Conversion of Bergstrom Air Force Base," Final Report, February 14, 1991.

City of Austin, Appropriations-Engineering Department, 1932–1933, 1934–1935, and 1937.

City of Austin, Engineering File Room, Land Acquisitions, Austin, Texas.

Civil Aeronautics Administration, War Training Records, Master Records. Center for American History, University of Texas at Austin.

Civilian Pilot Training Act, U.S. Statutes at Large 53 (1939), pp. 855 ff.

Deed Records, Office of the County Clerk, Travis County, Texas.

"Development Cost for Long-Term Expansion of Robert Mueller Municipal Airport." Austin: The Greiner Austin Team, 1987.

Docket No. 32143, April 17, 1978, Direct Exhibits and Testimony of the City and the Chamber of Commerce of Austin, Texas; April 27, 1978, Rebuttal Exhibits. Civil Aeronautics Board, Washington, D.C.

Doughtie, Venton L. "CAA Pilot Training, The University of Texas, September 1940 August 1944." Texas War Records, Center for American History, University of Texas at Austin.

The Economic Boom of the Austin Area. Austin: Angelou Economic Advisors, Inc., undated.

"Existing Facilities at Bergstrom Planned for Reuse." Bergstrom Air Force Base Collection, Austin History Center.

"Final Report, City of Austin, Citizens' Airport Task Force," November 15, 1984. Wasserman Library, Lyndon B. Johnson School of Public Affairs, Austin.

General and Special Laws of The State of Texas, Regular Session, Seventy-First Legislature, January 10, 1989 to May 29, 1989, State of Texas, S.B. No. 1707, pp. 4933–4934.

Governor Miriam A. Ferguson's Records, Archives and Information Services, Texas State Archives, Austin, Texas.

House Committee Report, H.B. No. 2848, pp. 1–2, Regular Session, Seventy-First Legislature, January 10, 1989 to May 29, 1989, State of Texas.

Katz, James E., and Richard T. McCulley. "The Safety of Robert Mueller Municipal Airport." Austin: Lyndon B. Johnson School of Public Affairs, 1986.

Keenan, Ray. Narrative, 9 April 2000, in Author's files.

Long, Walter E., Collection. Austin History Center, Austin, Texas.

Longhorn Flying Club Records. In possession of Morris S. Johnston, Austin, Texas.

"Master Plan for the New City of Austin Municipal Airport," Final Report, February 1990, Murfee Engineering Company, Inc., Page Southerland Page/Thompson Consultants International, and P&D Technologies. Samuelson Private Collection.

Minutes. City Council, City of Austin, Texas.

"Options Summary for the Austin Citizens' Airport Task Force." Austin: Bovay Engineers, Inc., 1984. LBJ School of Public Affairs Library, Austin.

"The Perryman Economic Forecast: Short-term Outlook for The United States, Texas, and the Austin–San Marcos MSA." The Perryman Group, Fall 1998.

Population Growth and Trends (1970–1994), City of Austin, Travis County, Austin MSA (Metropolitan Statistical Area), State of Texas. Austin History Center.

Records, Accounting Office, University of Texas at Austin.

"Regional Case Study, Texas or 'How to Create a Knowledge Economy.'" Research Study. Angelou Economic, Austin, Texas. Undated.

Reuben Rountree Report. Public Works Department, City of Austin.

"Robert Mueller Municipal Airport Redevelopment and Reuse Plan, Prepared by ROMA Design Group and Associated Consultants, Administrative Draft, October 14, 1997," Building Services Division, City of Austin, Texas.

Samuelson, David. Private Collection.

Servicemen's Readjustment Act of 1944, U.S. Statutes at Large 58 (1944): 284–294.

State Aircraft Pooling Act, H.B. No. 1146, passed March 28, 1979.

State of Texas, Department of Public Safety, Annual Financial Report, September 1, 1949, through August 31, 1950.

Student Pilots Log Book. Lloyd B. Fry Jr., Liberty Hill, Texas. On loan to the author.

Sunday Morning News, City Plan Supplement, Austin, Texas, February 12, 1928.

Texas War Records. Center for American History, University of Texas at Austin.

United States Congress, Senate, *Revisions of Air-Mail Laws,* Hearing before Committee on Post Roads, 73rd Cong., 2nd Sess., 1934.

University of Texas Presidents Office Records, T. S. Painter Records, Center for American History, University of Texas at Austin.

Secondary Sources

Books, Articles, Documents, and Theses

Air Force Bases: A Directory of U.S. Air Force Installations Both in the Continental U.S. and Overseas, with Useful Information on Each Base and Its Nearby Community. Harrisburg, Pennsylvania: Stackpole, 1965.

Airport Activity Statistics of Certified Route Air Carriers. Civil Aeronautics Board and Department of Transportation, Federal Aviation Administration.

Anderson, David. *The History of the United States Air Force.* New York: Crescent Books, 1981.

Austin, Texas: Building a High-tech Economy. Boston: Harvard Business School Publishing, 1998.

Austin Chamber of Commerce Annual Reports.

Bednarek, Janet R. *America's Airports: Airfield Development, 1918–1947*. College Station: Texas A&M University Press, 2001.

Bilstein, Roger, and Jay Miller. *Aviation in Texas*. Austin: Texas Monthly Press, 1985.

Blomquist, Albert E. *Outline of Air Transport Practice*. New York: Pitman, 1941.

Blum, John Morton. *V Was For Victory: Politics and American Culture during World War II*. London: Harcourt Brace Jovanovich, 1973.

Boyne, Walter J. *The Wright Flyer: An Engineering Perspective*. Washington, D.C.: Smithsonian Institution Press, 1970.

Bury, J. B. *The Idea of Progress: An Inquiry into Its Origin and Growth*. London: Macmillan, 1921.

Callander, Bruce D. "The Return of Kelly Field." *Air Force Magazine Online*, July 2001.

Civilian Pilot Training Act, (June 27, 1939, Ch. 244, 53 Stat. 855).

Corn, Joseph J. *The Winged Gospel: America's Romance with Aviation, 1900–1950*. New York: Oxford University Press, 1983.

Davis, R. E. G. *Airlines of the United States since 1914*. London: Putnam, 1972.

Daynes, Byron W., William D. Pederson, and Michael P. Riccards, eds. *The New Deal and Public Policy*. New York: St. Martin's Press, 1998.

Description of Airports and Landing Fields in the United States. Airways Bulletin No. 2. Washington D.C.: Department of Commerce, Aeronautics Branch, September 1, 1931.

Donald, David, General Editor. *The Complete Encyclopedia of World Aircraft*. New York: Barnes & Noble Books, 1997.

Emme, Eugene M. *Aeronautics and Astronautics: An American Chronology of Science and Technology in the Exploration of Space, 1915–1960*. Washington, D.C.: National Aeronautics and Space Administration, 1961.

Enplaning Airline Traffic by Community. Washington, D.C.: Civil Aeronautics Administration.

Foulois, Maj. Gen. Benjamin D. ". . . And Teach Yourself to Fly." *Reader's Digest*, October 1960, 50–54.

———, with Carroll V. Glines, *From the Wright Brothers to the Astronauts*. New York: Arno Press, 1980.

Fraser, Chelsea. *Heroes of the Air*. New York: Thomas Y. Crowell, 1930.

Gaskill, Melissa Pitts. "Private Wings on the Rise in Austin Business." *Austin*, November 1982, 19–23.

Gibbs-Smith, Charles Howard. *Aviation: An Historical Survey from Its Origins to the End of World War II*. London: Her Majesty's Stationery Office, 1970.

Glines, Carroll V. *The Compact History of the United States Air Force*. New York: Hawthorne Books, 1963.

Glynn, Gary. "1st Aero Squadron in Pursuit of Pancho Villa." *The American Legion Magazine*, November 1997, 50–56.

Goldberg, Alfred. *A History of the United States Air Force*. New York: D. Van Nostrand, 1957.

Gould, Lewis L. *Progressives and Prohibitionists: Texas Democrats in the Wilson Era*. Austin: University of Texas Press, 1973.

Haley, J. Evetts. *George W. Littlefield, Texan*. Austin: University of Texas Press, 1943.

Heider, Beverly. "Executive Air Travel." *Austin*, August 1981, 14–17.

Kane, Robert M., and Allan D. Voss, *Air Transportation*. Dubuque, Iowa: Kendall Hall, 1979.

Kennedy, David M. *Freedom from Fear: The American People in Depression and War, 1929–1945*. Vol. 9 of *Oxford History of the United States*. New York: Oxford University Press, 1999.

———. *Over Here: The First World War and American Society*. New York: Oxford University Press, 1980.

Kent, Richard J., Jr. *Safe, Separate, and Soaring: A History of Federal Civil Aviation Policy, 1961–1972*. Washington, D.C.: U.S. Department of Transportation, Federal Aviation Administration, 1980.

Knight, Robert S. "Financing of Small and Medium Size Aircraft." *Bulletin of the Robert Morris Associates*, vol. 43, no. 11 (July 1961).

Knock, Thomas J. *To End All Wars: Woodrow Wilson and the Quest for a New Order*. New York: Oxford University Press, 1992.

Komons, Nick A. *Bonfires to Beacons: Federal Civil Aviation Policy under the Air Commerce Acts of 1926 and 1938*. Washington, D.C.: U.S. Department of Transportation, 1978.

Laudan, Larry. *Progress and Its Problems: Towards a Theory of Scientific Growth*. Berkeley: University of California Press, 1977.

Leary, William M. *Aerial Pioneers: The U.S. Air Mail Service, 1918–1927*. Washington, D.C.: Smithsonian Institution Press, 1985.

Lebow, Eileen F. *Cal Rodgers and the Vin Fiz: The First Transcontinental Flight*. Washington, D.C.: Smithsonian Institution Press, 1989.

Lindbergh, Charles A. *We*. New York: G. P. Putnam's Sons, 1927.

Link, Arthur S. *American Epoch: A History of the United States Since the 1890s*, Vol. 1, 1897–1920. New York: Alfred A. Knopf, 1967.

Loeblein, John M. *Memoirs of Kelly Field, 1917–1918*. Manhattan, Kans.: Aerospace Historian Publishing, 1974.

Long, Walter E. *Something Made Austin Grow*. Austin: Austin Chamber of Commerce, 1948.

———. *Wings over Austin*. Austin, 1962. Private publication.

Mahoney, Tom. "The First Airman across America." *The American Legion Magazine*, March 1965, 20–51.

May, Ernest R. *The World War and American Isolation, 1914–1917*. Chicago: Quadrangle Books, 1959.

McFarland, Marvin W., ed. *The Papers of Orville and Wilbur Wright*. New York: McGraw-Hill, 1953.

Meyer, Henry Cord. *Airshipmen, Businessmen, and Politics, 1980–1940*. Washington, D.C.: Smithsonian Institution Press, 1991.

Miller, Jonathan. *Regional Case Study: Austin, Texas or "How to Create a Knowledge Economy."* Washington: European Union, 2001.

Mueller, Robert. *Air Force Bases*. Vol. 1, *Active Air Force Bases within the United States of America on 17 September 1982*. Washington, D.C.: Office of Air Force History, 1989.

Murphy, Vance E. "The Soaring Sixties." *Austin in Action*, June 1964, 28–29.

O'Neil, Paul. *Barnstorming and Speed Kings*. Alexandria, Va.: Time-Life Books, 1981.

Payne, Darwin. "The Feud That Built the World's Second Busiest Airport: Dallas vs. Fort Worth." *Legacies,* Spring 1999, 55–65.

———, and Kathy Fitzpatrick. *From Prairies to Planes: How Dallas and Fort Worth Overcame Politics and Personalities to Build One of the World's Biggest and Busiest Airports.* Dallas: Three Forks Press, 1999.

Powers, Pike. "Airport Task Force Seeks Citizen Input." *Austin Business Executive,* August 1984, pp. 20–24.

Propwash. January 1968. Newsletter of the Longhorn Flying Club.

A Quick Look at Aeronautical Activities in Texas. Austin: Aviation Division, Texas Department of Transportation.

Ragsdale, Kenneth B. *Wings over the Mexican Border: Pioneer Military Aviation in the Big Bend.* Austin: University of Texas Press, 1984.

Rapp, Jim. "The Austin Miracle." *TechWeb,* February 6, 1998.

Roseberry, C. R. *Glenn Curtiss: Pioneer of Flight.* Garden City: Doubleday, 1972.

Serling, Robert J. *Eagle: The History of American Airlines.* New York: St. Martin's/Marek, 1985.

Smith, Griffin, Jr. "The Most Dangerous Airports in Texas." *Texas Monthly,* April 1975, 64.

Smith, Myron J. *The Airline Bibliography: The Salem College Guide to Sources in Commercial Aviation.* Vol. 1, *The United States.* West Cornwall, Conn.: Locust Hill Press, 1986.

Still Flying High. San Antonio: Stinson Municipal Airport brochure.

Strickland, Patricia. *The Putt-Putt Air Force: The Story of the Civilian Pilot Training Program and the War Training Service, 1939–1944.* Washington, D.C.: Department of Transportation, Federal Aviation Administration, 1970.

Takeoff at Mid-Century: Federal Civil Aviation Policy in the Eisenhower Years, 1953–1961. Washington, D.C.: U.S. Department of Transportation, Federal Aviation Administration, 1976.

Tompkins, Col. Frank. *Chasing Villa: The Story behind the Story of Pershing's Expedition into Mexico.* [Harrisburg, Pa.]: The Military Services Publishing Company, 1934.

Vinson, R. E. "The University Crosses the Bar." *Southwestern Historical Quarterly,* vol. 42 (1939–1940).

Wilson, John R. M. *Turbulence Aloft: The Civil Aeronautics Administration amid Wars and Rumors of Wars, 1938–1953.* Washington, D.C.: U.S. Department of Transportation, Federal Aviation Administration, 1979.

Windsock. Newsletter, Marketing Division, Exxon Corporation, 1981.

Young, David, and Neal Callahan. *Fill the Heavens with Commerce: Chicago Aviation, 1855–1926.* Chicago: Chicago Review Press, 1981.

Your Rights and Benefits as a Displacee; Under the Federal Relocation Assistance Program. Washington, D.C., n.d.

Newspapers and Journals

Aero Digest

Aircraft Blue Book Price List, Fall 2000

Austin American

Austin American-Statesman
Austin Business Executive
Austin Daily Statesman
Austin Magazine
Austin Municipal Magazine
Austin Statesman
The Daily Texan (University of Texas student newspaper)
Fort Worth Star-Telegram
Progressive Architecture
Sunday American-Statesman
The Sunday Morning News, City Plan Supplement (Austin)
Texas Business Review